BTEC Tech Award

ENTERPRISE

Student Book

Second Edition

Cathy Richards

Helen Coupland-Smith

Andy Redfern

Published by Pearson Education Limited, 80 Strand, London, WC2R 0RL.

www.pearsonschoolsandfecolleges.co.uk

Copies of official specifications for all Pearson qualifications may be found on the website: qualifications.pearson.com

Text © Pearson Education Limited
Editorial by Just Content Ltd., Braintree, Essex
Typeset by PDQ Digital Media Solutions Ltd.
Original illustrations © Pearson Education Limited 2018
Picture research by Pearson CSC
Cover illustration by KJAArtists

22 21 20 19 18
9 8 7 6 5 4 3 2 1

First published 2018
Second edition published 2018

British Library Cataloguing in Publication Data
A catalogue record for this book is available from the British Library

ISBN 9781292279343

Printed in the UK by Bell & Bain Ltd, Glasgow.

Acknowledgements
The authors and publisher would like to thank the following individuals and organisations for their kind permission to reproduce copyright material.

Photographs
The publisher would like to thank the following for their kind permission to reproduce their photographs:

(Key: b-bottom; c-centre; l-left; r-right; t-top)

123RF: Jens Brüggemann 5,Wavebreak Media Ltd 27, 177, Denis Ismagilov 72, NejroN 94, Elnur Amikishiyev 178, Adilfitree Prapruetsutjarit 190; **Alamy Stock Photo:** Hero Images Inc 3, Alex Hinds 6, Robertharding 15, Eric Farrelly 16,Chris Cooper-Smith 39, JFP 43, Vibrant Pictures 45, Julia Hiebaum 51, Marco Kesseler 53, Lionela Rob 64, DCPhoto 69, etPhotos 81, Tetra Images 87, Steve Vidler 119, Errol Rait 126, Richard Levine 133, Steven May 184, Pewi 157; **Pearson Education Ltd:** 117; **Razan Alsous:**8; **Shutterstock:** Dmitry Naumov 35, Rawpixel.com 36, Wong Yu Liang 61, Daisy Daisy 77, Takasu 95, Imtmphoto 96, Monkey Business Images 99, Iadams 100, ESB Professional 105,163,Lucky Business 115, Magicinfoto 120, Tyler Olson 123, Es Sarawuth 141, Basileus 145, Marijus Auruskevicius 146, Fmua 149, pmphoto 151, Mike Flippo 155, MitchFOTO 165, Vinnstock 169.

Cover images: Front: londoneye / iStock / Getty Images, Back: Di Studio / Shutterstock.com

All other images © Pearson Education

Websites
Pearson Education Limited is not responsible for the content of any external internet sites. It is essential for tutors to preview each website before using it in class so as to ensure that the URL is still accurate, relevant and appropriate. We suggest that tutors bookmark useful websites and consider enabling students to access them through the school/college intranet.

Notes from the publisher

Pearson has robust editorial processes, including answer and fact checks, to ensure the accuracy of the content in this publication, and every effort is made to ensure this publication is free of errors. We are, however, only human, and occasionally errors do occur. Pearson is not liable for any misunderstandings that arise as a result of errors in this publication, but it is our priority to ensure that the content is accurate. If you spot an error, please do contact us at resourcescorrections@pearson.com so we can make sure it is corrected.

Contents

CONTENTS

About this book

This book is designed to support you when you are taking a BTEC Tech Award in Enterprise.

About your BTEC Tech Award

Congratulations in choosing a BTEC Award in Enterprise. This is an exciting and challenging course. It will help to prepare you for an enterprising future by studying and practising the knowledge, behaviours and skills related to researching, planning for, pitching and reviewing an enterprise. It will enable you to develop your technical skills – such as market research, planning, promotion and finance – using realistic work scenarios, and personal skills – such as monitoring your own performance, time management and problem solving – through a practical and skills-based approach to learning and assessment. All businesses need enterprising leaders and employees to drive their organisations forward, to have ideas and initiatives to promote growth, and to ensure that businesses survive in this fast-changing world. Enterprise is a key government focus, and is set to form an important part of the UK's global economic status, both now and in the future. Enterprise skills provide a fantastic progression pathway into a number of roles in an organisation, and are transferable into all businesses.

How you will be assessed

The qualification consists of three components that give learners the opportunity to develop broad knowledge and understanding of the enterprise sector and relevant skills. Components 1 and 2 are assessed through internal assessments. This means that your teacher will give you an assignment brief and indicate to you the deadline for completing it. The assignment will cover what you have been learning about and will be an opportunity to apply your knowledge and skills. Your teacher will mark your assignment and award you with a grade. Your third assessment, for Component 3, will be an external assessment. This will be a task that is set and marked by Pearson. You will have a set time in which to complete this task. The task will be an opportunity to bring together what you have learned in components 1 and 2.

About the authors

Cathy Richards has been a teacher of Business and Enterprise for more than 20 years, and has been writing about the subject since 2014. She has taught Business, Enterprise and Information Technology from pre-entry to Level 4, coaching and mentoring hundreds of students to go on and establish their own small enterprises. She gains great satisfaction in seeing them do well, and is particularly interested in the use of information technology to support newly established businesses and tools to help support creativity in entrepreneurs.

Helen Coupland-Smith graduated in Economics from Lancaster University. Before she became a teacher she worked as a trainee chartered accountant and in HR. She was Head of Business and ICT at a large secondary school in York until 2008 and has worked as a principal and senior examiner and moderator for a number of examination boards. She left teaching in 2008 to pursue her ambition to put her business and economics knowledge to the test in setting up her own business. She is the founder and managing director of Time2Resources Ltd, a company specialising in Business and Economic education. Helen is a well-respected trainer and conference speaker.

Andy Redfern is Deputy Director of Education for a large multi-academy trust in South Yorkshire. He has experience leading successful Business and Economics departments and teaching and learning across schools. Since 2012, he has worked as a Principal Examiner at GCSE level and has authored several text books and revision guides for his subjects. Andy lives in Sheffield with his wife and cockapoo, Willow.

How to use this book

The book has been designed in a way that will help you to navigate easily through your course. Each component from the course is covered in a separate chapter that makes clear what you are learning and how this will contribute to your assessment. There are opportunities for you to test your understanding of key areas, as well as activities that will challenge and extend your knowledge and skills. You will get the most from this book if you use each feature as part of your study. The different features will also help you develop the skills that will be important in completing your assignments as well as preparing you for your external assessment.

Features of the book

This book is designed in spreads, which means that each pair of facing pages represents a topic of learning. Each spread is about 1 hour of lesson time. Your teacher may ask you to work through a spread during a lesson or in your own time. Each spread contains a number of features that will help you to check what you are learning and offer opportunities to practise new skills.

Getting started A short activity or discussion that will introduce you to what you will be covering in the lesson.

Activity These will help you learn about the topic. You may be asked to work in pairs, groups or on your own.

Did you know? These include interesting facts that relate to what you're learning about.

Link it up This indicates where what you're learning about is covered in another part of the course.

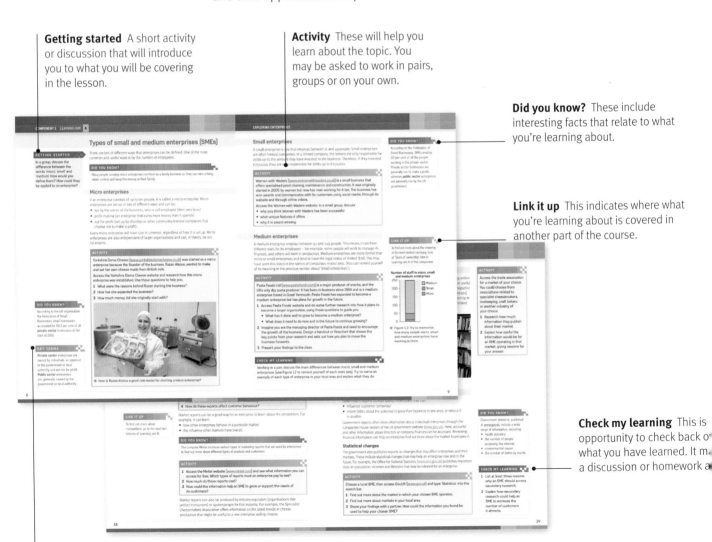

Check my learning This is opportunity to check back o what you have learned. It m a discussion or homework a

Key terms Important words or terms are defined.

At the end of each learning aim there is a section that outlines how you will be assessed and provides opportunities for you to build skills for assessment.

Checkpoint This feature is designed to allow you to assess your learning. The 'strengthen' question helps you to check your knowledge and understanding of what you have been studying, while the 'challenge' questions are an opportunity to extend your learning.

Assessment activity This is a practice assessment that reflects the style and approach of an assignment brief. In Component 3, tasks in the assessment activity features will be similar to those you should expect in your external assessment.

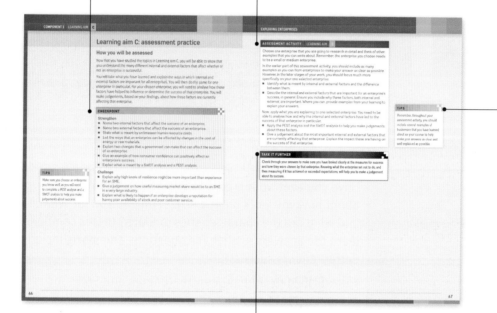

Tips A hint or tip that will help you with your assessment.

Take it further This provides suggestions for what you can do to build on the work you've done in the practice assessment.

01 Exploring Enterprises

Introduction

Have you ever wondered who owns all the different enterprises, or thought about how you work out the size of an enterprise? What does SME mean and what are the characteristics of SMEs? In this component, you will learn the answers to all these questions and more, including what makes entrepreneurs successful.

You will also explore how entrepreneurs and SMEs focus on what their customers need and how they meet these needs. You will develop your skills in market research and learn how competitors compare each other's businesses to make decisions for their future.

Finally, you will look at the factors that affect an enterprise from the inside and outside. This will include how enterprises make decisions, are affected by a decision and how this can help or prevent them from being successful.

LEARNING AIMS

In this component you will:

A	Examine the characteristics of enterprises
B	Explore how market research helps enterprises meet customer needs and understand competitor behaviour
C	Investigate the factors that contribute to the success of an enterprise

Examining the characteristics of enterprises

We often hear the word '**enterprise**' and may generally know what it means. However, just as people do, enterprises have **characteristics** that define them.

What is an enterprise?

Enterprise is the term used to describe a business or company. You need to understand:

- the features of different enterprises – known as characteristics
- what makes one enterprise different from another.

Carrying out activities

Enterprises carry out one or more activities. These activities vary depending on:

- the size of the enterprise
- its purpose.

Enterprises can offer **goods**, **services** or both.

- **Goods** are sold physically. For example, an enterprise may sell trainers or books to customers in person or online.
- **Services** are offered to anyone who needs them. For example, an enterprise may provide a cleaning service or serve food.

Offering goods and services

Some enterprises offer both goods *and* services. For example, an enterprise may sell a car to a customer and also have a workshop that offers services such as car repairs or maintenance.

Facing competition

Nearly all enterprises have to compete with each other because their goods and services are not **unique**. Other enterprises are called 'competition' and customers need to have a reason to go to one enterprise over another. This means that every enterprise needs to:

- decide on the features or characteristics that make its goods or services different from other enterprises
- ensure that customers are aware of what makes it different.

GETTING STARTED

Working with a partner, make a list of of five **small or medium enterprises (SMEs)** that you are familiar with. For each one, write down whether it sells goods, services or both. Compare your answers with another pair.

KEY TERMS

Enterprise is an organisation that provides goods or services.
Characteristics are features that are typical of a particular enterprise.
Goods are physical products that can be purchased.
Services are acts or tasks carried out by an enterprise that can be purchased.
Small and medium enterprises (SMEs) are enterprises with fewer than 250 staff.

ACTIVITY

1 For each type of enterprise listed below, decide whether it is possible to offer goods only, services only or both:
   - cleaning business
   - caravan park
   - bicycle shop
   - sweet shop.
2 Find an example in your area of a small or medium enterprise that matches each type listed above.

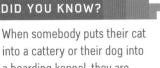

DID YOU KNOW?

When somebody puts their cat into a cattery or their dog into a boarding kennel, they are purchasing a service from an enterprise.

ACTIVITY

Compare the competition for three small enterprises in your area – for example, a coffee shop, a barber and a bakery. Try to ensure each enterprise is **independent** (not part of a larger **chain** or organisation). Then complete the following tasks.

1 List the characteristics of the enterprises you have chosen.
2 For each enterprise, state what it offers – goods, services or both.
3 Note down what makes each enterprise unique.
4 Now note down how much competition each enterprise has in the area.
5 Finally, make a list of the things you purchase from each enterprise.

Attracting customers and keeping them

Enterprises need to make sure they attract customers and **retain** them by meeting their needs and keeping them happy.

Newer enterprises may find it hard to attract customers for a variety of reasons.

- Customers may not be aware that the enterprise exists.
- The enterprise has not built up a **reputation**, so customers may not trust it yet.
- Customers may be loyal to another enterprise and not want to try a new one.

Smaller enterprises may also find it hard to attract new customers for a number of reasons.

- Advertising **budgets** may be small compared to larger enterprises, meaning it may be difficult to make people aware of their existence.
- Their goods or services may be more expensive than larger enterprises because it costs more to produce them.

Even if customers are convinced to buy goods or services from a new enterprise, they may not buy from them again if:

- they have not received a good service
- the quality of goods is not high enough.

It is important that customers are happy so that they are encouraged to use the enterprise again. In fact, many customers will pay more for goods and services from an enterprise that offers excellent customer service or is local, rather than going to a competitor that may be less expensive.

◻ **Why is it important for customers to be happy with the goods they buy?**

KEY TERMS

Unique means that something is one of a kind, so if an enterprise is unique it is the only one.
Independent businesses are those that are not part of a larger chain or organisation.
Chains are groups of businesses, such as hotels or coffee shops, owned by one parent company.
Retain means ensuring that a customer stays with an enterprise and does not take their custom to one of its competitors.
Reputation is the opinions that customers have about an enterprise.
Budgets are the amount of money put aside for a particular purpose (for example, advertising).
Profit is the amount of money earned minus the costs paid out.

DID YOU KNOW?

The more materials an enterprise buys to provide its goods or services, the cheaper they become. A small enterprise does not need to purchase as much to operate, so the things it buys are generally more expensive. This means it will have to sell its goods or services for more money in order to make a **profit**.

CHECK MY LEARNING

Note down the difference between goods and services. Give an example of each.

Customer service

As a customer, you always hope to receive good customer service. When you are buying goods or services, it is reassuring to feel that those selling them know their product and are as helpful as possible.

Keeping customers happy means ensuring they are offered the best service possible. There are four main reasons why having good customer service helps a business.

1 It attracts new customers to try the goods or services.

2 It encourages customers to come back and buy again.

3 It encourages customers to be loyal and not consider shopping elsewhere.

4 If customers are happy, they are more likely to share their positive experience with others. This will help improve the reputation of the enterprise and, also, attract more customers.

You will know what it feels like to be a customer when you go into a shop or buy something online. Customer service is about your whole experience before, during and after you make a payment. Customer service relates to both online and offline purchasing. This means it is important for enterprises to consider how they can provide support for customers at all times, even if they do not meet them in person or talk to them on the phone.

Service and loyalty

Good customer service can attract new customers because people hear about the service that others have had and want to experience it for themselves. This helps an enterprise to develop a good reputation and loyal customers.

Incentives

Customer **loyalty** can be developed by offering incentives or experiences that support customers, in addition to buying the goods or services themselves. Many smaller enterprises are able to compete with larger ones by using online methods. These include:

- **social media** promotions
- newsletters
- online comments or feedback
- loyalty cards or credits.

▪ Do loyalty cards encourage you to support any enterprises you use?

ACTIVITY

Good customer service is crucial for attracting and retaining customers. If an employee working in customer service is unhappy, they are unlikely to provide good service. Happy employees are therefore very important for making sure that customers are pleased with their experience.

1 In a small group, discuss the skills and qualities a good customer service employee should have in order to give the best possible customer service.

2 With your group, write down some answers and ideas for these questions.
  - What training do employees need to help them develop good customer service skills?
  - What should an enterprise do if an employee does not offer good customer service?

Creativity and innovation

Small and medium enterprises can be flexible and can change or adapt what they do to make sure their customers are happy. This is called being creative and **innovative**. To do this, the enterprise must strive to:

- fill any **gaps in the market** for the goods and services it offers
- develop new ideas for a service or goods that no one else is yet producing.

Ways to be creative and develop new ideas include:

- getting feedback from customers
- listening to, and acting on, what customers want.

Meeting customer needs

By listening to customer feedback, an enterprise can develop its services and improve the ways it meets the needs of its customers. This will also make customers feel they are being valued and cared for, and encourage loyalty to the enterprise.

ACTIVITY

CSSCloud (www.csscloud.co.uk) is a small business in Great Yarmouth. Access its website to find out about its goods and services.

1 How does the business use creativity and innovation to develop new goods and services for its customers?

2 What does its website tell you about the customer service it offers?

Why enterprises fail

Although many enterprises are very well thought out, there are reasons why small and medium ones sometimes fail. Figure 1.1 shows some examples of these reasons.

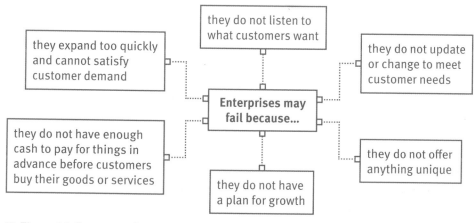

■ Figure 1.1: Reasons why enterprises may fail

CHECK MY LEARNING

Give a definition of what is meant by an enterprise, then list three things you have learned about why it is important to keep customers happy.

DID YOU KNOW?

According to the website www.smallbusiness.co.uk, the most common types of business enterprise to fail in the UK are property services, accommodation, food services and financial services.

Types of small and medium enterprises

GETTING STARTED

In a group, discuss the difference between the words 'micro', 'small' and 'medium'. How would you define them? How could they be applied to an enterprise?

There are lots of different ways that enterprises can be defined. One of the most common and useful ways is by the number of employees.

DID YOU KNOW?

Many people running micro enterprises run them as a family business so they can earn a living, retain control and keep the money in their family.

Micro enterprises

If an enterprise consists of up to ten people, it is called a micro enterprise. Micro enterprises are set up in lots of different ways and can be:

- run by the owner of the business, who is self-employed (their own boss)
- profit-making (an enterprise that earns more money than it spends)
- not-for-profit (set up by charities or other community interest companies that choose not to make a profit).

Every micro enterprise will have size in common, regardless of how it is set up. Micro enterprises are also independent of larger organisations and can, in theory, be run by anyone.

ACTIVITY

Yorkshire Dama Cheese (www.yorkshiredamacheese.co.uk) was started as a micro enterprise because the founder of the business, Razan Alsous, wanted to make and eat her own cheese made from British milk.

Access the Yorkshire Dama Cheese website and research how this micro enterprise was established. Use these questions to help you.

1 What were the reasons behind Razan starting the business?

2 How has she expanded the business?

3 How much money did she originally start with?

▫ How is Razan Alsous a good role model for starting a micro enterprise?

DID YOU KNOW?

According to the UK organisation the Federation of Small Businesses, small businesses accounted for 99.3 per cent of all **private sector** businesses at the start of 2016.

KEY TERMS

Private sector enterprises are owned by individuals, as opposed to the government or local authority, and are run for profit.
Public sector enterprises are, generally, owned by the government or a local authority.

Small enterprises

A small enterprise is one that employs between 11 and 49 people. Small enterprises are often limited companies. In a limited company, the owners are only responsible for debts up to the amount they have invested in the business. Therefore, if they invested £250,000, they are only responsible for debts up to £250,000.

ACTIVITY

Women with Waders (www.womenwithwaders.co.uk) is a small business that offers specialised pond cleaning, maintenance and construction. It was originally started in 2005 by women but now has men working for it too. The business has won awards and communicates with its customers using social media, through its website and through online videos.

Access the Women with Waders website. In a small group, discuss:

- why you think Women with Waders has been successful
- what unique features it offers
- why it is award-winning.

Medium enterprises

A medium enterprise employs between 50 and 249 people. This means it can have different roles for its employees – for example, some people will work to manage its finances, and others will work in production. Medium enterprises are more formal than micro or small enterprises and tend to have the legal status of limited (Ltd). You may have seen this listed in the names of companies in your area. (You can remind yourself of its meaning in the previous section about 'Small enterprises'.)

LINK IT UP

To find out more about the meaning of the term limited company, look at 'Types of ownership' later in Learning aim A of this component.

ACTIVITY

Pasta Foods Ltd (www.pastafoods.com) is a major producer of snacks, and the UK's only dry pasta producer. It has been in business since 1964 and is a medium enterprise based in Great Yarmouth. Pasta Foods has expanded to become a medium enterprise but has plans for growth in the future.

1 Access Pasta Foods' website and do some further research into how it plans to become a larger organisation, using these questions to guide you.
- What has it done well to grow to become a medium enterprise?
- What does it need to do now and in the future to continue growing?

2 Imagine you are the managing director of Pasta Foods and need to encourage the growth of the business. Design a handout or flowchart that shows the key points from your research and sets out how you plan to move the business forwards.

3 Present your findings to the class.

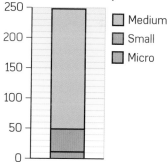

Number of staff in micro, small and medium enterprises

- Medium
- Small
- Micro

◘ Figure 1.2: Try to memorise how many people micro, small and medium enterprises have working in them

CHECK MY LEARNING

Working in a pair, discuss the main differences between micro, small and medium enterprises (use Figure 1.2 to remind yourself of each one's size). Try to name an example of each type of enterprise in your local area and explain what they do.

Characteristics of small and medium enterprises

LINK IT UP

To remind yourself of the sizes of SMEs, go back to the previous lesson 'Types of small and medium enterprises (SMEs)' in Learning aim A of this component.

KEY TERM

HMRC is Her Majesty's Revenue and Customs – the agency that works to collect taxes from individuals and businesses in the UK.

SMEs are run and owned by fewer people than large organisations, and have fewer employees. This gives them certain characteristics.

Running SMEs

As you have already learned, SMEs are often run by either a single person or a small team. These people are usually the owners of the enterprise. If one person is running the enterprise it is most common for them to be self-employed. This means they run the business themselves and take responsibility for it, whether it succeeds or not.

Running their own enterprise means that an individual can decide:

- when, how and who they do their work for
- the price they charge
- the quality of their service.

DID YOU KNOW?

As soon as you start working for yourself, you become self-employed and are classed as a sole trader. You will need to register with **HMRC** (Her Majesty's Revenue and Customs) so that you can pay the correct National Insurance and income tax.

Employees

The maximum number of employees in any SME is 249, and the minimum number is one person. This means there are fewer employees working for these enterprises compared to larger organisations. Having fewer employees means the owners or managers of the enterprise are able to develop close working relationships with their staff, especially if the business is very small. Employees who work for SMEs may have benefits such as:

- greater variety of work
- higher levels of responsibility – if there are very few employees, people may be encouraged to fulfil tasks and take on roles that they would not have had the opportunity to do if they were working for a larger company.

ACTIVITY

Working for an SME can have a range of benefits.

1 Working in a pair, think about part-time jobs or work experience you may have had with an SME. Alternatively, you can carry out some research online into an SME. Write down the benefits of working for the SME and turn your list into a poster.

2 In a small group, discuss the drawbacks of working for an SME.

3 Consider if you would like to run or work for an SME. Explain your answer to the rest of your group.

Type of ownership

Take a look at Table 1.1, which explains the types of ownership of SMEs.

◘ **Table 1.1: Types of ownership of SMEs**

Type of owner	Description	Legal definition
Sole trader	A sole trader is the legal owner of the enterprise. Often, sole traders only need a small amount of money to run their business. They keep all the profits of their enterprise after tax has been paid, but are also responsible for any losses. If they lose money and cannot pay their bills, they can be declared bankrupt as they have unlimited liability.	'Bankrupt' means a person cannot pay their debts. Their possessions may be sold to pay off the debts and they may be unable to work in certain professions – for example, as a company director. 'Unlimited liability' means that a person is responsible for the debts of themselves and others. They can lose their home or personal money if they cannot pay the debts of their enterprise.
Partnership	A partnership is two or more people who legally own the enterprise. Partners, like sole traders, have unlimited liability. Working as a partnership means the responsibility for business decisions is shared between the partners, and so are the debts and profits.	
Ltd (limited company)	Private limited companies (Ltd) have their own legal identity and are separate enterprises from their owners. This means they have limited liability. Limited companies have boards of directors and the owners of a limited company do not always run it – they may just invest in **private shares**, while other people are responsible for the daily operations of the enterprise.	'Limited liability' means the owners of the enterprise are not personally liable for the debts of the enterprise.

Location or operation

SMEs can be run from a wide range of physical, and sometimes virtual, locations, as Figure 1.3 shows. The enterprise's location will depend on:

- the type of business (whether it offers goods or services)
- the number of employees.

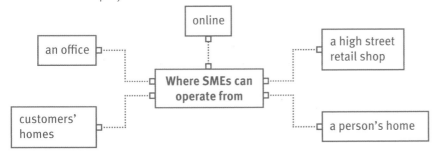

◘ **Figure 1.3: Can you think of any other locations for an SME?**

Customers can generally visit a physical (real) location in person, but they cannot do this with a virtual location such as an online store.

KEY TERMS

Private shares are a stake in a company, from which the shareholder receives a share of the profits (known as a dividend).

Entrepreneurs are people who set up a new enterprise in order to make a profit.

DID YOU KNOW?

A virtual location, such as an online shop, is a low-cost way for a new micro-business to start.

CHECK MY LEARNING

In a pair, discuss why an **entrepreneur** might decide their enterprise should become a limited company instead of operating as a sole trader. What are the benefits and potential risks of each option?

The purpose of enterprise

GETTING STARTED

If you had the opportunity to set up your own enterprise, what sort of business would it be? What would be your main reasons for doing it? Discuss your thoughts with members of your class.

The purpose of an enterprise can have a big influence on the way it is run and the business decisions it makes. One example of a purpose might be to make money. Its purpose can be present in its longer-term plans, as well as being the basis for the day-to-day objectives that the enterprise sets itself.

Aims

Aims are the overarching goals that an enterprise wants to achieve. They are statements that support the original purpose of the enterprise. An enterprise's aims set out what it wants to do in the future, such as make a profit, stay in business (survive), expand in size and increase profits, and be environmentally friendly.

Making a profit

Many SMEs have the primary aim of making a profit. This is because the owners are using the enterprise to make money for themselves and their families, as they are private enterprises.

DID YOU KNOW?

An SME's profits are used to calculate the amount of income tax the enterprise must pay to HMRC.

Surviving

When they start to trade (do business), many SMEs have survival as one of their key aims. This is because enterprises can fail soon after starting if they do not earn enough money. This might happen for a number of reasons.

- The SME's costs may be higher than expected.
- It may not have as many customers as it would like.
- It may not be attracting and keeping a sufficient number of customers.

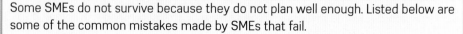

ACTIVITY

Some SMEs do not survive because they do not plan well enough. Listed below are some of the common mistakes made by SMEs that fail.

1 They do not have enough money to begin with.
2 Their costs are higher than expected.
3 They do not have the right skills.
4 They do not have enough customers.
5 They do not properly research their business sector.
6 They lack experience.
7 They do not provide adequate customer service.

For each of these points, note down what an SME owner or manager could do to ensure they avoid these common mistakes and are successful.

Discuss your answers in a group.

DID YOU KNOW?

According to www.smallbusiness. co.uk, only 40 per cent of SMEs are still trading after five years in business. The other 60 per cent often fail because they do not have enough money available to keep operating.

Expanding

Growing from a micro enterprise to a small or medium enterprise is often an aim, because being larger can mean higher profits. There are many different ways in which enterprises expand, such as:

- moving to a new location
- increasing their customers
- becoming involved in different types of **market**
- offering additional services to existing customers.

KEY TERM

A **market** is the type of customers an enterprise sells to.

Maximising sales

It is important for an enterprise to make the sales of its goods or services as high as possible. This can be done by:

- trying to make as many sales as possible
- making sure each sale is worth as much as possible.

All enterprises need to do this, but it is especially important for SMEs because they are trying to survive and make a profit, which can be difficult when they are starting out.

Being environmentally friendly and ethical

It is important that enterprises consider the environment and the materials they use when producing their goods and services. In order to attract and keep customers, they will need to run their enterprise in a way that is sustainable and **ethical**. Ideally, they should think about:

- where materials come from and the effect on the environment of removing them
- the workforce they use, making sure working conditions and pay adhere to the necessary ethical standards.

KEY TERM

Ethical is avoiding harm to others, animals or the environment

Providing a voluntary or charitable service

You have learned that many SMEs are set up to make a profit and are in the private sector. However, some SMEs are set up to provide voluntary or charity contributions to local communities or causes. These SMEs are often called social enterprises because they have a social impact or interest.

ACTIVITY

Your Own Place (www.yourownplace.org.uk) is a community interest company. Carry out research into what it does by answering these questions.

1 What are its aims?
2 What makes it different from other social enterprises?
3 What type of liability does it have?

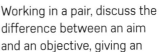

Figure 1.4: Try to remember what SMART stands for. Do you use these objectives yourself in your studies?

Objectives

Objectives work alongside aims because they are specific targets and timescales that enterprises set in order to achieve their aims. They are often turned into SMART objectives, which means they have to be:

- **S**pecific
- **M**easurable
- **A**chievable
- **R**ealistic
- **T**ime-related.

By having specific objectives that are SMART, enterprises can easily measure the progress they have made.

CHECK MY LEARNING

Working in a pair, discuss the difference between an aim and an objective, giving an example of each.

Discuss why you think setting SMART objectives might be useful for a business.

Social and political pressures influencing enterprises

SMEs can be affected by many pressures, whether their main aim is to make a profit or not. These pressures can come from the communities they work in, the politics of the local area and national politics. These influences are called **social pressure** and **political pressure.**

Social pressure

Social pressure affects all SMEs, as Table 1.2 shows.

■ Table 1.2: How social pressure affects SMEs

Type of social pressure	Effects on an SME
From purchasers of an SME's goods or services (customers)	The amount they buy (or not) can help a business to succeed or fail.
Changes in how general communities and customers behave	Trends in taste or fashion can affect sales, which can become very high or very low. These trends are sometimes called 'fads'. Fads are often short-lived, so an SME needs to establish itself on a short-lived basis in order to survive and grow. 'Pop-ups', for instance, are an example of how SMEs adapt to fast-changing trends.
Changing how a business should operate	If an SME is working in a way that damages the environment or does not seem ethical (but is still legal), it may need to change how it operates.

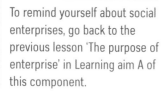
ACTIVITY

'Selfie sticks' (extendable poles that can be attached to cameras or phones to help people take better photos of themselves) sold at very high rates during 2014 and 2015. Hundreds were bought each week. By October 2016, sales had fallen by about 50 per cent. Many tourist destinations started to ban them because they were an annoyance to the general public.

1 Research selfie sticks to find out what social pressure was being placed on customers using them.

2 What could happen to an SME selling these sticks?

3 What could an SME selling selfie sticks do to protect itself for the future?

Social pressure within a community can also lead to social enterprises being set up – for example:

- to help older people
- to employ people who find it difficult to get work in other places.

ACTIVITY

Nemi Teas (www.nemiteas.com) was set up to help refugees moving to the UK by offering them employment and leadership roles.

Research how this social enterprise works and the social pressures that started it.

Political pressure

SMEs can be influenced by political pressure to change through:

- laws
- campaigns
- what is happening in local, national, European and international politics.

Policy changes

Political pressure is placed on SMEs when there are changes to:

- the way people are employed
- the amount of tax that must be paid
- other ways investment needs to be made – for example, by SMEs that operate in transport or technology.

Political pressure can influence SMEs through local authorities such as county councils and borough, town or district councils. Local enterprise partnerships can also add positive pressure and influence by offering grants. SMEs can apply for these grants, which can help them to expand (for example, by buying new machinery that they may need) and create more jobs in the local economy.

⬛ National and local political pressures influence the way that SMEs operate

> **ACTIVITY**
>
> The New Anglia Local Enterprise Partnership offers grants for enterprises in the East of England to help them create new jobs for people. SMEs can apply for grants of up to £500,000 to help them expand. Stokes Sauces (www.stokessauces.co.uk) is an SME that was given a grant by the fund. This allowed it to buy additional machinery to cook and produce its sauces. These sauces are sold to much larger businesses.
>
> 1 Find out more about Stokes Sauces' story and how being helped by the local enterprise partnership enabled it to expand and gain new customers.
>
> 2 In a small group, discuss why you think politicians and local councils want businesses like Stokes to benefit from grants and how this can, in turn, benefit their communities.

Broader ethical responsibilities

SMEs are influenced by what they need to do on a broader level by thinking about their business and its sustainability, honesty, fairness and responsibility to others. There are no written rules for how an SME behaves ethically; enterprises have to make these decisions themselves. Many SMEs are run by individuals or families, so the way they do business (for example, their respect for the environment and their staff, or whether they make charitable donations) is heavily influenced by the way they view these responsibilities.

> **CHECK MY LEARNING**
>
> Working in a pair, take turns to explain to each other, in simple terms, the difference between social and political pressure.

Range of goods and services

Enterprises offer a wide range of goods and services. Most of them will deal in the sort of things that are very familiar to you – from plumbing and car repairs to retail and manufacturing. Consider the examples below. Which of them do you already know about? Are there any that you were not aware of?

Enterprises selling services

Cleaning

Some SMEs offer cleaning services that can be general (for example, dry cleaning available for the public or commercial customers). They can also specialise in particular types of cleaning that may be unusual or targeted to certain customers (for example, cleaning tropical fish tanks).

ACTIVITY

Virtu Conservation Housekeeping Ltd (www.conservation-housekeeping.co.uk) offers specialist cleaning services through its micro enterprise. Find out more about this business, including its background and services.

Fitness instruction

Fitness instruction enterprises are often run by individuals who are self-employed. Some instructors run general fitness classes that are open to everyone. Others may work as a personal trainer with individuals to target specific fitness levels (for example, helping someone prepare for a competition) or with athletes specialising in a particular sport.

DID YOU KNOW?

The National Register of Personal Trainers (NRPT) (www.nrpt.co.uk) helps to check that people working as fitness instructors are properly trained and insured. Fitness instructors are added to the register if they agree to work according to the NRPT's code of ethics. The register can then match instructors to clients, based on their individual requirements.

IT consultancy

Consultancies specialising in IT come in all sizes, from sole traders upwards. A sole trader typically provides help to individuals (such as advising on and maintaining their personal computers and devices). Larger enterprises might also sell complicated and expensive hardware and software. IT consultancy may be offered through a partnership, which means that several experts could pool their knowledge together.

ACTIVITY

Century IT Services (www.century-it.co.uk) is a micro enterprise offering IT consultancy to other businesses. Its legal status is a partnership but it has a **limited liability partnership** called an LLP. Research and discuss this enterprise with a partner. What are the benefits of having a limited liability partnership for an IT consultancy?

Financial consultancy

Financial consultants offer advice and guidance to members of the public or businesses about how to improve their financial situation. Like fitness instructors, financial consultants can belong to a register to match them with potential customers. This helps them to:

- expand their business
- increase the level of trust and build up a good reputation.

Enterprises selling goods

Some SMEs, as you have learned, sell goods rather than services. Table 1.3 explores some of these.

☐ Table 1.3: Examples of enterprises that sell goods

Type of enterprise	Goods it sells
Food stall	Sells a range of different popular foods. These are often micro enterprises that start in the kitchens of people early in their careers.
Newsagent	Sells newspapers, magazines, sweets and stationery. These enterprises can be independent businesses in local neighbourhoods or on the high street.
An artist selling online	Sells the work the artist produces in their own home or studio. Often, artists and craftspeople sell through their own websites or specific platforms that allow them to be supported and promoted more widely.

Entrepreneurs

GETTING STARTED

Reflect on your experience of businesses from visits, work experience or a part-time job. How much would you enjoy being your own boss or having people work for you? Discuss your thoughts with a partner.

'Entrepreneur' is the name given to a person who sets up their own enterprise. Entrepreneurs are drawn from a wide range of people who have different experiences and reasons for why and how they set up their own enterprises.

Reasons for starting your own enterprise

Enterprises are set up every day in the UK by people wishing to start a new business, begin a new career or make a social change. There are many reasons people may want to start an enterprise, as Figure 1.5 shows.

DID YOU KNOW?

The word 'enterprise' comes from a French word, 'entreprise', meaning 'undertaking'.

DID YOU KNOW?

According to Start Up Britain (http://startupbritain.org), which offers advice to entrepreneurs, more than 400,000 enterprises were started during the first half of 2017.

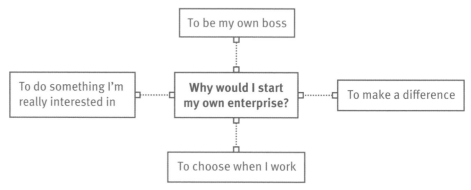

■ Figure 1.5: Do you think you could be an entrepreneur?

Being your own boss

Entrepreneurs often start their enterprises because they want to be in control of their career and act as their own boss. By being the boss, they are able to make all the decisions. Someone may want to become an entrepreneur because they were made redundant (their job role was no longer needed), were dismissed (asked to leave) or decided to leave their previous job. They may feel they will gain greater job satisfaction and be more successful if they are in charge of their own work.

DID YOU KNOW?

Startup (www.startupnow.org.uk) is a charity that helps ex-offenders and disadvantaged young women to set up their own enterprises through funding, support and mentoring.

ACTIVITY

In a small group, discuss if and why you would like to be your own boss. What would the advantages be? Can you think of any disadvantages?

Pursuing a hobby

Some entrepreneurs turn their hobby or interest into an enterprise, which they are then able to earn money from. By basing their enterprise around a hobby or interest, an entrepreneur is able to enjoy what they do, as well as benefiting from it financially.

ACTIVITY

I Heart Buttons (www.iheartbuttons.co.uk) was set up as a new business by Lesa Simons so that she could earn money from her hobby of making 'button bouquets' for weddings and other occasions.

Use her website to research the background to her business. How did it start and what did she need to do to be successful?

If an entrepreneur chooses to turn their hobby into their business, they must be sure their passion has the potential to become a successful enterprise. Making it successful will involve a lot of hard work and careful planning to ensure they do not invest their money in the business only to have it fail.

◻ Handicrafts can be turned from a hobby into a business, but it is important to develop a clear plan to minimise risk when trying to make money from any hobby

> **ACTIVITY**
>
> In a small group, discuss and write down your hobbies or interests. Then try to answer these questions.
>
> 1 Could any of these be turned into an enterprise?
>
> 2 How much skill do you have in this area?
>
> 3 How easy do you think it would be to establish an enterprise from your hobby or interest?
>
> 4 How much money would you need to support setting up an enterprise?
>
> 5 Is there much competition from something similar in your area?

Having flexibility

Being an entrepreneur gives a person more flexibility to choose how they work and run their business. This means they can:

- decide how much time they will spend working (and how much leisure time they will have)
- choose their working hours – for example, it may be better for them to work in the evenings after their children have gone to bed, or at weekends when they have the support of others at home
- combine other responsibilities – for example, caring for a relative or looking after their children
- decide the pace and intensity of their work – for example, they might work very hard for several weeks, so that they can work fewer hours for a period afterwards.

Making a difference

Sometimes entrepreneurs start an enterprise because they want to make a difference to society. Generally, these businesses are called social enterprises and the people who start them are called social entrepreneurs. The purpose of the enterprise might be to:

- employ people from different backgrounds
- be ethical
- consider sustainability and/or local communities.

Social entrepreneurs

Social entrepreneurs start their enterprises with a cause or idea as their first priority, and making a profit is secondary. Making money is still important to them, but usually because it can then be put back into their business (reinvested). This helps them to continue working to achieve their original idea.

> **ACTIVITY**
>
> How It Should Be (http://hisbe.co.uk) is a social enterprise supermarket set up in Brighton. It seeks to be fairer, more responsible and sustainable in the food industry. Its products are sourced and sold according to its key values – ethics, welfare, reducing waste and protecting nature.
>
> 1 Use its website to research the work it does. Explain three ways it makes sure its key values are upheld.
>
> 2 Are there any goods or services that don't currently exist that you think should? What are they? Would they be suitable to start a new enterprise? Explain your answers.

> **CHECK MY LEARNING**
>
> Name one disadvantage of an entrepreneur turning their hobby into their business.

> **LINK IT UP**
>
> To remind yourself about social enterprises, go back to earlier lessons ('The purpose of enterprise' and 'Social and political pressures influencing enterprises') in Learning aim A of this component.

Mind-set of an entrepreneur

GETTING STARTED

On your own, think about your personal mind-set. How do you approach challenges and work for your course? Are you positive and forward thinking? What could you do to be more like this?

Your mind-set is how you view the world. Starting an enterprise requires a special way of thinking and a lot of energy. Entrepreneurs need to be strong-willed to make sure their enterprise is successful. They need to be positive and have a 'can do' attitude.

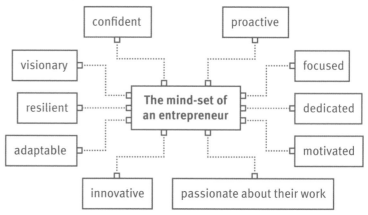

■ Figure 1.6: Do you have the mind-set of an entrepreneur? What else could you add to these qualities?

ACTIVITY

Think of a time when you had something important to do (perhaps at home or for your course) but were distracted and did not complete the task. What stopped you from completing it? What could you have done differently to avoid being distracted?

Being focused

Setting up a new enterprise can be very difficult. If entrepreneurs are not focused enough, they may be distracted by other activities and life events that are happening around them. Here are some ideas about what being focused means.

DID YOU KNOW?

Many entrepreneurs start their enterprises at home, especially when they are micro enterprises. This means they must be careful to focus on their business when they need to, but also learn how to focus on their personal life, in order to find a healthy balance.

Having passion

Having passion for what they do and for the product they provide is extremely important for an entrepreneur. They will often have to persuade others that their goods or services are top quality and worth buying.

ACTIVITY

Parravani's Ice Ceam (www.parravanis.co.uk) was set up in 1898 by its first owner, entrepreneur Giuseppe Parravani. Using its website, find out more about how Giuseppe set up his enterprise, and about the passion that led to his business becoming a favourite producer in Norfolk and Suffolk.

LINK IT UP

To remind yourself about how customer service should ideally work, go back to an earlier lesson, 'Customer service', in Learning aim A of this component.

Showing motivation and dedication

Working for yourself or with a small team requires hard work to improve the enterprise and make it a success. An entrepreneur needs:

- motivation (wanting to make something different or better)
- dedication (putting in effort to ensure the enterprise does well).

Being innovative or inventive

Developing a new idea or a new way of offering something that already exists is important for any entrepreneur. If an enterprise offers something different or the service is better than that provided by other businesses, customers are more likely to spend their money there. This means the business generates profit and has more chance of being successful.

Being proactive

Entrepreneurs constantly need to make improvements to their enterprise. This could be by:

- selling something different
- thinking about new ranges/services
- reviewing the existing goods or services on offer.

Being proactive means always looking to make changes or improvements, rather than waiting for things to happen and then reacting to them. It is an important quality in entrepreneurs, because it enables them to improve their business and be prepared for a variety of situations.

Having confidence

Developing confidence is a very important skill. Often, entrepreneurs will need to present their ideas to others, and they must show they are organised, capable and in control – even if sometimes they do not feel that they are. They must be able to show the belief they have in their product, and they must make others feel confident about them as well. Confidence will help to persuade:

- customers to buy from them
- investors to give them money to keep the business running.

Being flexible, adaptable and resilient

The best entrepreneurs are able to be flexible, adaptable and **resilient**. This means they can change an idea quickly for something better, if necessary, to improve their services and constantly keep their customers happy, which, in turn, means the customers will keep returning.

Setting up an enterprise is hard work. You will need to be resilient, which means not giving up if faced with problems. Managing your own business without the help of others can be hard, especially after a setback, so an entrepreneur needs to be able to pick themselves up quickly and get back on track. Failures can have advantages, too, and many entrepreneurs will be able to recount how their failures have gone on to help their enterprises become successful.

Being visionary and inspirational

Having vision means having a plan for the future and being able to share that plan with others. Entrepreneurs do not always have a vision for the long-term future, but they must be able to inspire other people to want to buy from, or invest in, their enterprise.

ACTIVITY

Hannah Banana Bakery (www.hannahbananabakery. co.uk), which produces cakes and brownies, was established in 2011. This bakery has some differences from other bakeries. Check its website to find out more about what Hannah offers and what makes her bakery different.

DID YOU KNOW?

In most areas around the UK, chambers of commerce (which aim to help businesses) organise networking events where entrepreneurs can discuss their business ideas and learn from each other.

CHECK MY LEARNING

Explain what is meant by the term 'proactive' and why it is important for an entrepreneur to have this mindset.

Skills for success

KEY TERMS

Industry means an area of goods or services that are being sold – for example, the computer repair industry.

Sector is a part of the economy – for example, the IT sector, which consists of several related industries.

ACTIVITY

Think of a local enterprise near to you. In a small group, discuss the skills and knowledge the entrepreneur would have needed to start their enterprise. How important is it for that enterprise to keep its staff up to date with their skills? What would happen if it did not?

LINK IT UP

To remind yourself about why enterprises can fail, go back to an earlier lesson, 'Customer service', in Learning aim A of this component.

It is important that entrepreneurs understand the **industry** or **sector** they are working in and have the right skills to do a good job. Some entrepreneurs can learn skills for themselves. Others need specialist training or qualifications to set up their business.

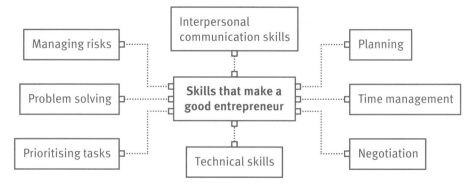

◻ Figure 1.7: These skills are important to succeed in business. Can you think of any others?

Interpersonal communication skills

Interpersonal communication skills relate to dealing with other people, and are required when:

- talking to others face to face
- making a phone call or video call
- speaking to people via email.

Part of growing an enterprise is persuading others they should buy from you. Being able to communicate well as an entrepreneur gives others confidence, shows that the person is competent and establishes trust with their customers.

Planning

Planning is a key skill that all entrepreneurs must have. They need to be able to plan for the:

- *short term* – handling daily occurrences and making sure customers are looked after immediately, which ensures money is constantly coming into the enterprise
- *medium term* – thinking further ahead about the goods and services on offer, making sure they are still useful
- *long term* – planning how to retain customers, reviewing sales and income (how much is sold and bought by customers) and how the enterprise can develop.

Time management

Being skilled in time management means that time is not wasted and is spent productively. Entrepreneurs need to make sure they plan how to produce and deliver their goods and services in the most effective way. This could be by choosing particular timeslots when:

- deliveries are made or services are offered
- existing customers are cared for
- plans are made to develop the business and attract new customers.

Negotiation

When an enterprise is new, it needs to establish itself within its industry and community, and aim to make as much money as it can as early as possible. This means entrepreneurs need the skill to **negotiate**:

- the best price for materials that need to bought for the business
- the best price from the customers.

If an entrepreneur cannot get the right price or number of goods they may not be able to offer their customers what they want. This could lead to lower sales than required to keep the business running.

◩ Figure 1.8: Negotiation is important. It allows entrepreneurs to get the best deal for their enterprise

Prioritising tasks

Entrepreneurs are always busy, but it is important that they are able to prioritise tasks. This means they work out which tasks must be done first and which can be done later. For some types of enterprise it is essential that goods are in stock or services can be offered at a certain time, so these would be a main priority.

Problem solving

All businesses experience challenges and problems, but entrepreneurs may not be able to predict in advance what these are likely to be. Sometimes there will be unexpected changes that could not have been planned for. For example, changes in weather may create higher or lower demand for some goods or services, such as types of clothing or holidays. Entrepreneurs need to develop the skills to look for solutions and make different plans when problems arise.

Managing risks

Entrepreneurs face many risks and need to work out how to balance these risks to make sure they are successful. They may need to:

- invest a lot of their own money and time
- trust the advice they have been given by others about whether their business can succeed
- find investors who can give financial backing.

Entrepreneurs weigh up the risk of setting up their business against the possible rewards they would get if it is successful.

Learning aim A: assessment practice

How you will be assessed

Now that you have studied the topics in Learning aim A, you will be able to show you have found out more about what is meant by an enterprise, the type and characteristics of enterprises, their purpose, and the role of an entrepreneur – including the skills and mind-set they need to be successful.

You will now take what you have learned and carry out research into real enterprises by comparing two contrasting local enterprises. You will also need to describe and analyse the entrepreneurial characteristics and skills that the entrepreneurs running those enterprises have demonstrated. This will help you decide how successful you think they have been in achieving their aims.

CHECKPOINT

Strengthen

- What is an enterprise?
- How is the size of an enterprise measured?
- What are three characteristics of an enterprise?
- What are an enterprise's purpose and aims?
- Explain two reasons why an entrepreneur might choose to set up their own enterprise.
- Give an example of one element that an entrepreneur must have in their mind-set to be successful.
- Explain two skills that an entrepreneur should demonstrate for their enterprise to be a success.

Challenge

- Why might an enterprise fail?
- Give a suggestion for how the success of an enterprise could be measured.
- Explain what is likely to happen if an entrepreneur is not proactive or confident when carrying out their role.

TIPS

Make sure you choose enterprises that have a lot of information about them published or that you know well. This means you will be able to access all the information that you need.

ASSESSMENT ACTIVITY | LEARNING AIM | A

Choose two local enterprises that you can write about and compare. They need to be very different, so one might be a local micro enterprise and another a limited company.

- Describe, for each enterprise, its purpose and how it achieves this purpose.
- Now describe the characteristics of each enterprise, including the type of ownership, which goods or services it offers and how it delivers customer service.
- For each entrepreneur, describe their characteristics, including the mind-set and skills that they have.
- Explain how the characteristics of each enterprise and entrepreneur help them to be successful in what they do.
- Now choose one of the enterprises and analyse how the skills and characteristics of its entrepreneur(s) have supported its purpose, and make a judgement about how successful you think they have been overall in achieving what they set out to do.

You should include as many examples as you can from each of the enterprises to make your answer as clear as possible.

TIPS

When choosing your enterprise, do not forget you could choose an online business, one that has a physical outlet or both.

TAKE IT FURTHER

Look through your answers to check that you have made clear links between the characteristics and the success of the enterprise. There may be more than one characteristic that has helped the enterprise. See if you can link the two and make sure you include which characteristics you think were most important to the success of the enterprise, giving reasons for your answers, and examples, as much as possible.

Market research: anticipating and identifying what customers want

KEY TERMS

Customer needs are the wants or requirements a customer has for goods or services.

Market research is the process of gathering information about customers, including what they want and what they need – for example, the number of people who might wish to buy a product.

Stock is another word for the amount of goods an enterprise has immediately available for sale, without having to order more from its supplier.

LINK IT UP

To remind yourself about the challenges of attracting new customers, and how important it is to keep existing customers, go back to Learning aim A of this component.

Customers are vital to any business – without them, a business could not exist. It is, therefore, extremely important that an enterprise makes meeting the needs of customers (ensuring they are happy) one of its aims. One way of finding out about **customer needs** is through **market research**.

There are two key elements of customer needs that are important for any enterprise.

1 Working out in advance (anticipating) the needs of a customer.
2 Identifying the needs of a customer.

Anticipating customer needs

Anticipating customer needs means working out:

- how many customers are likely to buy from the enterprise
- the market the enterprise will be operating in
- when customers are likely to buy
- what customers are likely to buy.

For example, small enterprises have to forecast (judge) when they think sales of certain products will be highest and when they will be lowest. Judging these levels of demand means that the right amount of **stock** can be bought at the right time and at the right cost.

DID YOU KNOW?

Many retail enterprises start planning their Christmas sales about 18 months beforehand to make sure they have the right campaigns, plans and stock levels to get the highest profits. This means that planning for Christmas 2019 might begin as early as the summer of 2018!

ACTIVITY

In a small group, think about the information an SME would require to create its customer forecast if it were:

- an ice cream producer
- a car wash owner
- a dog kennel owner.

Write down three key points that each of these SMEs should focus on.

Identifying customer needs

An enterprise needs to think carefully about how many customers it has and when they are likely to buy something. It will also need to consider what its customers actually want and need.

- Working out what a person wants or needs, and providing it, is likely to lead to sales.
- Offering a customer something they do not want could mean the enterprise invests money in goods or services that will not sell. However, offering something a customer needs but did not previously know they wanted can be a good way of gaining their loyalty.

Identifying customer expectations

As well as establishing what customers want or need, it is also important for an enterprise to work out what customers expect to receive. Enterprises can often offer their goods and services in basic or more expensive versions – a customer who pays a higher price for something is likely to have higher expectations about the quality of the product or service. Knowing what customers expect means an enterprise can avoid there being a difference between what customers think they want and what they actually get. Failure to meet expectations is likely to lead to unhappy customers and create problems for the enterprise.

◻ An unhappy customer could damage the reputation of an SME

Offering value

Customers often want what is called 'good value'. This means they receive what they feel is good quality for the amount they have paid. This does not mean that it is the cheapest product; it means the customer believes the service or goods they receive is worth the money they have spent.

Responding rapidly to enquiries

Experiencing good customer service is also essential for customer satisfaction. This means enterprises should reply to any enquiries or complaints promptly and efficiently, to ensure customers feel they have been treated well. Customers are more likely to return to a business if they receive a quick response because:

- they feel they have been listened to
- the enterprise has shown it values them as a customer
- they have increased confidence in the enterprise.

If a customer does not get an answer, or feels they have not been listened to, they may choose to go to another enterprise, meaning potential future sales are lost.

◻ Figure 1.9: How long would you be prepared to wait for an SME to answer your queries?

Providing clear and honest information

Clear, truthful information is very important to customers. A customer is unlikely to buy from an enterprise again if:

- they do not understand what the enterprise is offering
- the goods or service do not match what they were expecting.

There are also legal reasons why enterprises need to make sure the descriptions and advertising of their products are accurate. If the information they provide is false or misleading, they could be:

- fined
- taken to court
- sent to prison.

ACTIVITY

Think about the needs of customers for an ice cream parlour, car wash or dog kennel. How could these be anticipated?

CHECK MY LEARNING

Explain the difference between anticipating and identifying customer needs. Discuss why each is important.

Market research and ongoing customer needs

A customer's needs do not end once they have bought a product. They may need to stay in touch with the enterprise for advice, repairs or even upgrades. This means enterprises need to continue thinking about customer needs, and ensuring they are happy, even after a sale has happened.

After-sales service

After-sales is the support an enterprise offers after the initial purchase or service has taken place. After-sales service can cover a range of things depending what the enterprise is selling.

Customer satisfaction

After-sales service can be as simple as contacting a customer to:

- find out how happy they were with the service or goods they purchased
- check if they can be helped in any way.

This could be done through one or more of the methods shown in Figure 1.10.

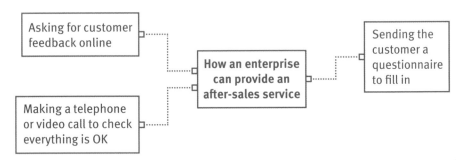

□ Figure 1.10: Can you think of any other kinds of after-sales services?

Some customers may decide to rate their satisfaction levels publicly online using a star system (with five stars being excellent and one star being very poor) or writing a short message about their experience. Receiving customer feedback in this way can act as a form of research that an enterprise can use to improve its services in the future.

ACTIVITY

SMEs do not always have a large budget to collect data about customer satisfaction.

1 Think about the potential benefits and disadvantages of each of these methods of evaluating customer satisfaction levels:
  - telephone calls
  - email questionnaires
  - questionnaires given out in person
  - website ratings
  - online chat forums
  - feedback on social media platforms
  - video calls
  - text messages.

2 Consider the SMEs below. Which of the methods above is most likely to suit each type of enterprise, and why?
  - IT consultant
  - fitness instructor
  - sweet stall on a market
  - cleaning business
  - ice cream producer.

Repairs or maintenance

For some goods, an enterprise may provide an after-sales service which offers repairs or maintenance. For example, a garage may offer:

- a free follow-up service for a car after purchase
- a discount on future work on the car.

Delivery information

For some products, an after-sales service can include:

- giving information about how and when the goods will be delivered after a sale has been made
- providing tracking information so that a customer knows what time of the day to expect delivery
- checking the delivery went smoothly, arrived on time and that the goods were not damaged in any way.

Guarantees

Sometimes an enterprise will offer a guarantee for a product. This is an agreement that it will pay for repairs for a specified amount of time after the sale, or even provide replacement goods in some circumstances. An enterprise may also offer an exchange of goods if:

- the goods are faulty
- a customer changes their mind within a certain number of days after purchasing.

DID YOU KNOW?

Customers have rights if they want to exchange goods or get their money back. The UK government sets out how enterprises must follow the law on its website (www.gov.uk). Search for 'Accepting returns and giving refunds: the law' to find out your rights as a customer.

Linking products to customers

Another way enterprises can meet customers' needs is by linking them to different types of products (goods or services) according to a range of factors, as Figure 1.11 shows.

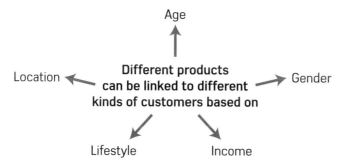

■ Figure 1.11: How do you think enterprises benefit from linking products to customers?

Matching a customer to a product according to these factors is very useful for enterprises. It enables them to:

- make sure they are communicating with the right types of customers
- advertise and promote their products in the correct places.

This prevents an enterprise from using time and resources promoting products that are not relevant to a certain category of customers, and decreases the likelihood that it will spend money on things it will not benefit from.

CHECK MY LEARNING

Name two ways that an enterprise can increase sales by offering customers good after-sales service.

LINK IT UP

To find out more about target markets and how this applies to a small enterprise, go to Learning aim A of Component 3.

Using market research to understand customers

Market research can be carried out in many different ways, some of which you have learned about already. Here, we will look at two important types of research that SMEs must consider before they start collecting data: **qualitative research** and **quantitative research**.

Qualitative research

Qualitative research can be very useful to an SME. This type of research collects information about ideas, feelings and thoughts on a particular product. The way the information is collected will depend on:

- the type of enterprise doing the research
- the resources available to collect the information.

For example, small enterprises may not have enough staff or time to collect research information easily. Table 1.4 shows how an enterprise could use this method of research.

Table 1.4: Methods of qualitative research and the data they produce

Method of research	How research data is collected and produced
An enterprise puts together a small group of customers to talk about their opinions or ideas about goods or services.	• Customers are asked for their permission to take part in this kind of research. • The enterprise collects data from written notes or a video of the group discussion. • The results of the group discussion are then analysed.
An enterprise interviews an individual customer to learn their views, thoughts and feelings about a service or goods.	• Consenting individuals (people who have agreed to take part) could be interviewed in person or over the phone. • The individual is often asked **open-ended questions**. • The enterprise takes notes on, or records, what the individual says. • The results are then analysed.
A potential customer is observed when they are buying goods or receiving a service.	• The enterprise observes the reactions of potential customers. • It considers how things could be changed to improve the customer's overall experience. • A set of notes is written up giving lots of description, which is then used for review.

ACTIVITY

1 In a pair, create a list of the types of qualitative information a small enterprise would find useful.

2 Working individually, explain how an enterprise selling each of the following products could collect qualitative information.
- Online cleaning products, where customers never visit the enterprise in person.
- Goats' cheese, where customers go to the farm to buy the cheese directly.
- Antique furniture, sold on a market stall every Sunday.
- Bread and cakes, sold from a small high street bakery six days a week.

Now discuss your ideas with your partner. Are your answers different from or similar to theirs?

ACTIVITY

1 Working in the same pair as the last activity, select a product that one of you has purchased in the past. Choose one person in your pair to be the interviewer and one to be the customer. Write a list of questions the interviewer could ask the customer about that product in order to get the best qualitative information.

2 Share your questions with the class, explaining your reasoning for including them.

Quantitative research

Quantitative research is more easily measured than qualitative research. This is because it is designed to provide a set of statistics. These statistics are used to:

- spot patterns
- identify trends.

Quantitative research has one major disadvantage: it can tell you how many times something happens, but not why it does so. Table 1.5 shows how an enterprise could use this method of research.

■ Table 1.5: Methods of quantitative research and the data they produce

Method of research	How research data is collected and produced
An enterprise compiles a survey or questionnaire about something specific for individuals to answer.	• Surveys are made available online, via email or in a hard copy format for individuals to fill in. • Questions are often 'closed', so that responses can be measured – for example, 'How many times...?', 'How often...?' and so on. • Data is gathered from the surveys or questionnaires, which will often show patterns or trends.
The enterprise interviews a range of individuals.	• Interviews can take place online, by phone or in person. • Questions are designed so that responses can be measured and compared. • Individuals could be asked to rate something – for example, 'On a scale of 1 to 5 (with 5 being high), how would you rate...?' • Data is gathered and information compared.
The enterprise collects statistics while observing customers.	• Customers are observed buying goods or using a service. • The enterprise notes down information on, for example, how many times a customer does something in particular. • It notes down anything else that can be measured. • It compares data between customers.

DID YOU KNOW?

Sometimes, researchers are only looking for a 'yes' or 'no' answer to a question. This type of question is known as a 'closed question'. If you fill in online questionnaires, you may notice that the questions are mainly 'closed'. They are likely to be short and, generally, do not ask about feelings or thoughts. Have a go at writing three closed questions that an enterprise might use when conducting research.

ACTIVITY

Find a set of statistics in a newspaper or on a website that would help an SME in your area.

1 Produce a graph of those statistics, either by hand or using a computer.

2 Explain what the quantitative data shows.

3 Note down how the data could be used by the SME to help them in the future.

CHECK MY LEARNING

Name two types of quantitative data and two types of qualitative data that an enterprise could use.

Primary research: questionnaires, visits and observations

Primary research involves collecting research directly from the customer. It does not use research collected or published by others. This type of research is considered 'first-hand' research.

Why primary research is important

Primary research is important for an SME, because it can:

- help the enterprise gain new customers
- gather information from existing customers about how they can be encouraged to stay loyal to the enterprise
- gather information from existing customers about how they can be encouraged to spend more money with the enterprise.

Primary research is collected first hand. In other words, it is collected by the enterprise itself. This gives the enterprise a source of important information about how it can:

- improve its overall performance
- continue to satisfy its customers
- create new markets
- increase its profits.

Primary research can have many benefits for an SME. However, it may also have some disadvantages, as Table 1.6 explains.

◻ Table 1.6: The benefits and drawbacks of primary research

Benefits of primary research for an SME	Drawbacks of primary research for an SME
• Helps an enterprise to hear the 'voice of the customer' • Tailored to the specific needs of the enterprise • Source and date of the data collection are known • Data is owned by the enterprise and may not be shared • The enterprise is in control of the research	• Can be expensive to collect • Can take a long time to collect • May not be accurate • May not include the right questions • May be biased (an enterprise may word questions to get particular answers in its favour)

As we have seen in previous lessons, primary research can be collected in several different ways – including online and offline. Nowadays, online research methods are frequently used because:

- the cost of collecting the data has reduced
- the process of collecting the data has become easier.

However, it can still be difficult to find enough of the right people (those who can provide the enterprise with the kind of information it seeks) to take part in the research.

Your assessment

Primary research methods that you need to learn about and apply to your assessment include:

- questionnaires
- visits and observations
- interviews and **focus groups**
- surveys.

In the rest of this lesson, you will learn about questionnaires, visits and observations. In the next lesson, you will learn about interviews and surveys.

Questionnaires

Questionnaires are commonly used by SMEs to ask both quantitative and qualitative questions. Questionnaires can be completed:

- on paper
- online.

Questionnaires are usually:

- given directly to customers when they are purchasing a product
- filled in with a customer in person
- completed over the telephone
- sent in the post.

Increasingly, questionnaires are linked to websites. They are often sent to customers through social media or by email.

Visits and observations

Visits or observations are another way of collecting primary research. Watching how a customer reacts to a product or how they use it in their home or business can provide an enterprise with a lot of data. For example, it can provide data on:

- how to improve a product
- how often a customer interacts with a product
- whether changes need to be made to meet customer expectations.

Visiting a customer or observing their behaviour provides information that could lead to higher sales. An enterprise might evaluate video recordings of customer behaviour in its shop to work out which product displays attract the most attention. It could then learn which products might require more promotion or advertising, in order to increase sales.

Consent

Customers should be asked for their consent if they are going to be observed. However, if they know they are being watched, it might influence how they behave. Therefore, a researcher needs to be very skilled to carry out this type of work. Enterprises use several different methods of gaining consent, including:

- putting up information messages
- distributing forms that customers read and then sign, to show they have agreed to take part.

For example, a business might display a sign telling visitors to its shop that market research is being carried out.

KEY TERM

Focus groups are group interviews during which people are asked for their views and opinions about different ideas that are suggested to them – for example, a proposal for a new product or enterprise.

DID YOU KNOW?

Questionnaires sent via email can be tracked by an enterprise. This means the enterprise will know how many people have opened it and when. This information helps an enterprise to find out more about its customers.

ACTIVITY

In a small group, discuss questionnaires. Use the questions below to guide your discussion.

1 How many of your group have completed a questionnaire?

2 What did it feel like for the person (or people) completing the questionnaire?

3 How truthful were they when responding?

4 Were the questions mainly open-ended or mainly closed?

5 How useful do you think the answers would be to an SME?

CHECK MY LEARNING

1 Write a definition of 'primary research'.

2 Describe at least two methods of primary research that an SME could use easily and cheaply.

Primary research: interviews, focus groups and surveys

GETTING STARTED

With a partner, make a list of all the different types of interview you have heard of. What type of information do you think an interview could provide as part of primary research?

In the previous lesson, you looked at how you can do primary research using questionnaires, visits and observations. The lessons looks at interviews, focus groups and surveys.

Interviews and focus groups

Do you like giving your opinions about things you have bought or intend to buy? Enterprises find this kind of information very useful. In fact, one method of collecting primary research is by interviewing people directly. Interviews with individuals or focus groups are designed to find out more about the views of those people.

Interviewing individuals

Individual interviews can take place with customers, prospective customers or even the general public, if the interviewer has permission to collect this information. Carrying out individual interviews can provide a lot of information about what specific individuals want from an enterprise. During these, people are encouraged to give their thoughts, views and opinions. These observations can be used by the enterprise to consider:

- what it does well
- what areas it could improve in
- the goods or services a customer might want to buy.

LINK IT UP

To find out more about the importance of recording interviews with individuals or focus groups, go to Learning aim A in Component 2.

ACTIVITY

Primary research can be expensive to collect. This is because an enterprise needs people to collect the research. It may also need certain materials or resources, such as the internet.

Write a list of the resources (people, materials and technology) an SME would need if it decided to collect primary research using interviews in person.

DID YOU KNOW?

Sometimes an enterprise will use a target group for its research. This means the enterprise has identified what it wants to know more about and the specific group of people who can provide that information. Factors such as the size of the target research group, and the gender, age or interests of the participants, depend on what the enterprise wants to find out.

Setting up focus groups

Focus groups are small groups of people who are brought together to give their views about something, such as a particular product or service. An enterprise can then use their views to decide what works successfully and what is less successful.

Focus groups can be carried out in person, at locations such as village halls or supermarkets. However, they can also be carried out online, using technology such as video calls or group messages.

Surveys

Surveys, like questionnaires, require customers, potential customers or members of a target research group to answer particular questions.

The difference is that questionnaires often ask about thoughts and opinions, as well as numerical information. Surveys tend to ask questions that only provide numerical information.

Paper-based or online?

Surveys can be filled in online or on paper. Table 1.7 gives more details about both of these.

◘ Table 1.7: The characteristics of paper-based and online surveys

Paper-based surveys	Online surveys
Can be given out in person or through the post	Can be added to a website or sent via email
Incur printing costs for the paper and ink	Have low costs of distribution but may take time to set up using the technology
Need to be added up or scanned to work out the total number of completed surveys	Can be tracked easily, and the responses can be evaluated as and when they are received
Tend to have a higher response rate (the number of people who fill them in) as they are harder to ignore – especially if a customer receives them in person	Tend to have lower response rates as they are easier to ignore
Can be targeted at specific individuals	Can be targeted at specific groups of people and their responses using technology – e.g. opening the email or starting the survey can be tracked

◘ What are the advantages and disadvantages of surveys like these?

Secondary research: online research and company materials

Secondary research is research that has been collected by someone else. It is research that already exists and has been bought or used by an enterprise to save time and money doing its own research.

Advantages of secondary research

The main advantages of secondary research include the following.

- The research already exists and is instantly available (so an enterprise doesn't need to take the time to carry it out itself).
- It is publicly available and is often free to use.
- Details of how the research was collected are often included. This can help the researcher to understand the challenges that were involved in collecting the data.
- Trends or ideas in a particular market can be seen through information that has already been published.

Disadvantages of secondary research

The main disadvantages of secondary research, and concerns relating to its use, include the following.

- It may not be possible to check the quality of the research.
- The questions that were asked may not be relevant for every enterprise.
- The research may be out of date or no longer relevant.
- The methods or sources may not be included or may not be reliable.

▣ Secondary research may be available at little to no cost; it can also help an enterprise find out more about potential customers

Online research

Online research using statistics, information or any other published material helps SMEs to find out more about their markets. Online research can involve:

- reviewing websites for ideas
- comparing statistics for sales or the use of a website
- carrying out searches to identify trends or themes in a market
- checking the use of particular words to see which ones are the most popular, as happens with AdWords
- reviewing information published online, such as prices or types of products, to compare them.

ACTIVITY

1 Carry out online research into the price of a pair of your favourite shoes or trainers. Do a search to see how many different websites have the item for sale – try to focus on those that are SMEs.

   a) Note the differences in price and marketing.

   b) Note the differences in the cost of sending the item or picking it up in store.

2 a) Write a mini review about the pricing of the pair of shoes or trainers.

   b) Explain your findings to other members of the class.

3 Carry out an online search for one of the following types of enterprise, or a type of your own choice, in your local area:

   - IT consultant
   - cleaning services
   - food stall.

   For the type of enterprise you have chosen, how many operate in your local area? What makes each one unique?

DID YOU KNOW?

When AdWords was first launched, there were about 20 million searches a day on Google. By 2017 the number of searches had risen to 3.5 billion a day.

Company materials

Materials that companies write about themselves, or the markets they operate in, are widely available online. These can provide a lot of useful information for an SME starting up or thinking about expanding. Enterprises can also use this material to find out as much as possible about their **competitors**. This kind of information could help an SME to work out if there are any gaps in the market that it could fill.

Many larger enterprises publish their accounts and other key information about their markets online. This can be beneficial to SMEs because:

- they can work out which markets the larger businesses are not operating in
- they can try to increase their sales within these markets.

KEY TERM

Competitors are businesses that sell similar goods or services to your enterprise. You should take their products into consideration when deciding things like pricing and target markets.

CHECK MY LEARNING

1 Write a definition for 'secondary research'.

2 Give two examples of how this kind of research can be carried out.

Secondary research: market reports, government reports and the media

GETTING STARTED

In pairs, write a list of the published information that would help you if you were thinking of setting up a small enterprise in your area providing dog walking services.

Reports that have already been published can provide enterprises with many types of research data that might be useful to them. For example, the UK government produces reports on the weekly prices paid for fruit and vegetables.

Market reports

Market reports can come from a variety of places.

- The type of report depends on who it is aimed at.
- Even articles in magazines give some information about a market – for example, different types of aftershave or lifestyle products.
- Some types of market reports give information about reviews that have been carried out on goods and services.
- Reports may also be produced by companies, such as Which?, that carry out reviews of goods and services. They then publish the reasons why customers like one product over another and make recommendations.

ACTIVITY

Access the Which? website (www.which.co.uk) and look at the type of market information available there.

1. What type of information is freely available on the site?
2. What kind of reports must be purchased from the site?
3. How could an SME use this information? How would it help that enterprise to meet the needs of its customers more effectively?
4. How do these reports affect customer behaviour?

LINK IT UP

To find out more about competitors, go to the next two lessons of Learning aim B.

Market reports can be a good way for an enterprise to learn about its competitors. For example, it can learn:

- how other enterprises behave in a particular market
- the influence other markets have overall.

DID YOU KNOW?

The company Mintel produces various types of marketing reports that are used by enterprises to find out more about different types of products and customers.

ACTIVITY

1. Access the Mintel website (www.mintel.com) and see what information you can access for free. Which types of reports must an enterprise pay to see?
2. How much do these reports cost?
3. How could this information help an SME to grow or support the needs of its customers?

Market reports can also be produced by industry regulators (organisations that protect consumers) or spokespeople for that industry. For example, the Specialist Cheesemakers Association offers information on the latest trends in cheese production that might be useful to a new enterprise selling cheese.

Reports in trade journals and magazines

Trade journals and magazines are produced for people and businesses working within a particular trade or market. They often contain reports and information that are useful and relevant for enterprises in that market or trade. For example, *The Grocer* magazine (www.thegrocer.co.uk) offers a wide range of reports and webinars (online seminars) giving information to small, independent retailers (sellers) about what is happening in different markets that affects them. One useful piece of information might be related to changing trends in the breakfast market.

▣ How do you think trade journals and magazines can help an enterprise?

Government reports

Government reports contain useful information that can:
- influence customer behaviour
- inform SMEs about the potential to grow their business in one area, or reduce it in another.

Government reports often show information about individual enterprises through the Companies House section of the UK government website (www.gov.uk). Here, accounts and other information about directors or company finances can be accessed. Reviewing financial information can help an enterprise find out more about the market it operates in.

Statistical changes

The government also publishes reports on changes that may affect enterprises and their markets. These include statistical changes that may help an enterprise now and in the future. For example, the Office for National Statistics (www.ons.gov.uk) publishes important data on population, incomes and lifestyles that may be relevant for an enterprise.

ACTIVITY

Choose a local SME, then access Gov.UK (www.gov.uk) and type 'Statistics' into the search bar.

1 Find out more about the market in which your chosen SME operates.

2 Find out more about markets in your local area.

3 Share your findings with a partner. How could the information you found be used to help your chosen SME?

Understanding competitors: price and quality

Most enterprises will have competitors – businesses that sell similar products or operate in similar ways. An enterprise will always need to keep an eye on what its competitors are doing, so that it is less likely to lose any of its own customers to them. In other words, a successful enterprise needs to understand its competitors and how it can use this information to improve itself.

Main features that make products competitive

Enterprises need to be competitive – they have to make sure their products can compete successfully with other similar products in the market. The main **features** that will help them to do this are shown in Figure 1.12.

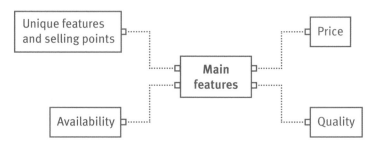

◼ **Figure 1.12: Why do you think these features make goods or services competitive?**

For the rest of this lesson, the focus will be on two of these features: price and quality.

Price

Pricing is one of the first ways a service or goods offered by different enterprises can be compared. Being the cheapest is not necessarily the best approach. Sometimes customers might decide to buy more expensive goods or services if they:

- offer the best all-round value
- have something that makes them stand out – a unique feature or **unique selling point**.

In fact, in some instances customers will avoid buying something if they think it is too cheap. They may feel that a low price indicates low quality.

GETTING STARTED

In a small group, think about why you would buy one type of mobile phone over another, if you had the choice. What makes each mobile phone different? Why do you prefer one over the other?

LINK IT UP

To remind yourself about competition and what makes one enterprise different from another, go back to Learning aim A of this component.

KEY TERMS

Features are aspects or elements of a service or goods.
Unique selling points (USPs) are features that make one product different from any other product.

LINK IT UP

To find out more about unique features or unique selling points, go to the next lesson of Learning aim B.

ACTIVITY

You may have heard the phrase 'Buy cheap, buy twice'. When people say this, it means they think that cheap goods and services will not last and will need to be replaced or purchased again.

1   In a small group, discuss whether you agree that buying cheap leads to having to buy again. You can use the following questions to help your discussion.

   a)   Have you had personal experience of buying cheap products and then finding they were not very good?

   b)   Have you ever paid a lot of money for something and then regretted it?

2   Consider how the idea of goods or services being 'too cheap' could affect the way an enterprise chooses its pricing.

Being too cheap

Most SMEs cannot compete with larger companies when it comes to costs. Often, they cannot sell their products as cheaply as a larger competitor. If they did, they would struggle to make a profit. This means they have to rely on other features to ensure that customers buy from them.

Being too expensive

It is also important for an SME to make sure its goods or services are not so expensive that people will not buy from it at all. The highest possible price that could be paid for a product is called the ceiling price. If an enterprise cannot make a profit on the ceiling price, it is not going to do well in the future.

Finding the best fit

Often, enterprises will need to consider the price being offered by competitors and then compare their own prices to see where they fit. This can be done by:

- completing a competitor analysis, where the enterprise considers all the other businesses offering similar goods or services
- comparing their prices to everyone they compete against
- finding out whether their prices are nearer to the top or lower end of that market.

> **LINK IT UP**
>
> To find out more about pricing and break-even analysis, go to Learning aim C of Component 3.

Quality

The quality of a product is another important feature that can encourage a customer to choose one over another. It is sometimes linked to price because it can be an indicator of:

- how long something might last
- the outcome of a service that has been received.

Measuring quality

A high-quality meal in an expensive restaurant is likely to be made from the best ingredients. A quality service, such as gardening, will offer the best results for the customer after the service has been carried out.

Often, potential customers use the internet to find out more about the quality of goods and services, based on ratings and reviews from previous customers.

> **ACTIVITY**
>
> Think of a product you would like to buy. Research prices for it on different websites.
>
> 1 What is the most expensive price and the cheapest price you can find for it?
>
> 2 List possible reasons why some websites might be offering it more cheaply than others.

> **ACTIVITY**
>
> Go to the TripAdvisor website (www.tripadvisor.co.uk). Search for a small or medium-sized independent restaurant in your area and look at the ratings for that restaurant. What do the reviews say? Do the opinions of the reviewers affect whether or not you would choose to go there? Why?

> **CHECK MY LEARNING**
>
> Give an example of when an enterprise might choose to compete on quality rather than price.

Understanding competitors: availability and unique features

GETTING STARTED

Imagine it is a sunny day today and you want to buy some new sunglasses. Unfortunately, the shop you'd prefer to buy from is out of stock and won't have any more sunglasses until next week. In a pair, discuss what you would do in this scenario. Then discuss how you think your decision would affect a small or medium enterprise.

Understanding how its competitors work will give an enterprise the information it needs to improve its own performance. The previous lesson looked at how the price and quality of products can help with this. This lesson will look at how availability and being unique can do the same.

Availability

As you will have seen from the 'Getting started' task, the availability of goods and services is extremely important to both customers *and* enterprises.

Availability of goods means:
- being in stock
- having a short or fast delivery time.

Availability of services means:
- being bookable at the time a customer wants
- being easy to book – for example, online through a website or by phone.

Will loyal customers wait?

The impact of availability on an enterprise depends on:
- the type of products they are offering
- the customers they attract.

Some customers are very loyal. This means they will wait for something to be offered by a specific enterprise or for goods to come through. Other customers might not see a reason to be loyal – if they are unable to get what they want on a particular day, then they will go to another enterprise to meet their needs.

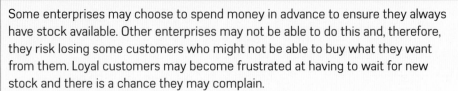

ACTIVITY

Some enterprises may choose to spend money in advance to ensure they always have stock available. Other enterprises may not be able to do this and, therefore, they risk losing some customers who might not be able to buy what they want from them. Loyal customers may become frustrated at having to wait for new stock and there is a chance they may complain.

1 Using this information, carry out research into:
   - the benefits for an SME of having high levels of stock available for customers to buy
   - the drawbacks for an SME of having high levels of stock available.
2 Think of examples where:
   - high stock levels of goods are essential for an SME
   - low stock levels are important. How could an SME ensure customers are not dissatisfied if they have to wait for their goods?

Goods that are made to order or are very large, like furniture, may not be held in stock by an enterprise. The time between a customer ordering an item like this and having it delivered is called the lead time.

◪ If your favourite supermarket had nothing to sell, would you wait until it got new stock?

Sometimes customers may be willing to wait for something – even if it takes several days or weeks. They may wait this long because they find it difficult, or even impossible, to get that product anywhere else. Services that fall into this category are called 'specialist services' and are often offered by smaller enterprises.

Unique features and selling points

Goods and services can both have features and selling points that make them unique. This might be a particular flavour of tea, a rare clothing material, or a service that is different from anything else you can find. Being unique means:

- offering something no other businesses supply
- being the only enterprise in the area selling a particular thing
- offering a new 'twist' on something people are already familiar with.

ACTIVITY

The Ambershop (www.ambershop.co.uk), in Suffolk, offers a unique experience. Customers can buy amber jewellery from the shop and visit the museum attached to the shop, free of charge. This small business offers specialist services providing advice about amber jewellery, while also selling amber goods in its shop and online.

1 In a pair, find out more about this shop and what makes it unique.

2 Think of an SME in your area that is the only one that sells a particular product. Why do customers choose to buy from it? What makes it unique and different from competitors?

3 Choose one product from this shop. Spend a few minutes thinking about it, then try to sell it to a partner. Make sure you emphasise what makes it unique.

Being unique can also mean taking something from one geographical area and introducing it to another – for example, classic French food in Southampton or a Lebanese bakery in Salisbury. Both of these might be unique in those areas because they offer types of food that no other local business does. The same is true for services. Can you think of any examples in your area?

If an enterprise is offering something that is unique, then it has more freedom when deciding at what level to set the price that customers must pay for that product.

LINK IT UP

To find out more about the importance of having a unique idea when you create your own micro enterprise, go to Learning aim A of Component 2.

DID YOU KNOW?

Tiny House® UK (www.tinyhouseuk.co.uk) makes very small houses that people can buy and live in. This enterprise's USP is the small size of its mobile houses and it has won awards for its designs.

CHECK MY LEARNING

'Having products available is essential for any enterprise.' In a pair, discuss whether you agree or disagree with this statement. You should give reasons for your thinking.

Identifying competitors

GETTING STARTED

Imagine you are setting up an ice cream parlour. List all the other places in your area where you can already get ice cream. These places would all be your competitors.

One of the key priorities of an enterprise is to identify its existing competitors. This will allow the business to make careful decisions about marketing, pricing and after-sales services, all of which can boost its profits and help the business be successful. Identifying competition will also provide information to help it stand out from others in the market.

Researching competitors

Before an enterprise launches, it is very important that it carries out research into its competitors. Using secondary research is a good way to do this. This can involve:

- looking online
- visiting the local area to see who is selling similar goods or services.

There are many different ways to collect information on competitors. One way is to produce a competitor analysis table (like Table 1.8 below), which shows how enterprises differ from one another.

ACTIVITY

1 Carry out research, using your own knowledge and the internet, on enterprises that sell second-hand furniture in your area. Compile a list. How many did you find? Which ones sell online? Which ones have a physical shop?

2 Write a statement for each enterprise about what it offers. Why do you think customers might choose to use each enterprise?

◻ Table 1.8: An example of a competitor analysis table

	Enterprise 1	Enterprise 2	Enterprise 3
Location			
Goods on offer			
Quality			
Price			
Reputation			
Opening hours			
Purchase online or offline			
Website/social media			
Type of customer			
Delivery charges			

ACTIVITY

1 You are about to put your first piece of secondary research on second-hand furniture sellers into action. In a small group, and using your list of second-hand furniture sellers, draw and fill in a competitor analysis table. You may need more than three columns for your enterprises, so adjust your table to fit your research.

2 Now, choose a service that is offered in your area and repeat this activity. You will need to change the questions in the table to fit the service you choose.

3 For both of your competitor analysis tables, try to identify any gaps in the types of goods or services that are on offer for customers.

   a) If there are gaps, could this be a market for an enterprise?

   b) If there are no gaps, how do the different enterprises make themselves unique? Which features do they have that persuade customers to keep returning?

Making products stand out

For any enterprise to be successful, it needs to do something to stand out in its market. This will encourage customers to purchase its goods or services.

◘ How do you think these chocolates stand out in their market?

ACTIVITY

Choccywoccydoodah (www.choccywoccydoodah.com) is a unique chocolatier operating in London and Brighton. This enterprise combines art with chocolate to create unique gifts and cakes that can be shipped all over the world. Its products stand out because they are very different from the goods that are offered by other chocolatiers.

1 Carry out research into the size of this enterprise and what it offers. Are all of its goods and services unique and unusual, or only some? Why do you think this business has been successful?

2 Now, think about goods and services on offer in your area.

a) Outline whether it would be possible to offer something as unique as Choccywoccydoodah in the area.

b) Select one product on offer near you. Create a mind map showing the skills, ideas and goals you would need to make this product stand out in its market.

CHECK MY LEARNING

1 Explain what is meant by:

- pricing
- competition
- unique selling point.

2 Explain one method you would use to research your competition.

Learning aim B: assessment practice

How you will be assessed

Now that you have studied the topics in Learning aim B, you will be able to show that you have explored market research, and that you know how it helps enterprises to meet the needs of customers and better understand customer behaviour.

You will now take what you have learned and carry out research into **two real local** small or medium enterprises. You will need to investigate how the two SMEs carry out their market research and how they are affected by customer behaviour.

CHECKPOINT

Strengthen

- What are customer needs and why are they important?
- Name two common expectations that customers will have of any SME.
- What is the difference between qualitative research and quantitative research?
- How can primary research methods be used to collect data?
- When is it useful to use secondary research and how is it used?
- Explain what is meant by the 'purpose' and 'aims' of an enterprise.
- Explain what is meant by 'USPs' and why these are important.
- What is a competitor?
- What is meant by 'competitor behaviour'?
- Give an example of when quality could be more important for a customer than price.
- Explain how having poor levels of availability impacts an SME, using examples from both goods and services to explain your thinking.

Challenge

- What is meant by 'good-value products' and why are they important to a medium enterprise?
- Give a judgement about the importance of after-sales service for a micro enterprise.
- Explain the importance of government reports to an enterprise owner when planning their market research.

ASSESSMENT ACTIVITY | LEARNING AIM | B

Choose two local SMEs that you can write about and compare. You will need access to information about their market research methods and findings, so ensure they are happy to share this data with you, whether this is online or through government statistics.

For each enterprise, describe:

- the type of market research information they collect and why they collect that information
- how those enterprises use this information to understand the needs of their customers
- how the enterprises use this information to understand the behaviour of their competitors.

For each enterprise, discuss how they use both primary and secondary research, and how market research methods are designed to find out as much as possible about the needs of customers (from both quantitative and qualitative data). Discuss how this research helps the SMEs to understand the behaviour of other enterprises they compete with.

Choose one of the enterprises and make a judgement about how effective its market research is for enabling it to understand the needs of its customers and the behaviour of its competitors.

Using as many examples as you can from each of the enterprises, produce a competitor analysis table to review the behaviour of competitors and make judgements about them.

TIPS

Make sure you choose two local enterprises that are going to be able to share their information with you. Remember, they must be small or medium enterprises.

TAKE IT FURTHER

Look through your answers to check you have:

- described all the market research methods used by the two enterprises
- discussed the reasons why you think those methods are appropriate (or not).

If you feel there are better methods for them to use, include this in your thinking. You may do this by comparing the methods your enterprises have used to methods used by their competitors.

TIPS

When choosing your enterprises, remember you could choose an online business, one with a physical shop, or both.

The impact of internal factors on costs: markets and customer satisfaction

GETTING STARTED

In a small group, think of an SME that used to offer products in your area but has now closed down. Discuss the factors that you think led to its closure.

'Costs' are everything an enterprise needs to pay for in order to produce, market and sell its products. Sometimes an enterprise can control its costs internally – as will be shown in this lesson and the next one. However, often costs are controlled or influenced by external factors, as will be discussed later on in this learning aim.

Understanding internal factors

Internal factors that affect costs can be controlled by an enterprise. These factors include, for example, how to understand the market it sells in and how to keep its customers happy. Happy customers lead to sales, which will balance out the costs an enterprise has.

Understanding the market

For an enterprise to be successful, it must understand the market it is operating in. It needs to know:
- what makes its products unique
- what its customers want.
- who its competitors are

LINK IT UP

To remind yourself of the creativity and innovation required by SMEs, and how important it is for an enterprise to understand its market to change for the future, go back to Learning aim A of this component.

ACTIVITY

1 a) In a small group, choose two of the following types of goods and services:
- handmade greeting cards
- dog walking
- recycling plastic or glass bottles
- pet photography
- second-hand books and DVDs
- ironing
- vintage clothing
- hair oil.

Make sure your group is considering different types to other groups.

b) Carry out some basic research on the rest of your class members to find out if there is a market among them for your two chosen goods or services. Use the questions below to help you.
- Would students in your class pay for any of these goods or services?
- If 'yes', how much would they be willing to pay?

2 a) Explain how you would work out the size of the market in your area and online for any of these goods and services.

b) Using the list above, discuss with your group which market for new customers you think would be the largest.

One way an enterprise can learn about its market is through research. This will help it to find out which customers may want the goods that are being offered and whether there is a competitor selling these already, either locally or online.

An entrepreneur can use secondary research as:
- a useful way of identifying competitors
- a method to ensure there is space in the market for another enterprise.

Researching the market

Properly researching its market and competitors will allow a business to keep its costs down by:
- avoiding spending money on ventures that are unlikely to be successful
- establishing how much it can expect customers to pay for goods or services, compared to how much it will cost to provide them.

LINK IT UP

To remind yourself of what secondary research is and how it works, go back to Learning aim B of this component.

For example, if an enterprise has an idea for a new product, researching to see whether similar products exist will mean it can judge the amount of potential competition before paying to produce goods.

Take a look at Figure 1.13, which shows a scenario where an entrepreneur might not have done sufficient research into their potential competitors.

■ Figure 1.13: Are all of these shops likely to survive in such a competitive market?

Keeping customers satisfied

Even in markets with a lot of competition (like the scenario in Figure 1.13), it is possible for an enterprise to succeed. As Table 1.9 shows, there are six ways an enterprise can outdo its competitors to keep its customers satisfied. This will help an enterprise to make a profit, manage its costs efficiently and be successful.

■ Table 1.9: Six ways an enterprise can outdo its competitors

1	Quality of product	Matching the quality of products to what customers are willing to pay is important. • If the quality is too low, the customer is unlikely to return. • If it is too high, the resulting higher price may put them off.
2	Price of product	Customers look for value for money. This does not always mean a product is cheap. It means the customer feels the product is worth what they pay for it.
3	Unique features and selling points	These are the elements that make the product different from what competitors are offering. Customers are often attracted by something that is new or different.
4	Customer service	Smaller enterprises can often provide more personal service or local knowledge.
5	Availability	Having products available at the right time can help to retain customers. • Customers who are unable to get what they want, when they want, may shop somewhere else if the product is widely available. • However, some customers may be prepared to wait if the enterprise sells something unique that cannot be bought anywhere else.
6	Convenience	Convenience could include: • offering a service in the evenings and at weekends, as well as during the day • having parking available close to the enterprise.

LINK IT UP

To remind yourself of how to compile a competitor analysis table, go back to Table 1.8 in Learning aim B of this component.

ACTIVITY

Think back to the first activity you did in this lesson.

1 Carry out research into the most popular market you identified.

2 Practise your skills at identifying the competition by producing a competitor analysis table. The information in your table will help you to answer the questions below.
   a) How much competition is there in your area?
   b) How much competition is there online?
   c) If this type of enterprise was established in your area, do you think it would be successful? Why?

CHECK MY LEARNING

Make a list of the reasons why an enterprise needs to understand its market.

The impact of internal factors on costs: planning, financing and marketing

The previous lesson looked at how an enterprise can control its costs through understanding the market and keeping its customers happy. This lesson examines how enterprises can manage their costs for planning, marketing and human resources.

Effective planning and financing

Many SMEs fail because they do not effectively plan how to produce and sell their product, even though the product itself may be a brilliant idea. This type of failure is due to internal factors – how the enterprise itself has operated – but can be avoided if the enterprise is willing to change how it works.

Effective planning

Effective planning includes:

- choosing how and when customer orders can be taken – for example, in person or online
- being organised in terms of time management and ensuring that stock is checked regularly
- making sure that bookings are placed correctly
- taking into account travelling time (for example, how long it takes to get from the office to a customer's home when offering a service such as dog walking) so that customers are not kept waiting.

Another way of planning is to work out how many customers want products at certain times of year – for example, for their summer holidays. Some services have high peaks in **demand** at certain points in the year and low demand at other times. An enterprise that plans for this can sell more products. It can also avoid:

- having *too much* stock at the wrong time of year, which could result in having to lower prices and, therefore, lose profit
- not having *enough* stock at the right time of year, which could mean losing out on sales and the opportunity to bring money into the business.

Effective financing

Planning the **financing** and how money flows into and out of an enterprise is also crucial for its success. Without money, an enterprise cannot buy the materials or stock it needs to trade and may have to close down. A business needs to consider how much it is spending, or will spend, on internal factors, including:

- paying staff their wages
- marketing and advertising.

These factors must be planned for and balanced against the money the enterprise is hoping to bring in.

Marketing and promoting the enterprise

Controlling marketing and promotion is another internal factor that an enterprise can manage itself. Some smaller enterprises do all of their marketing through word of mouth – see Figure 1.14.

Advertising and promotion can be very expensive. Smaller enterprises have to make sure the amount they are spending gives them value for money, by being effective in creating more customers and extra sales.

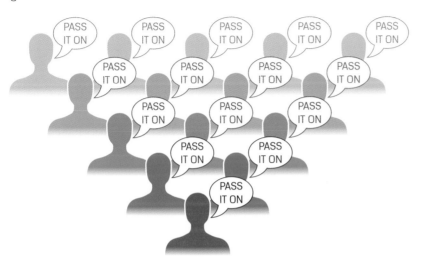

Social media platforms, such as Twitter and Instagram, make it possible for enterprises to advertise and promote themselves for free – for example, by sending out tweets or setting up feeds for customers to follow. It is also possible for enterprises to encourage customers to review and rate their goods or services online.

Unforeseen human resource costs

An enterprise always needs to have a **contingency plan** when it comes to human resources. In other words, it needs to:

- plan for the things it hopes will not actually happen – for example, a key member of staff being unable to work for several weeks because of illness
- have money available for unexpected costs – for example, having to pay someone else to help while the staff member is ill, while also continuing to pay the sick person's wages.

Sometimes a member of the enterprise's team may decide to leave their position for another job. If this happens, the enterprise will need to:

- advertise for a new team member
- ensure managers take time out of their busy schedule to interview new staff
- pay for any training requirements a new team member may have.

■ Why might an enterprise need to reduce the price of its summer products?

DID YOU KNOW?

Social media sites such as Facebook offer SMEs the ability to do 'cost per click' advertising. This means an enterprise only pays for an advert when a customer clicks to look at the products, meaning that this is a highly cost-effective method of advertising.

KEY TERM

A **contingency plan** is a back-up plan for when things go wrong for an enterprise.

LINK IT UP

To find out more about contingency plans, go to Learning aim A in Component 2.

ACTIVITY

Read the following review that a customer has left on a review website for a small café owner.

Terrible service (1 star)

We ordered our food and ended up waiting for over an hour. All the other customers got their food and when our order finally arrived it had items missing. Our table was dirty. We had no knives or forks, salt or pepper. Not one member of staff came to check we were OK. There was no WiFi available and the drinks were very expensive.

How do you think the business owner should respond?

CHECK MY LEARNING

List three reasons why effective planning is important for an enterprise.

The impact of external factors on costs

GETTING STARTED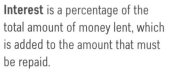

Sometimes an enterprise is affected by factors that are beyond its control. In a pair, think of three external factors that might affect any enterprise.

As you have learned, an enterprise can control the effect of internal factors. However, this is not the case with external factors. When an enterprise is affected by external factors, it will need to work out quickly how to overcome them.

What happens when costs change

Enterprises can be affected by many different factors that they will not be able to control. These factors can help them positively, or can have a negative effect. You have already learned that effective planning and contingency plans can help an enterprise to overcome the impact of internal factors, which are individual to that enterprise. However, external factors may end up having an impact on many enterprises. An example of this is a rise (or fall) in costs, which includes things such as:

- energy costs – gas, electricity and oil
- costs of raw materials – the items an enterprise needs to produce its product
- the cost of borrowing money – the enterprise may have a bank loan that it pays **interest** on
- rates of renting premises – the enterprise may pay an individual or organisation to use the space it works in.

The rising and falling of costs is known as **fluctuation**. Enterprises need to be prepared for costs to fluctuate and should understand the effects this might have.

Raw materials

Raw materials are all the elements that go into making goods or offering services. They include anything that is needed to create the products or services that you are going to sell. Think of a flower stall owner. Their raw materials would include:

- the flowers themselves
- water to keep the flowers in, so they do not wilt or die
- wrapping paper, to wrap flowers in when they are sold.

Counting the cost of raw materials

Raw material prices are important because if they go up, costs go up too. Enterprises will always aim to make a **gross profit**. If their costs increase, but the amount they charge does not increase as well, they will make less money. This means an enterprise needs to be able to make adjustments to its prices, if necessary.

KEY TERMS

Interest is a percentage of the total amount of money lent, which is added to the amount that must be repaid.

Fluctuation is variations such as rises and falls in prices or costs.

DID YOU KNOW?

The price of oil can change daily, according to supply and demand. If the global price of oil rises, then the cost of electricity is likely to rise (become more expensive). If the global price of oil drops, then electricity prices are likely to drop as well. Use the internet to find out how much oil costs today compared with yesterday.

KEY TERM

Gross profit is the money made from selling a product (sales revenue) after the cost of sales has been deducted. It is calculated before tax has been taken off – profit after tax is called net profit.

LINK IT UP

To find out more about gross profit and costs, go to Learning aim B in Component 3.

ACTIVITY

Imagine you are an entrepreneur making sandwiches. Your most popular sandwich is cheese and tomato and it sells for £1.50. To make each sandwich you spend: 10p on bread, 30p on cheese, 5p on butter and 20p on tomatoes. However, a recent global shortage of tomatoes means the cost has risen 25 per cent.

1 In a group, calculate:
   a) the gross profit each sandwich made before the cost of tomatoes increased
   b) the new gross profit each sandwich will make, due to the increase
   c) the difference this increase in cost of raw materials makes, per sandwich.

2 Discuss with your group what you should do about the increase in the cost of raw materials. List your ideas.

Borrowing

An enterprise can sometimes borrow money from a lender such as:

- a bank
- a building society
- an investor.

When an enterprise borrows money, it will pay an interest charge on the amount it has been lent. This is a percentage of the total amount of money, which is added to what it must pay back. However, interest rates can sometimes rise and fall, and these changes are beyond the control of an enterprise. They are external factors.

- If the interest rate goes down, then an enterprise will pay back less on the money it has borrowed (its **loan**).
- If an interest rate rises, then an enterprise will pay back more.

Premises

Many enterprises rent the space they work in. This means they pay an individual or an organistion for using their premises. Rent is often paid at least one month in advance. Like other external factors you have looked at, rent is often beyond the control of an enterprise. This means it can be raised by the owner, sometimes with very little notice.

Micro enterprises often trade from home to avoid these costs.

◩ If an enterprise's rent increases, why might it have to increase the price of its goods or services?

ACTIVITY

1 Carry out research to find examples of one of the following types of premises available for rent in your local area: industrial unit, retail shop or market stall.

2 Work out what would happen to an enterprise trading in each of these locations if it had the following increases in rent: one per cent, ten per cent and 20 per cent.

3 Discuss the questions below in pairs.
   a) How likely would it be that the enterprise would need to raise prices?
   b) What would happen if it did not raise prices?
   c) What might happen if it did?

LINK IT UP

To remind yourself of the impact of a USP and customer loyalty, go back to Learning aim B of this component.

CHECK MY LEARNING

Make a list of all the raw materials that you think would be used by a bakery and a cleaning enterprise. Compare them.

The impact of external factors: marketing, selling and regulations

As you have seen, fluctuations in costs are often external factors, beyond the control of enterprises, which can, nevertheless, have a big impact on them. This lesson looks at how marketing and selling are affected by rising costs, and what the law and regulations can mean for enterprises.

Changes in marketing costs

One of the vital tasks an enterprise will undertake is marketing its products. As with other costs you have read about, the costs of marketing and advertising may also rise. In these instances, enterprises will need to consider whether they can change how they do their marketing and advertising so that they can reduce costs. Generally speaking, enterprises will use the following sources to do their marketing. Some of these cost a lot of money, some are low cost and some are free:

- advertising on social media platforms
- advertising on other websites such as eBay
- using a blog
- flyers and brochures
- newspaper/magazine advertising
- vehicle advertising
- radio advertising
- email shots or campaigns
- trade shows
- business cards.

An increase in price for any these marketing methods will affect the the enterprise's gross profit.

Changes in selling costs

Costs of selling a service or goods can include the following.

- Paying the wages of everyone who helps to run an enterprise – even if an entrepreneur is the only person running a micro enterprise, they will still need to take a salary.
- Delivering the goods – for example, packaging and postage or courier costs.
- The cost of travelling – an enterprise delivering a service to the home (for example, a gardener) will need transport. Travelling costs include the transport itself, vehicle insurance, fuel and general maintenance of the vehicle.

Changes in government regulations

Some increases in price, such as the cost of motor insurance, happen because of an overall increase in the number of accidents. In these instances, the motor insurance industry has to pay by raising its charges. This means that buyers of insurance then have to pay more.

At other times, the UK government makes changes, usually on a yearly basis, to **regulations** that can increase the costs an enterprise must pay. Here are two examples.

Example 1:

The government sets an hourly rate on the minimum amount of money a business must legally pay its staff. When this amount rises, an enterprise will need to find the extra money to pay its staff the correct amount.

Example 2:

From 2018, the General Data Protection Regulations mean that businesses must store the personal data of their customers correctly to keep it safe. Setting up the new data protection system could cost an enterprise extra money. However, it will need to pay this cost in order to avoid breaking the law – if a business does not comply with this regulation, it could face a fine or the owner could be given a prison sentence.

> **DID YOU KNOW?**
>
> Employees younger than 25 are legally entitled to a minimum hourly wage. Employees over 25 are legally entitled to the National Minimum Wage. Use the internet to find out what both of these amounts are.

> **LINK IT UP**
>
> To remind yourself of how politics and social pressure as a whole can affect the way an enterprise operates, go back to Learning aim A of this component.

◻ Figure 1.15: All employees aged 25 and over should be paid the National Minimum Wage under government regulations

Changes in taxation

A third example of how government regulations can affect an enterprise is a change in **taxation**.

Governments set the amount of tax that is paid. This amount can change from one year to the next.

- An enterprise can generally earn a small amount of money without paying tax on it. This is known as an allowance.
- The enterprise then pays tax on everything above this amount.
- Enterprises and entrepreneurs pay National Insurance contributions on behalf of their employees and for themselves. National Insurance contributions go towards paying people's pensions when they retire and covering medical expenses provided by the NHS.

As with all the other cost increases you have learned about, any changes made by the government will eventually find their way to the customer. In other words, when a cost is raised, the fees an enterprise charges have to be raised to pay for it.

> **KEY TERM**
>
> **Taxation** is the amount of money an enterprise or entrepreneur must pay the government each year. Enterprises and entrepreneurs are taxed on the amount of money they earn from running their business.

> **ACTIVITY**
>
> When direct taxes such as value added tax (VAT) increase, an enterprise has to pay higher costs for its raw materials or energy. This means that the price increase needs to be passed on to customers, via higher charges, or there needs to be a smaller difference between revenue and costs.
>
> With a partner, consider the following questions.
>
> 1 What happens if the cost of raw materials goes up very quickly, at a time when customers cannot afford to pay higher prices?
> 2 If there is a VAT reduction, should an enterprise pass this saving on to the customer? If not, what else could it do?

> **CHECK MY LEARNING**
>
> Write a list of as many costs as you can think of that an enterprise has to pay. Consider what might happen to the enterprise if every one of these costs increased.

The impact of external factors on revenue

'Revenue' is how much an enterprise earns from selling its goods or services. Just like costs, this income can also be affected by external factors that an enterprise cannot control.

Changes in revenue

Changes in revenue happen when the amount of money an enterprise receives goes up or down because of something happening outside the enterprise. It is not always possible for an enterprise to stop or influence others making changes. However, how it responds to changes is very important.

Competitors

As well as having to consider rising costs and how this impacts on the price of products, an enterprise needs to know what its competition is doing. This might be:

- existing competitors the enterprise already knows about
- new enterprises coming into the market.

A new enterprise can have an impact on an existing enterprise by attracting its customers – for example, by running promotions or special offers that are appealing. Existing competitors may also decide to run special offers to try and gain customers from other businesses.

Competition can sometimes become very fierce and turn into a price war, with enterprises trying to outdo one another by offering the lowest possible price. This could lead to problems, or even failure for some of the enterprises, because lower prices mean lower revenue for the businesses involved. Reduced revenue will affect cash flow and can leave businesses struggling to pay bills. Figure 1.16 shows what can happen in a price war.

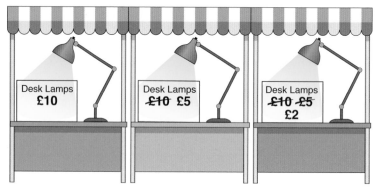

◻ Figure 1.16: Can you think of any recent price wars that have been in the news?

Consumer confidence

Consumer confidence means the confidence that existing and potential customers have in the UK **economy**.

If the economy is experiencing **growth** (doing well) and most people have jobs, consumers are likely to:

- feel confident about the future
- spend their money – which leads to increased sales for enterprises.

If the economy is experiencing a **recession** (doing badly) consumers are likely to:

- lose confidence about the future
- worry about whether their jobs are safe
- only spend money on essential things, which can lead to lower sales for enterprises.

DID YOU KNOW?

Some products are affected by consumer confidence more than others. During a recession, when confidence is low, expensive and luxury products such as jewellery sell less well. However, during growth periods, when confidence is high, sales of luxury goods increase.

Consumer behaviour

Consumer **tastes** can have a big impact on sales. For example, trends in fashion can show what is and what is not popular at a certain time. Many consumers will not buy things that are not 'on trend'. This is a form of social pressure that can affect many kinds of enterprise.

An enterprise may open a new business when consumer demand is high for a particular product – for example, an electronic gadget that everyone wants. However, when consumer tastes change, and the gadget is no longer popular, the enterprise will either have to change and adapt, or risk failing.

ACTIVITY

Between 2010 and 2012, there was a high demand for fish spa treatments. Many salons opened all over the UK and they became very popular. However, this trend only lasted for a short amount of time.

1 Working individually, find out more about fish spa treatments, why they became popular and why they closed again.

2 In a group, create a list of any other enterprise ideas you can think of that started, were very popular and then closed due to loss of popularity.

Consumer legislation

The final external factor that can have an impact on revenues is any change in **legislation**. Sometimes things that have previously been allowed are:

- banned – they are no longer permitted to exist
- changed in terms of how they can be used or sold – for example, how goods can be packaged
- changed in terms of how they can be advertised or promoted.

Such bans and changes can have a considerable impact on sales. Customers may stop buying something because of a change in the way it is labelled or displayed. Similarly, if a product is banned, it becomes illegal to buy or sell it without facing serious consequences.

CHECK MY LEARNING

Explain the difference between consumer confidence and consumer behaviour. Give one example of each.

KEY TERMS

Economy is the system by which a country's money and goods are produced and used.

Growth is when the number and value of goods and services produced in an economy is going up. This usually results in consumer confidence.

Recession is when the number and value of goods and services produced is going down. This may be followed by a lack in confidence and people buying less because they are concerned about the future.

Tastes are the trends or fashions that a consumer may follow, relating to what they like, dislike and are interested in.

Legislation relates to the laws of a country, which everyone must obey.

LINK IT UP

To recap your knowledge about social pressures influencing enterprises, look back at Learning aim A of this component.

DID YOU KNOW?

In the UK, tobacco goods can no longer be publicly displayed and their packaging has been changed. In 2007, the legal minimum age to buy cigarettes was also increased from 16 to 18. These changes were made to try to discourage customers from buying them.

Understanding situational analysis: SWOT

GETTING STARTED

List all the internal and external factors you can think of that can affect an enterprise. Compare your list with others in the class.

Situational analysis literally means the process of analysing (or studying) a situation. An enterprise that uses situational analysis will be able to study its position in the market, and assess how it could be affected by trends and developments.

SWOT analysis

There are two common tools an enterprise can use to help it make a situational analysis. The first one is known as SWOT and the second is known as PEST. In this lesson, you will look more closely at SWOT.

SWOT stands for:

Strengths

Weaknesses

Opportunities

Threats.

How to carry out a SWOT analysis

An enterprise will be able to use a SWOT analysis when it has identified all the internal and external factors it needs to review (much like you did in the 'Getting started' activity). The analysis will help the enterprise to make judgements on how each factor can have an impact on it.

A SWOT analysis can be made using a table like the one shown in Figure 1.17. The enterprise lists all the internal and external factors it has identified and decides whether they are strengths, weaknesses, opportunities or threats. Here are some examples.

Strengths

Strengths are things the enterprise is very good at. They could include:

- maintaining a high number of customers
- having a good reputation
- offering quality service.

Weaknesses

Weaknesses are areas where the enterprise needs to improve. Examples of these could include:

- lack of training provision for staff
- not enough resources that would improve trade
- goods or services that are not selling as well as others.

Opportunities

Opportunities are developed from both the strengths and weaknesses of the enterprise, and aim to set out ways that the enterprise can consider new areas or aspects to improve on. If a product is not selling well, there is an opportunity to offer a different one or consider stopping selling it altogether. If an enterprise is good at something, an opportunity could be to start selling in a new location or to new customers.

Threats

Threats are anything that is likely to prevent the enterprise from being successful. Examples include:

- changes in customer taste
- new competitors entering the market
- existing competitors changing what they are doing or increasing their marketing
- existing or new competitors lowering their prices to negatively affect the enterprise.

DID YOU KNOW?

A SWOT analysis can be applied to every type of SME. It is often included in business plans when considering the future of the enterprise. SWOT analysis could be used to think about specific areas of the business that might require extra finance, or to consider ideas for marketing. (A business plan generally also includes information about finances, marketing and human resources.)

The café in Figure 1.17 lists many more strengths and opportunities than it does threats, which suggests the enterprise is doing well. It looks as though it currently has a **competitive advantage**. If an enterprise has too many weaknesses or threats, it is likely to be at a disadvantage and will need to do something to change its situation.

One thing all enterprises need to remember is that a SWOT analysis is only useful if it is done regularly and updated to show any changes that have happened. If a SWOT analysis is out of date, it will not be helpful going forward.

Strengths	Excellent customer service. Very loyal customers. 5 star hygiene rating from local council. Experienced staff working at the café for more than two years. Only café on the high street offering scones and jam. Good reputation locally. Excellent advertising with a local magazine, with high take-up of special offers and vouchers. Value for money prices.
Opportunities	Increase the number of tables in the café by taking over the empty shop next door. Increase the number of tables by rearranging the furniture to make best use of space. Recruit another weekend cook to reduce waiting times. Include new types of cakes and pastries to increase the number of customers.
Weaknesses	Not enough tables available on a Saturday morning, due to high numbers of customers. Waiting times can be 30 minutes at busy times, due to having only one cook.
Threats	The empty shop next door may be taken by another café and this could affect customer numbers. A new restaurant is opening at the other end of the high street and this may affect trade. Other cafés may start offering scones and jam.

◻ **Figure 1.17:** A completed SWOT analysis for a small café. How well do you think this enterprise is doing?

ACTIVITY

1. In a small group, choose two local enterprises you know well that are in very different industries. Complete a SWOT analysis for each enterprise, making sure you include as much information as possible.

2. When your SWOT analysis is complete, share it with another group to exchange ideas and compare what you have found out.

KEY TERM

Competitive advantage is the advantage gained by offering superior goods or services to those of competitors or offering cheaper prices.

CHECK MY LEARNING

Write out what SWOT stands for. Then note down briefly why it is important for an enterprise to use this tool regularly.

Understanding situational analysis: PEST

GETTING STARTED

Think about all the political, economic, social and technological aspects you have learned about that affect enterprises. List as many as you can remember, then share your list with others in your class to create a class mind map of all these factors.

LINK IT UP

To remind yourself about political and social pressures, go back to Learning aim A of this component.

LINK IT UP

To remind yourself about external factors, go back to the lessons 'The impact of external factors on costs', 'The impact of external factors: marketing, selling and regulations' and 'The impact of external factors on revenue' in this learning aim. These can all be used to form a PEST analysis.

The previous lesson looked at how an enterprise can benefit from using a situational analysis tool called SWOT. Now you will take a look at a situational analysis tool known as PEST.

PEST analysis

PEST stands for:
- **P**olitical
- **E**conomic
- **S**ocial
- **T**echnological.

An enterprise will be able to use a PEST analysis when it has identified all the internal and external factors it needs to review. This analysis will help the enterprise to make judgements on how each factor identified can have an impact on it. Many of the factors identified in a PEST analysis are likely to be external.

How to carry out a PEST analysis

A PEST analysis can be made using a table like the one shown in Figure 1.18. The enterprise lists all the factors it has identified and categorises them as either political, economic, social or technological.

Political

Political influences include:
- any changes or factors happening with government policies and laws
- any changes in government, such as a new leader of a political party being appointed
- the effect of pressure groups
- the effect of wars
- the effect of taxation
- the effect of changes in the environment
- relationships with other countries
- factors relating to the European Union (EU), especially as the UK undergoes the process of leaving it.

Economic

Economic means factors that relate to the economy as a whole, such as:
- employment levels
- exchange rates, which can change the price of raw materials
- wage levels
- interest rates, that enterprises may have to pay for loans
- the amount of money people in the UK have to spend.

Social

Social is anything to do with lifestyles, cultures and how people spend their time. This could include:
- changes in trends and fashion
- ethical concerns – for example, buying Fairtrade goods

How do you think apps to book a table at a restaurant could help an enterprise?

- environmental concerns – for example, the impact some products can have towards climate change
- welfare concerns – for example, thinking about how farm animals are cared for
- customer demographics - for example, their typical age and whether or not that age group is increasing, gender and potential growth of that gender in purchasing
- attitudes towards work and jobs affecting income
- education - the level of education of customers and how this affects sales.

Technological

Technology changes all the time. Enterprises need to consider how technological changes might affect them in the future and what they can do to keep up with these changes. Technological factors include:

- developments in computers and the internet
- developments in mobile technology, such as smartphones
- the introduction of machines to replace human workers, such as self-service checkouts in supermarkets
- increases in the amount of online buying.

Some of these factors might overlap and fall into more than one category – for example, an increase in the purchasing of eBooks could be due to both technological and social changes. It is important for enterprises to be aware of all of these kinds of changes and how they might affect their business.

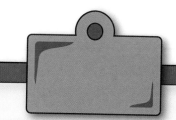

Political
- Small business grants are being given to local enterprises if they take on more staff.
- Tax increases are predicted in the next 6 months.
- The National Minimum Wage is increasing in the next 12 months.
- A ban is being considered on the car wash soap that is being used by the majority of car washing businesses because there are concerns about some of the ingredients in it.

Economic
- Unemployment is going down so more people are in work and likely to have their cars washed.
- The cost of sponges and cleaning materials is rising as they are imported; the exchange rates mean that the value of the pound is going down, so imports are more expensive.
- Interest rates on the loan to set up the business are going down, so the payments will be lower.

Social
- Local people are earning more money as unemployment is lower and demand for car washing is going up.
- More people in the area have higher levels of education and better paid jobs. They want their cars washed at the weekend so they can spend their time on other leisure activities.

Technological
- An app has been developed to allow drivers to book a time for the car wash instead of sitting and waiting. A competitor has started to use this app.
- Waiting customers are asking to be able to link to WiFi and wish to have access to online movies or gaming while their cars are being washed.

◘ Figure 1.18: A completed PEST analysis for a car wash business. What does this enterprise need to think about for its future?

Reasons an SME is successful

GETTING STARTED

Think back to the start of this component and the aims that all enterprises have. Write a list of those aims. How many can you remember?

As you will have seen throughout this component, there can be many reasons for the success, or failure, of an SME. However, the main reasons come from the aims it sets out to achieve.

LINK IT UP

To remind yourself about setting objectives and aims in order to achieve something, go back to Learning aim A of this component.

Top four aims

Many SMEs have common aims. The top four are:

- surviving
- breaking even
- making a profit
- meeting customer needs.

In this lesson, you will take a look at each of these in turn.

Surviving

Survival means continuing to operate for a long time – four to five years is a common benchmark – after the enterprise started. About 90 per cent of small businesses survive their first year. However, after five years many of these enterprises begin to struggle. Generally, only 40 per cent will still be running at this point.

Breaking even

Breaking even is the point at which an enterprise can evenly balance its costs and revenue. The enterprise is not making a profit, but it is not making a loss either. For some new enterprises just getting to this point is a success, especially if they are in their early years and hoping to build up a customer base for the future.

ACTIVITY

Think back on what you have learned so far about the reasons why enterprises fail.

1 In a small group, discuss why you think enterprises are able to survive for one year but might struggle or fail after five years. Consider cash flow, competition, reputation, industry and other factors you have come across in this component.

2 Share your thoughts with other groups to create a class mind map outlining your ideas.

LINK IT UP

To learn more about how to work out break-even, and the calculations of costs and revenue that relate to this, go to Learning aim C of Component 3.

Making a profit

An enterprise will generally want to make a profit. Profit is the amount of money left over after all the costs have been taken away from all of the revenue (income). Making a profit is an essential measure of success for most privately owned enterprises. In fact, it is the key reason many enterprises trade. For social enterprises, this profit is called a surplus. The surplus is reinvested in the venture or given to charity in order to help causes the enterprise feels are important.

LINK IT UP

To remind yourself of the different ownership types and how they are defined, go back to Learning aim A of this component.

LINK IT UP

To remind yourself how enterprises can satisfy the needs of customers, go back to Learning aim A of this component.

Meeting customer needs

A further measure of success is that customers are happy and satisfied. Meeting the needs of customers ensures they remain loyal to the enterprise and keep buying from it.

Reasons for the success of SMEs

As well as thinking about their original aims, SMEs are often successful due to hard work, high levels of resilience and **perseverance**. Take a look at Figure 1.19, which offers some more reasons.

KEY TERM

Perseverance is not giving up and continuing to work at something, despite difficulties encountered along the way.

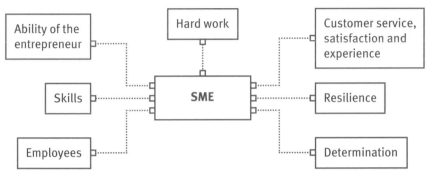

◘ Figure 1.19: A combination of many different elements will increase an enterprise's chance of success

ACTIVITY

1 Choose three successful micro or small enterprises in your area. Try to answer these questions about each one.
   a) What makes these enterprises successful?
   b) Why do customers use them?
2 Check against each of the elements in Figure 1.19 to see what each enterprise does that matches these areas of success.

Maintaining success

Even when an SME reaches a point at which it considers itself a success, it will need to continue working hard to ensure it stays that way. Some methods of maintaining success are shown in Table 1.10.

◘ Table 1.10: How an SME can maintain success

Area	Maintaining success
Motivating, developing and training employees	Employees in smaller enterprises often have more responsibility and are relied on to help the business grow. Motivating them and making sure they have the highest level of training are key reasons for success, now and in the future.
Customer service and satisfaction	Good customer service helps any enterprise to be successful. An SME should continue to monitor its customer service and satisfaction to keep it at a high level.
Experience of operating in that market or similar markets	Enterprises that are successful often have experience of working in the market. An entrepreneur may already have had market experience before they joined the enterprise, and so bring this knowledge to the role. Staying in touch with how the market(s) operate, and being aware of any new or potential changes, will help the SME in the future.

CHECK MY LEARNING

Explain the difference between breaking even and making a profit. Then explain why this difference is important.

Measuring the success of an SME

Knowing what success means is just one part of being successful. Being able to measure success will allow an enterprise to understand what it does well, any changes it might need to make and what it should endeavour to do in the future.

Methods of measuring success

There are six key ways in which success can be measured, as Figure 1.20 shows.

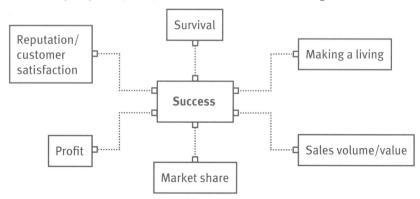

◘ Figure 1.20: How do you think measuring success in these six key ways can help an enterprise?

Method 1: survival

Measuring survival is based on the number of years an enterprise has traded. You have already learned in an earlier lesson that the first five years of business are usually the most challenging. The longer an enterprise trades for, the more successful it has been.

Method 2: making a living

You have learned about the many reasons why an entrepreneur starts up their business. Often, one of their main goals will be to create a comfortable and happy life for themselves and their family. Being able to provide for the family and make money shows the enterprise is a success.

Method 3: sales volume/value

The number of customers and value of those customers are also measures that demonstrate success.
- The sales volume is the *number* of sales that have been made. These can be measured through the number of customers or transactions taking place.
- The value is the *amount* each customer spends. The higher the value, the more likely it is that the enterprise is doing well.

Enterprises often have the objective of increasing the value of sales per customer. This is one way to be even more successful. It is often easier to encourage a customer who already knows the enterprise to spend more, rather than trying to gain a new customer.

Method 4: market share

Market share is the percentage of a market that an enterprise controls. For example, if an enterprise has £10,000 worth of business per year of the car washing market, in an area where the market is worth £100,000 a year, they have ten per cent of that market.

◘ How could you gauge this enterprise's success?

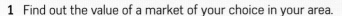

ACTIVITY

1 Find out the value of a market of your choice in your area.

2 How large is that market?

3 How many enterprises operate in that market?

4 Work out the market share that each enterprise has.

DID YOU KNOW?

According to the Management Consultancies Association, the management consultancy market in the UK is worth around £10 billion and, of this, 28 per cent is technology consultancy.

Method 5: profit

Measuring profit shows the success of an enterprise. There are many different **liquidity ratios** you need to know to be able to measure this. As profits go up, the enterprise is demonstrating success.

However, it is also important for it to have enough cash available. An enterprise can sometimes find itself in a situation where, even though it is making healthy profits in the long term, there is not enough cash in the bank in the short term. This would usually be because it has had to pay for things like raw materials and the energy needed to run the enterprise before its customers have paid for their goods or services.

LINK IT UP

To find out more about the many different ways to measure liquidity and profitability, go to Learning aim B of Component 3.

KEY TERM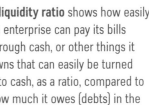

A **liquidity ratio** shows how easily an enterprise can pay its bills through cash, or other things it owns that can easily be turned into cash, as a ratio, compared to how much it owes (debts) in the next year. Cash and debts should be at least equal or, ideally, there should be more cash available than debts; for example, 2:1.

Method 6: reputation/customer satisfaction

Measuring customer satisfaction and the reputation of the enterprise can help an SME to work out if it is successful or not.

- If the enterprise is doing well, it is likely to have a good reputation and customers will tell their friends and family to buy there or use its services.
- If customers are unhappy and tell others, it may lead to them avoiding the enterprise. This could lead to sales going down and cause serious problems for the business.

LINK IT UP

To remind yourself of the methods that could be used to collect primary and secondary research on how customers feel about products, go back to Learning aim B of this component.

ACTIVITY

1 In a pair, choose a local enterprise. Produce a survey, or other method of collecting primary research, to measure customer satisfaction for that enterprise and think of a way to measure its reputation.

2 With your partner, use your survey to collect data about the enterprise. Share your findings with your class.

3 As a class, discuss the following questions.
   a) How easy was it to do this task?   b) How useful was your data?

CHECK MY LEARNING

List three different methods of how an enterprise can measure success. Explain how an enterprise would know whether or not it was successful from these methods.

Learning aim C: assessment practice

How you will be assessed

Now that you have studied the topics in Learning aim C, you will be able to show that you understand the many different internal and external factors that affect whether or not an enterprise is successful.

You will take what you have learned and explain the ways in which internal and external factors are important for all enterprises. You will then do the same for one enterprise in particular. For your chosen enterprise, you will need to analyse how these factors have helped to influence or determine the success of that enterprise. You will make judgements, based on your findings, about how these factors are currently affecting that enterprise.

CHECKPOINT

Strengthen
- Name two internal factors that affect the success of an enterprise.
- Name two external factors that affect the success of an enterprise.
- State what is meant by unforeseen human resource costs.
- List the ways that an enterprise can be affected by changes in the cost of energy or raw materials.
- Explain two changes that a government can make that can affect the success of an enterprise.
- Give an example of how consumer confidence can positively affect an enterprise's success.
- Explain what is meant by a SWOT analysis and a PEST analysis.

Challenge
- Explain why high levels of resilience might be more important than experience for an SME.
- Give a judgement on how useful measuring market share would be to an SME in a very large industry.
- Explain what is likely to happen if an enterprise develops a reputation for having poor availability of stock and poor customer service.

TIPS

Make sure you choose an enterprise you know well, as you will need to complete a PEST analysis and a SWOT analysis to help you make judgements about success.

ASSESSMENT ACTIVITY | LEARNING AIM | C

Choose one enterprise that you are going to research in detail and think of other examples that you can write about. Remember, the enterprise you choose needs to be a small or medium enterprise.

In the earlier part of this assessment activity, you should include as many examples as you can from enterprises to make your answer as clear as possible. However, in the later stages of your work, you should focus much more specifically on your one selected enterprise.

- Identify what is meant by internal and external factors and the difference between them.
- Describe the internal and external factors that are important for an enterprise's success, in general. Ensure you include why these factors, both internal and external, are important. Where you can, provide examples from your learning to explain your answers.

Now, apply what you are explaining to one selected enterprise. You need to be able to analyse how and why the internal and external factors have led to the success of that enterprise in particular.

- Apply the PEST analysis and the SWOT analysis to help you make judgements about these factors.
- Give a judgement about the most important internal and external factors that are currently affecting that enterprise. Explain the impact these are having on the success of that enterprise.

TIPS

Remember, throughout your assessment activity, you should include several examples of businesses that you have learned about on your course to help make your answers as clear and well explained as possible.

TAKE IT FURTHER

Check through your answers to make sure you have looked clearly at the measures for success and how they were chosen by that enterprise. Knowing what the enterprise set out to do, and then measuring if it has achieved or exceeded expectations, will help you to make a judgement about its success.

02 Planning for and Pitching an Enterprise Activity

Introduction

The BBC TV show *Dragons' Den* has brought the challenges and the triumphs faced by entrepreneurs into sharp focus. Could you be a dragon in the den in years to come? How will you have made your fortune and what types of enterprise would you invest in?

In this component, you will have the opportunity to plan and pitch your own business enterprise. What type of business have you always dreamed of owning? Do you have what it takes to be a successful entrepreneur?

You will learn how successful entrepreneurs and innovators need to have not only great ideas, but also the ability to develop strategies to put these ideas into practice. Turning an idea into a reality is a challenge. You will find out how enterprises must plan how to gain and make the most of physical, financial and human resources.

You will also build on the research knowledge gained in Component 1 to develop, plan, pitch and evaluate a micro enterprise of your own. You will need to come up with an idea, plan its set up and funding, and then pitch your plan to an audience. This will involve improving your communication, co-operation and problem-solving skills. Even well-planned ideas can have setbacks, so you will need to monitor your progress and think of solutions to problems as they arise.

Finally, after pitching your plan, you will reflect on your pitch and performance. This is a great opportunity to consider your skills and strengths, and identify areas for improvement.

LEARNING AIMS

In this component you will:

A	Explore ideas and plan for a micro-enterprise activity
B	Pitch a micro-enterprise activity
C	Review own pitch for a micro-enterprise activity

Generating ideas for a micro enterprise activity

Have you ever thought about running your own business? Do you believe you would be up to the challenge? In this component, you will come up with an idea for your own micro enterprise and work to make it a success.

Generating ideas

The starting point for any enterprise is the idea. What makes an entrepreneur is the willingness to take the risk and act on that idea. Ideas can come from a variety of sources, including:

- solving a problem
- thought showers
- importing an idea from abroad
- professional skills or experiences.

Ideas can involve:

- **innovation** of goods or services
- provision of goods or services in a new context
- provision of goods or services to new markets.

Innovation of goods or services

Innovation involves bringing new goods or services to market, normally with the goal of making a profit. This could be a new product (for example, a video game such as Splatoon™ 2) or a new service (for example, an app such as Deliveroo or Snapchat).

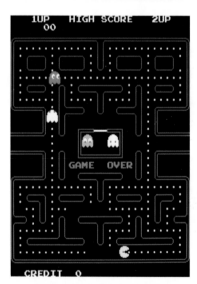

■ Much has changed since this computer game was an innovation in the 1980s. Can you think of any new goods and services that have been launched in this market in the last 12 months?

Provision of goods and services in a new context

Entrepreneurs can take an existing idea and change the context in which it is sold. This could include:

- a new use or new way of viewing the product
- how often we use a product.

Below are two examples of new contexts.

Glamping

Camping holidays have been popular for a long time. Traditionally, they were seen as 'cheap and cheerful' holidays with no luxuries. A new context for this type of holiday is 'glamping' (glamorous camping). Glamping is considered more upmarket than camping because it offers luxuries such as electricity, beds with proper mattresses and even hot tubs.

Porridge

A bowl of porridge is traditionally thought of as a breakfast product, but recently it has been promoted as a filling and healthy food for any time of the day. It can also now be easily purchased in one-portion pots.

Imagine, as a micro enterprise, setting up a stall selling piping hot pots of porridge outside a busy railway or bus station. Do you think it would be successful?

Provision of goods and services in a new market

Entrepreneurs can take an existing idea and change the market in which it is sold. This could be by:

- targeting a new geographical area of the UK or abroad
- creating a new market.

Below are two examples of new markets.

Bubble tea

Entrepreneur Assad Khan first tried bubble tea – a Taiwanese tea-based drink – in a small café in New York. He was so impressed with it that in 2011 he opened the UK's first bubble tea shop (Bubbleology®). He now has bubble tea cafés throughout the UK, the Middle East and Europe.

Adult colouring books

Colouring books are usually seen as a way of keeping children entertained. Some enterprises saw an opportunity to move into a new market by introducing adult colouring books. Supported by research showing that colouring can reduce stress, these books have now become extremely popular in the UK.

ACTIVITY

You should carry out tasks 1 and 2 of this activity as a whole class.

1 Discuss the advantages and disadvantages of working as a team to set up a micro enterprise.

2 Think about the characteristics and skills you would look for in team members.

Based on your reflections from tasks 1 and 2, you should now carry out task 3 either in pairs or individually.

3 Note down as many ideas for a micro enterprise as you can think of. Try to include both goods and services. Remember at this point that no idea is a bad idea.

CHECK MY LEARNING

1 Note down where new ideas can come from.

2 List the different types of ideas.

3 Individually, or in a pair, visit the website of a large online store, such as a supermarket or toy retailer. What examples can you find of new business ideas – for example, new goods or services? Where do you think these ideas came from? How could you improve on any of these goods or services?

Selecting an idea

Sometimes entrepreneurs are referred to as serial entrepreneurs. This means they have lots of ideas and start many different businesses. However, to begin with, most entrepreneurs will select just one idea to focus on.

Choosing from a list of ideas

When selecting an idea, there are a number of factors to consider. An idea may seem good but might be unrealistic due to a number of constraints. The 'best' idea is one that:

- is achievable given the resources available
- has a potential market.

It is also important to remember that sometimes there is a good reason why there is a gap in a market – other entrepreneurs may have already discovered that it is not possible to make a profit in this area.

▣ How can you make sure you select the best idea for your micro enterprise?

Table 2.1 outlines the issues to consider when planning your business idea.

LINK IT UP

To find out more about how to promote a new idea and make financial forecasts, go to Learning aim A of Component 3.

◼ Table 2.1: Issues to consider when selecting a final business idea

Factors	Issues to consider
Resources available	**Human resources** ● What job roles will be needed? ● How many staff will be needed and at what hours? ● Will additional staff be needed or can the work be managed by the team? **Financial resources** ● Where will start-up finance come from? ● How will day-to-day activities be paid for in the early days of trading? **Physical resources** ● What equipment will be needed? ● What facilities will be needed?
Financial forecasts	● Will there be sufficient cash to cover day-to-day expenses? ● Does the enterprise have the ability to 'break even'? ● Will the enterprise make a profit or a loss?
Costing and pricing	● What will it cost to set up the business – for example, to rent premises and purchase equipment? ● How much will it cost to provide the goods or service? ● How much will customers be willing to pay? Will this be enough to cover costs?
Methods of communication and promotion	● How will the enterprise be launched? ● How will the enterprise be promoted so that customers are aware of its existence? ● What will be the core message of the enterprise?
Potential customers	Who is the target market? (Consider, for example, age, gender, income and spending habits.)
Skills of people in the group	● What skills do individual team members have? ● How can these be utilised most efficiently? ● Are there any gaps in the group's skill sets? If so, how can these be addressed?

KEY TERM

Break-even is the point where income and expenditure (total money spent) are equal.

ACTIVITY

On your own, look back at the business ideas you produced in the previous lesson.

1 Colour code your ideas using a traffic light system:
   ● red for ideas you should stop considering
   ● amber for ideas that have possibilities
   ● green for ideas that could work well and be developed further.
2 Compare the ideas you have coded green with others in your team.
3 Work as a team to narrow down these ideas and write a shortlist of your three favourite ideas. From this shortlist, your team will decide on its final micro enterprise idea.

CHECK MY LEARNING

1 Note down the resources you should consider when selecting an idea.
2 Outline why it is important to consider sources of finance and financial forecasts when selecting an idea.
3 List any other factors that need to be considered.

Doing a skills audit

GETTING STARTED

Working individually, draw a table with two columns. In the first column, list your own skills. In the second column, list the skills you think the person next to you has. Compare lists with each other. Do you agree with the skills they have identified for you? Do they agree with the skills you have identified for them?

Entrepreneurs often have similar characteristics and skills. It is these skills that play a large part in the success of the enterprise. Do you think you have the necessary skills to become an entrepreneur?

Skills audit

A **skill** is when an individual is able to do something well. For example, you could be skilled at dribbling the ball when playing football. A **skills audit** is the process of assessing your own skills and those of others in relation to what is required for the task. A skills audit for enterprise should consider:

- leadership, personal and communication skills
- technical and practical skills.

A skills audit normally involves assessing skills against a range – for example:

- using numbers, such as 1–5, from 'no experience' to 'extensive experience'
- using levels, such as 'competent', 'adequate' or 'needs development'.

KEY TERMS

A **skill** is the ability to perform an action well.

A **skills audit** is the process of identifying what skills are needed and matching them to current skills to identify training and development needs.

Identifying gaps

An important part of a skills audit is to:

- recognise any gaps in skills
- look for ways to address these gaps.

Take a look at Figure 2.1 to see the process involved in a skills audit. Then look at Table 2.2, which explains why certain skills are so important in an enterprise.

LINK IT UP

To remind yourself about the skills needed to become a successful entrepreneur, go back to Learning aim A of Component 1.

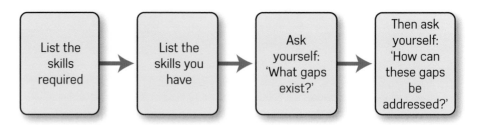

□ Figure 2.1: The skills audit process

DID YOU KNOW?

'Soft skills' is the term used to describe skills such as communication and teamwork that enable individuals to succeed in organisations. It is estimated that, by 2020, soft skills will contribute £109 billion to the UK economy. It is thought that this will increase to £127 billion by 2025.

◻ Table 2.2: The role of key skills in an enterprise

Skill	Role in enterprise
Leadership	• Leadership is the ability to motivate others to achieve goals. • Leaders must be able to gain the trust of employees and share a common sense of direction. • A leader must have the ability to encourage and inspire all members of the team to achieve the goals and do their best. • Leaders are often said to lead by example, acting as positive role models for others.
Personal	• Personal skills enable an individual to succeed in the workplace. • These skills are normally linked to a positive attitude. • Personal skills include problem solving, being able to interact with others, reliability, flexibility and being highly motivated.
Communication	• Communication involves the ability to share information with others. This has to be done in a way that conveys the correct message in a manner that is easy to understand. • Communication is a two-way process – the ability to listen is just as important as talking. • In enterprise, communication will take place both internally (among team members and employees) and externally (with customers and suppliers).
Technical	• Technical skills include specific knowledge of tools, such as computer software. • Examples include project management (the ability to plan, prioritise and monitor the use of resources), data handling and use of social media.
Practical	• Practical skills are the ability to perform specific tasks – for example, provide customer service or make goods. • These skills vary between enterprises – for example, the practical skills required to run a café are different from those needed to set up a horse stable.

ACTIVITY

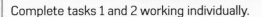

Complete tasks 1 and 2 working individually.

1 Write a list of all the skills you think will be required to make your enterprise a success.

2 Next to each skill, decide whether you and/or members of your team can perform that skill.

Complete task 3 working together with your group.

3 Identify any gaps in skills you have noticed. How can your team address these?

CHECK MY LEARNING

1 Explain what a skills audit is.

2 List the types of skills required in an enterprise.

3 Use the internet to find an online leadership skills test. Complete this to assess your own leadership skills.

Planning for a micro enterprise activity

When you began your BTEC Tech Award Enterprise, did you have any targets or ideas of what you wanted to achieve? Why is it important to set targets both at college and at work? What targets do you think entrepreneurs are likely to set when they first start up an enterprise?

Aims of micro enterprises

Aims are the targets that an enterprise wants to achieve, normally within a specified period of time. These help to motivate the entrepreneur towards achieving their goals. An aim should be SMART: Specific, Measurable, Achievable, Realistic and Time-related.

Aims can be split into:

- financial aims
- non-financial aims.

LINK IT UP

To remind yourself of the purpose of an enterprise, including its financial aims, go back to Learning aim A of Component 1.

Financial aims

Plans that involve meeting money-based targets are called financial aims. These could be linked to the amount of sales **revenue** to be achieved or the desired level of profits. Two examples of financial aims are to:

- make a profit
- achieve break-even.

To make a profit, an enterprise must achieve a total revenue that is higher than its total costs. For example:

Total revenue (money coming in)	£400,000
Total costs (money going out)	– £350,000
Profit	**£50,000**

This will leave a profit, or surplus, that can be used to improve the business, reward the entrepreneur or support a good cause.

If the total revenue is equal to the total costs, then the business will have reached break-even. For example:

Total revenue (money coming in)	£400,000
Total costs (money going out)	– £400,000
Profit	**£0**

At this point the enterprise is not making a profit or a loss.

Setting realistic aims

New enterprises may find that setting an aim to achieve a profit may be too ambitious in the short term. It may be more realistic to focus on making a profit later on, once the business has been established for a while. Most new enterprises are more likely to set an aim to survive – to achieve break-even.

LINK IT UP

To find out more about profit, break-even and how to calculate each of them, go to Learning aim C of Component 3.

Non-financial aims

Aims that do not involve meeting money-based targets can be grouped together as non-financial aims. These could be linked to other aspects of the business, such as becoming a recognised brand or to behaving in an ethical way. Two examples are:

- customer satisfaction
- social aims.

◨ **How can a social enterprise such as a nursery, a recycling and repair business or a café help to meet the needs of a local community?**

Customer satisfaction is achieved when the needs of customers are met before, during and after a transaction. This is important because it avoids complaints and builds a good reputation for an enterprise. This will help it to gain brand loyalty and repeat custom, which will, in turn, lead to an increase in sales.

Not all enterprises are set up purely to make profits. An enterprise may also have social aims, such as meeting the needs of the community or providing support for a charitable cause. Enterprises with a social aim use the surplus of revenue over costs (their profit) to support their identified aim. For example, a coffee shop may use its profit to provide education and training for disadvantaged young adults.

ACTIVITY

Complete tasks 1 and 2 working individually.

1 Identify an example of each of the following in your local area:
- a for-profit enterprise
- a social enterprise.

2 For each enterprise, write a list of their aims.

Now complete tasks 3 and 4 working as a whole class.

3 Share the aims you identified with the class and group them under two headings:
- 'For profit'
- 'Not for profit'.

4 Discuss how the aims vary depending on whether the enterprise is primarily for profit or not for profit.

CHECK MY LEARNING

1 With the use of an example for each, explain what is meant by:
- a financial aim
- a non-financial aim.

2 Suggest one SMART aim for your own micro enterprise.

Goods and services

All enterprises must have goods or services that they will sell to customers. Getting the goods and services right is key to the success of the enterprise. What goods or services will your micro enterprise supply? Why will people be willing to pay for them? How will you stand out from your competitors?

Goods or service to be sold

When setting up an enterprise it is important to have a clear understanding of:
- the goods or services to be provided
- how these will meet customers' needs.

For example, just saying you are a bakery that will supply cakes is insufficient. The customer needs to know the types of cakes, their unique selling points, why they should choose your cakes over another bakery's, how much they will cost and so on.

Planning features, benefits and USPs

An enterprise needs to plan the features, benefits and unique selling points of its products, as shown in Table 2.3.

◘ Table 2.3: Understanding features, benefits and USPs

Planning products	
Features	These could include the core features – that is: • what the product is • what the product does well • any additional features. For example, if describing the features of a men's jumper, the enterprise might give details such as: *has a hood*; *zip front*; *side pockets*; *available in three colours and four sizes*; *made of cotton*; *machine washable*.
Benefits	These are what the customer can expect to get from owning the product. For example, benefits of the men's jumper might include: *fashionable*; *warm*; *easy to care for*; *high-quality material*; *long-lasting*.
Unique selling points	These are what make the product different from its competitors – that is, its unique features. For example, USPs of the jumper might include: *it can be personalised with an individual or team name*; *it can be personalised with a logo or image*; *it is a specific brand*.

Planning costings and pricing

An enterprise will need to plan the costing and pricing of its products carefully.

Costings cover all of the costs associated with the provision of the product. This will include:
- fixed costs (costs that do not change according to changes in output) – such as electricity and water bills, rent or insurance costs
- variable costs (costs that change according to changes in output) – such as the raw materials that make up the product.

For example, if an enterprise plans to make jumpers, it may need to rent space in a factory or buy sewing machines. It would also need to buy fabric, zips, cord, labels and so on.

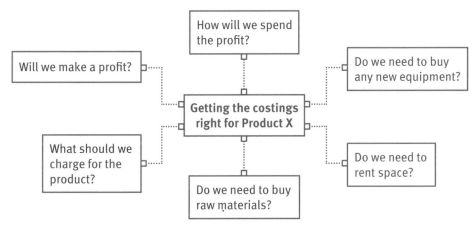

How will we spend the profit?

Will we make a profit?

Do we need to buy any new equipment?

Getting the costings right for Product X

What should we charge for the product?

Do we need to buy raw materials?

Do we need to rent space?

◻ **Figure 2.2: How will you approach costings for your own enterprise?**

It is important to understand all of the costs involved before making pricing decisions. An enterprise needs to ensure the price is high enough to cover the costs and (depending on the enterprise's aims) make a profit. Take a look at Figure 2.2 to see some of the questions you should consider when deciding on costings for your product.

Pricing models

It can be difficult for a new enterprise to set prices for its products or services that will both cover its costs and be at a level that potential customers are happy to pay. The different methods that enterprises typically use to set prices include:

- *cost-plus pricing* – calculating the cost of creating the product or service, then adding on a percentage
- *competition-based pricing* – looking at what competitors charge for the same sort of product or service and charging a similar price
- *skimming* – charging a high price initially to 'skim off' profits, before dropping the price later (this often happens with new technology)
- *penetration* – charging a low price initially to appeal to more customers ('penetrating the market'), before raising the price over time.

Competitors

When it comes to recognising the potential competition, a new enterprise is likely to research:

- the number and relative size of competitors
- the range of products offered by competitors
- the prices charged by competitors
- whether any competitors are offering products that are the same as, or similar to, theirs.

This information will help the new enterprise to find a gap in the market where it can offer its product, perhaps with a USP. Understanding the degree of competition is important when assessing the **feasibility** of an enterprise (how likely it is to be successful).

ACTIVITY

1 Draw a mind map to outline all the aspects of the goods or services that your micro enterprise will offer. Remember that the more detail you can provide, the easier it will be to tell customers about your products. Think about which aspects can be considered USPs.

2 Show your mind map to someone else in your class who does not know a lot about your idea. Give them two minutes to study your mind map and then explain your idea back to you. Have you provided enough information for them to fully understand your idea? Add to your mind map if necessary.

CHECK MY LEARNING

1 List three things an enterprise should include in a product description.

2 Explain why it is important for an enterprise to understand:

- costings
- the degree of competition in the market.

Identifying the target market

It is not always possible or beneficial to target all customers, especially if an enterprise is small. Therefore, enterprises often choose to aim their goods or services at a specific market. An important question to ask is: how will they reach that market?

Market segmentation

Market segmentation is the process of dividing the market into groups of customers with similar characteristics. For example, a **market segment** for sportswear might be girls aged 12–16 with an interest in athletics. This allows an enterprise to tailor (match) its products and communications to this specific segment of the market. Types of market segmentation include:

- **demographic** – based on age or cultural background
- geographic – based on the country, region or local area where you live
- psychographic – based on personality and attitude
- behavioural – based on interests or needs.

Appealing to the target market

Identifying the characteristics of the **target market** for the product will help inform marketing decisions within an enterprise. This will include:

- where to sell the product
- what price customers are willing and able to pay
- how best to attract the interest of the target market through promotional techniques.

Reaching the target market

Once the enterprise has identified its target market, it can decide the best way to reach that market. This will include where to sell the goods and services – for example, the type of store, its location and whether online options are available.

- If the target market is an older demographic, then goods and services may be offered in local shops.
- If the target market is high-paid city workers, then goods and services may be located at busy railway stations around London or other large cities.

Try adding some more options to this list. If your class was the target market of an enterprise, where would be a good place for it to locate its goods or services?

Physical and virtual market places

A key consideration is whether to sell in a physical or virtual market place.

- A physical market place is one where the buyers and sellers come together to trade face to face – for example at food stalls, in shops and at trade fairs.
- A virtual market place is one that makes use of the internet. Many enterprises now use ecommerce, either for part or all of their trading. This is often cheaper to set up and allows greater convenience to the customer, who can access the store at any time and from the comfort of their own home, their office or on a mobile device.

Mixing platforms

Enterprises can use a combination of both physical and online stores to reach their target market. Small enterprises are also able to reach their target market through third-party websites such as Notonthehighstreet, eBay, Amazon and Etsy. These have the advantage of being well-established platforms known by consumers. However, an enterprise must take into account that these platforms take a percentage of all sales revenue.

◘ **Why might it be easier for a micro enterprise to reach its target market through a third-party website?**

ACTIVITY

1 In a pair, select one of these categories: watches, sports bags or chocolate bars. Alternatively, choose a category of your own that is similar to these.
   a) Research at least four different products within your chosen category.
   b) Explain how each of the products you have selected meets the needs of a specific target market.

2 Think about whether you can identify a gap in the market for any of your products. Is there a group whose needs are not being met? How would you adapt a product to meet their needs?

Target sales

Understanding the buying habits and needs of the target market will help an enterprise to establish sales. However, an enterprise needs more than one-off or short-term sales. It must continually meet the needs of the customer in order to achieve its own goals. This will involve:

- attracting new customers
- gaining customer loyalty to achieve repeat sales.

To sustain this, an enterprise must regularly revisit customer needs and the target market to make changes as necessary. For example, if a new competitor enters the market, the enterprise may have to review its pricing decisions.

CHECK MY LEARNING

1 Identify three ways of segmenting a market.

2 Explain why it is important for an enterprise to understand its target market.

3 Briefly explain two ways a product can reach its target market.

4 Explain the importance of sustaining sales, as well as establishing them in the first instance.

Methods of communicating with customers

How many methods of communication have you used today, and how many of these involved using technology? Have any enterprises communicated with you today? For example, did you pass any billboards, receive any texts or see an advert on TV?

Selection of communication methods

Enterprises need to communicate with customers to:

- keep them informed – for example, by letting them know about new goods and services
- try to increase sales – for example, by reminding customers about what they sell and through special offers such as reductions in price.

An enterprise has a large range of communication methods to choose from, as Figure 2.3 shows.

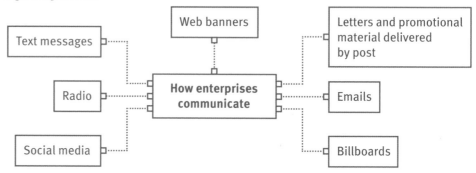

■ Figure 2.3: Can you think of any other ways that enterprises communicate?

If an enterprise chooses to advertise its goods or services, it needs to decide on the most appropriate communication method. The method must appeal to the target audience and present the right message. Small enterprises will often have small budgets. It is therefore important that they think carefully when deciding how best to communicate with their target market.

An enterprise can advertise in two main ways, which have both advantages and disadvantages.

Advertising through third parties

It can use the services of a third party, such as a newspaper, magazine or television broadcaster.

- *Advantages*: adverts such as these provide wide coverage and reach many people.
- *Disadvantages*: it is expensive to advertise in this way. A micro enterprise, for instance, may not be able to afford an expensive TV advertisement.

Internal promotions

It can choose an internal method such as social media or point of sales displays.

- *Advantages of social media*: social media (such as Twitter, Instagram and Facebook) is likely to generate two-way communication between the enterprise and the customer. This can be very efficient because a customer can communicate on behalf of the enterprise by sharing information with their own contacts.

- *Disadvantages of social media*: an enterprise does not have complete control of the content of social media. Dissatisfied customers may share messages that are damaging to the enterprise's reputation.
- *Advantages of point of sale*: point-of-sale displays appear in places where customers are in a buying frame of mind.
- *Disadvantages of point of sale*: customers may have become so used to seeing them that they ignore them.

ACTIVITY

In a pair, discuss the social media sites you use. Make a list of the ways that enterprises communicate with you via a social media platform.

When deciding how to communicate, enterprises need to consider aspects such as cost effectiveness. This means looking at whether the communication:
- achieved the desired outcome (increased customer numbers or awareness)
- was financially worthwhile (increased its sales).

In other words, if a large amount of money was spent on an advert but this didn't increase sales, then it was not cost effective.

Measuring response

It can be difficult to measure the exact response to a particular advert. Has a business ever asked you: 'How did you hear about us?' This question allows it to measure response rates to the types of communication it uses and to understand what method of communication works best.

How to design promotional material

When designing **promotional material** it is necessary to consider two key things:
1. the appropriateness of content
2. the appropriateness of appearance.

If the correct information is not presented in a way that is easily understandable, the communication may be wasted. Take a look at Table 2.4 for a checklist of what to include.

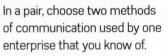 Table 2.4: Checklist for designing promotional materials

Appropriate content	Appropriate appearance
What is the message the enterprise wants to share with the customer?	
• Is it accurate (for example, does it give correct information about the features of the product or the benefits it offers)?	• Is use of colour appropriate for the target market? (For example, bright, bold colours may appeal more to a child while darker or softer colours may give an impression of an upmarket product.)
• Is it complete? Does it provide customers with everything they need to know, such as cost and contact/location details?	• Do the visual features add to or subtract from the clarity of the message? (For example, if a promotion is too busy or confusing it may be difficult to take in the core information from it.)
• Is the information clear and easy to understand? Or is it likely to confuse someone?	• Do images (the photographs of the product) support the message?
• Is it needed? Or is some of it 'waffle'?	• Do logos support the image the enterprise is trying to portray? Do they build on the brand?
	• Is the text easy to read? Or is it difficult to see because of images and colour?

DID YOU KNOW?

Point of sale means the place where you pay for your product. Point-of-sale (or POS) advertising materials are often used in shops and stores as part of a display. Take a look next time you pay for something in person. Can you spot any? Is there any point in using POS advertising when you pay for something online?

LINK IT UP

To find out more about the important aspects of communication, the message and the medium, go to Learning aim A of Component 3.

ACTIVITY

In a pair, choose two methods of communication used by one enterprise that you know of.

1. Make notes about these methods and identify why the content and appearance are appropriate to the target market.

2. If you had to recommend two ways of improving each method, what would they be and why?

CHECK MY LEARNING

1. State two examples of methods of communication.
2. State two reasons for communication.
3. State two factors to consider when choosing a method of communication.
4. Define what 'cost effective' means.
5. Explain two considerations when designing promotional materials.

Resources required

One of the roles of an entrepreneur is to organise resources. Sometimes, even straightforward tasks can involve lots of resources. Consider the resources involved in delivering today's lesson – are there more being used than you first thought?

Types of resources

Any enterprise will require a range of resources. These will include:

- physical resources
- financial resources
- human resources.

Physical resources

Physical resources are the tangible items an entrepreneur will need to start the enterprise. For a micro enterprise, the resources available are likely to be limited, particularly when it is just starting out. For example, it would not be realistic to assume you have the resources to set up an airline or compete with an online platform that allows you to watch films and TV programmes. The main physical resources are summarised in Table 2.5.

◾ Table 2.5: The physical resources needed by an enterprise

Resource	Use
Location	This is where the enterprise will operate from. This could be premises such as a warehouse, factory, office, shop or market stall. Alternatively, for an online business this could be where the webpage will be hosted and the domain name.
	Many micro enterprises will initially be located at home to save on costs. For example, an entrepreneur importing goods from abroad may set up an office area in their house, sell products online and store stock in the garage.
Materials	These could be the raw materials used to produce goods or provide services, or additional materials needed to operate. Examples include window display materials, point-of-sale promotions and sundries, such as bags and price tags.
Equipment	This is the machinery needed to produce goods and serve customers. This could include:
	• production machinery, such as ovens or conveyor belts
	• kitchen equipment or display equipment, such as fridges
	• small-scale equipment, such as scissors
	• point-of-sale equipment, such as cash registers.
Fixtures and fittings	These are the resources used within the premises, such as shelving and display materials, desks or tables and chairs.
Information technology	This could include:
	• IT equipment such as computers and printers
	• resources to access the internet (for example, a router)
	• software (for example, design or accountancy packages).
Stock	Depending on the nature of the enterprise, stock could include raw materials, work in progress and finished goods. The enterprise needs to hold enough stock to be able to meet customer needs, but not too much that it risks products becoming outdated.

Financial resources

Financial resources means the money an enterprise will need. The main financial resources are included in Table 2.6.

◪ **Table 2.6: Financial resources and why they are needed**

Resource	What it is and why it is needed
Sources of finance	These are needed to fund all other resources. They could include personal savings, loans from friends and family or a bank loan.
Start-up costs	These are the costs needed to actually start trading – for example, initial stock, promotions and premises.
Running costs/fixed costs	These are general costs incurred in the running of the business – for example, paying **wages** and paying utility bills, such as heating and electricity.
Production costs/cost of sales/variable costs	These are the costs directly involved in the production of the goods or provision of the service (for example, raw materials if a product is being made, or stock if finished goods are being sold).

Human resources

Human resources are the people an enterprise will need. This will include the employees who help to run the enterprise.

- A micro enterprise may consist of just one person – the entrepreneur who started it – if they have all the skills required.
- Other enterprises may need employees for a number of roles and skills – for example, to serve customers, make goods, provide a service or provide additional support such as web design or accounting.

Some employees may require training and development to allow them to stay up to date with the latest technological advances. Resources will be required to ensure they are equipped with the skills they need to carry out their roles effectively.

KEY TERMS

Wages are usually calculated hourly to pay for work that has been done.

ACTIVITY

1 Draw a picture to show the resources a micro enterprise such as a restaurant, barber shop or food manufacturer will need. Label the resources, using different colours to show physical, financial and human resources. Some resources may fall into two categories. For example, stock could be a physical resource as well as a financial resource.

2 Challenge a partner to spot a resource you have not included. Briefly discuss what the resource is and why it would be useful.

CHECK MY LEARNING

1 Identify five of the physical resources your micro enterprise will need.

2 Distinguish, with the use of an example, the difference between start-up costs and running costs.

3 Explain why an enterprise needs human resources.

4 What other resources will your micro enterprise will need?

5 Decide which of the resources you have identified in your answers to questions 1 and 4 are essential, which are important and which are desirable.

Risk assessment

GETTING STARTED

As a class, consider the new enterprises in your local area. Are there any that have closed down? Why do you think this may have been? What risks might new enterprises face?

KEY TERM

Risk averse is avoiding or being unwilling to take risks.

LINK IT UP

To remind yourself of skills needed by an entrepreneur for success, go back to Learning aim A of Component 1.

LINK IT UP

To find out more about how unexpected costs impact on cash flow, break-even and profitability, go to Learning aim C of Component 3.

Entrepreneurs are often described as risk takers. This is because, unfortunately, many micro enterprises do not manage to succeed. What is your attitude to risk? Would you say you are a risk taker or **risk averse**?

Understanding risk assessment

A risk assessment is the process of:

1 identifying potential risks to a business

2 considering the likelihood of these risks turning into problems

3 judging whether or not the benefits of something outweigh the potential risks associated with it.

This can help owners prepare for risk and allow entrepreneurs to take more decisive action when faced with risks.

Risks faced by enterprises

Take a look at these risks commonly faced by enterprises. Are there any others you can think of?

Lack of entrepreneurial skill

The entrepreneur does not have enough experience. As a result, they may make poor decisions such as:

- choosing the wrong location for their enterprise
- not communicating effectively with customers.

Competitor actions

A new enterprise will pose a threat to existing enterprises. These competitors may take action to maintain their market share such as:

- lowering prices in the short term
- increasing promotional spending or advertising budgets.

It would be difficult for a new enterprise that does not yet have a customer base to compete with this. Equally, other new enterprises may enter the market as well, increasing the degree of competition.

Unexpected costs of production

It is easy to miss something, no matter how carefully costs are forecast and resources are planned. Costs may be higher than expected, meaning break-even cannot be achieved and the survival of the enterprise is threatened. An unexpected rise in costs might be due to a supplier who decides to charge more for materials, or due to poor planning by the entrepreneur.

Sourcing raw materials

Without all the necessary resources, an enterprise will be unable to meet the needs of its customers. If these cannot be found then an enterprise may be left with nothing to sell. This can be especially challenging if the enterprise is looking to source materials that are in short supply or come from abroad. Even a time delay in sourcing supplies can be critical to the survival of an enterprise.

Quality control issues

A new enterprise needs to gain a good reputation as quickly as possible. It will also want to attract new customers through word of mouth. Unfortunately, the opposite can also happen. The enterprise must ensure that the goods and services it provides are of high quality and meet or exceed customer expectations. If customer needs are not met because of quality control problems, a reputation can be destroyed before it is properly established, and potential customers will be discouraged from using the business. If quality issues arise, a new enterprise may not have enough money to:

- rework faulty goods
- pay fines or legal fees (if they are challenged legally or officially about quality control issues).

Lack of customer interest

Sometimes the risk can simply be that the enterprise is trying to sell something that not enough people want. This may be because:

- the original idea was poorly thought out
- the target market has been misunderstood
- the market already has too many similar enterprises.

During the planning stages, market research can help reduce this risk, but cannot eliminate it completely.

Contingency plans

When an enterprise identifies its main risks, it should produce a contingency plan. This is a plan of how to react to unexpected events. Writing a contingency plan involves:

- identifying all the potential risks
- putting into place procedures for how to deal with those risks.

This does not reduce the risk, but does mean an enterprise can make better informed decisions when faced with a threat. This is why your school or college will have fire drills, for example, so that it can monitor what needs to happen if there was a real fire.

ACTIVITY

In pairs, discuss what might happen to a new grocery shop if only half of its shelves are filled with food. Do you think an enterprise could survive if it is not fully stocked when it first starts trading?

◾ What are the risks involved in running fitness classes as an enterprise?

ACTIVITY

1 In a pair, select an idea for an enterprise – such as a new bakery.
   a) Draw a mind map to identify all of the potential risks.
   b) Use a traffic light system of red, amber and green to highlight the severity of each risk, with red being the most severe.
2 a) Write your enterprise idea, plus its top three risks, on the board.
   b) Discuss, as a class, whether the top risks everyone has identified would be the same regardless of the type of business.

CHECK MY LEARNING

1 Identify two financial risks to an enterprise.
2 Identify one thing that could be done to reduce risk to your micro enterprise.
3 Devise a contingency plan for your micro enterprise.

Pitching for a micro enterprise activity

At this point in your studies, you should have undertaken enough research to produce a fully developed plan for your micro enterprise. Now is the time to share this with an audience.

Sharing your plan with an audience

Before you share your plan with an audience, you should consider:
- who might be interested in it
- why they might be interested in it.

Take a look at Table 2.7 to help you.

◻ Table 2.7: Who might be interested in a business plan and why

Who might be interested	Why they might be interested
Investors deciding whether to provide finance	They will be particularly interested in the validity of the idea and the financial forecasts.
Target market who may buy your goods or services	They will be particularly interested in the goods or services being sold, their features, benefits and USPs.
Suppliers who will provide resources	They will be particularly interested in the quantity you will require and when.
Community who will be affected by your enterprise	They will be particularly interested in how it will affect them – for example, whether it will cause a disruption, and whether a local interest group, such as a charity, will benefit from it.
Employees who will be providing human resources	They will be particularly interested in what their roles will be and whether they will receive any training.

What a pitch includes

A pitch must include a summary of the micro enterprise plan, which should take the audience's needs and interests into consideration. It should contain:
- clear communication of the developed idea
- a logical structure of the content of the plan.

Tips for communicating your developed idea clearly

Your pitch will be easier for your audience to digest if you bear in mind the following points.
- Start with a clear and precise explanation of what the enterprise will do, its aims and its goods or services.
- Use bullet points to summarise key points. Expand on these in your explanation, not in writing.
- Use diagrams to illustrate points. A picture of your product will be much easier to explain than using text.
- Use props or visual aids, such as an example of promotional material or a mock-up of a store.

Tips for logical structure of the content of your plan

Think about the order you use to cover the main points.

- Your pitch should have a logical structure.
- Think about it as telling a story with a clear start, development and end.
- Start with your aims. Tell a story of how you will achieve these aims and finish with the outcome (for example, the financial forecasts).

Tips for considering the audience's needs and interests

Your pitch may need to be more or less formal, depending on the audience.

- Consider your audience. Who are they? What are their interests?
- Be wary of using jargon or terms your audience may not understand – for example, USP. If you must use technical terms, ensure you explain them fully.
- Think about how you can engage and interact with your audience.
- Consider using presentation software such as PowerPoint® or Prezi.
- Consider using cue cards with notes to prompt you.
- Practise your presentation in front of others (perhaps family or friends) or in front of a mirror so you will be able to deliver it smoothly.
- Be prepared to welcome questions at the end of your presentation.

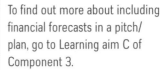

LINK IT UP

To find out more about including financial forecasts in a pitch/plan, go to Learning aim C of Component 3.

ACTIVITY

Working individually, look back at the top tips you discussed as a class at the start of this lesson. Use these, plus the content covered throughout this learning aim, to design an observation sheet to be used when watching the presentations. Include points such as:

- what the presenter does well
- whether the presentation explains what the aims of their micro enterprise are
- constructive feedback – for example, anything that they could do to improve their presentation.

CHECK MY LEARNING

1 Identify two potential members of your audience and their interests.
2 Explain why it is important to communicate your plan clearly.
3 Draw a flow chart to show a logical structure for your presentation.

Learning aim A: assessment practice

How you will be assessed

Now you have studied the topics in Learning aim A, you will need to demonstrate that you know how to select, plan and pitch an idea for a micro enterprise. The evidence you produce will focus on a specific idea for a micro enterprise activity. You should first consider a range of ideas and how feasible each one is in relation to your own skills.

CHECKPOINT

Strengthen

- Identify how ideas for enterprises are generated.
- Explain how and why you selected your final idea.
- Identify your skills.
- Outline the essential components of a plan for an enterprise activity.

Challenge

- Explain how your skills match those required to run your micro enterprise activity.
- Justify why your enterprise idea is likely to be successful.
- Explain what makes a successful pitch for a micro enterprise activity.

TIPS

- Keep your idea realistic.
- Organise your plan and pitch in a logical and easy-to-follow way. Using subheadings helps make it clearer.

ASSESSMENT ACTIVITY   LEARNING AIM   A

To complete this task you must work individually to create your plan and pitch. You should then work in teams of up to six people to select one of the pitches to run the enterprise for Learning aim B.

1 Explain a range of ideas considered.

2 Identify and justify why you chose your final idea.

3 Give reasons why your skills match those required to make your enterprise a success.

4 Produce a plan to put your micro enterprise activity into practice.

5 Carry out a pitch of your developed plan.

TAKE IT FURTHER

When presenting your idea, both in your plan and pitch, try to support your decisions with evidence – for example, a pricing decision backed by market research findings. To achieve higher assessment criteria, you need to be able to justify, as well as describe, key decisions.

The micro enterprise pitch

Search online for someone making a persuasive speech - it could be a politician, or a sporting coach.

1. How did they grab your attention?
2. How did they make the speech persuasive?
3. What was the message they were trying to get across?

If you have an idea for a business or product, it's likely you will want to 'sell' that idea to other people via a pitch so that they will invest in your business or buy your product. You have now developed an idea for a micro enterprise and explored various aspects of starting a small business. Your next task is to prepare and give a pitch.

Pitching

A business **pitch** is a presentation by one or more people to an investor or group of investors. It can also be a written pitch, an email, letter or even a passing conversation. The purpose of a pitch is to provide a potential investor or lender with information about the enterprise and convince them that it will be a success. A range of techniques can be used to communicate information, such as presentations using images, a speech to grab people's attention, facts about the enterprise and demonstrations of products or services. A pitch may last from two to ten minutes and usually ends with the opportunity for the audience to ask questions.

DID YOU KNOW?

An elevator pitch is a short description of an enterprise idea, product or oneself that conveys the concept in an exciting way that can be understood in a short period of time. The name comes from the idea that the pitch should be short enough to be delivered in the time it takes an elevator (lift) to get from the bottom to the top floor!

ACTIVITY

Watch clips of two pitches from a recent episode of the TV programme *Dragons' Den*. Don't watch the questions posed by the *Dragons*. Watch each pitch and discuss the following in small groups:

1 How persuasive was the pitch?

2 What information did the entrepreneurs share with the *Dragons*?

3 Which did you think was the best pitch? Which would you invest in?

Finish by watching the questions posed by the *Dragons* to see which pitch they thought was the best. Did you agree with them?

KEY TERM

Pitch – the presentation made by an entrepreneur about the nature and details of an idea or start-up to persuade a person or business to invest in the enterprise, or loan capital to start up the enterprise.

Delivering a persuasive pitch

Over the next few lessons you will learn about the contents of a successful pitch, along with the techniques and skills to deliver an effective pitch for your micro enterprise activity. Table 2.1 outlines a range of techniques that can be used during a pitch to grab your listeners' attention and persuade them of the suitability of your idea.

■ **Table 2.1: Techniques that can help to hold attention and persuade**

Tell a story	Everyone likes to hear a story. Stories grab people's attention and allow you to put your idea into context. For example, tell a story about someone using your product or service, or how you came up with the idea.
Focus on the problem being solved	Your product or service may have lots of features. It is important that your audience understand these features, but it is most important that they understand how these features benefit them. For example, how do they make life easier or solve a problem?
Rhetorical questions	A rhetorical question is one that does not need answering. Instead, a rhetorical question will make people think and reflect on their own attitudes, opinions and feelings. Using rhetorical questions can be an effective technique when trying to persuade your audience. For example, 'can you really live without this product in your lives?'
Repetition	After your pitch, you want people to remember a few key messages. To help make your pitch memorable, try repeating some key phrases, such as your enterprise strap line or the main reason your idea is unique.
Use the rule of three	People find it easier to remember things in threes. Therefore, when thinking about the benefits of your idea, the reasons people should invest, or the things that make your idea unique, always have three.

ACTIVITY

To get the ball rolling with your micro enterprise pitch, come up with your own elevator pitch for a product you can find in the classroom. The pitch should be no more than 30 seconds, and will help you practise some pitch techniques.

CHECK MY LEARNING

Give:

1 three reasons why someone might give a pitch?

2 three things that might be included in a pitch?

3 three ways to make a pitch persuasive?

The contents of your pitch

◘ **How would you pitch for a car wash business?**

It's important that your pitch conveys essential information about your new micro enterprise. Your audience needs to be clear about what you plan to do – and how..

What to include in your pitch

In Learning aim A, you learned how to plan for a micro enterprise activity. The purpose of a pitch is to share important information about your micro enterprise. Therefore, it is important to share aspects of your plan with your audience. The following aspects of running a micro enterprise will be included in your planning and may also be shared with your audience during your pitch.

- **Overview (opening the pitch)** A clear, concise explanation of your enterprise. It is important that your audience understand the concept of your enterprise from the outset. If they don't understand it within the first minute, they will not take in any information about the detail, such as your target market, promotion or finances.
- **Aims** What do you aim to achieve? Do you aim to make a profit, break even or meet the needs of the local community?
- **Your product or service** This will be covered in your overview or opening, but your audience needs to understand the features of your product or service, its benefits, and how it will be different from competitors.
- **Target market** Who is your product or service aimed at? How does it meet their needs and how will it appeal to them? This part of your pitch might be delivered at the point you outline the details of your product or service.
- **Competition** No doubt your micro enterprise activity will have some competition. This might be direct competition or a substitute that customers may opt to spend their money on. During your pitch you must convince your audience that your enterprise will be better or unique in some way.
- **Methods of communication** You have planned how to promote your micro enterprise activity. Which methods of promotion will you use to reach your potential customers?
- **Resources** Your pitch may also include a breakdown of the resources you will require to make your enterprise work. This will include materials, equipment, technology, a business location and any human skills. This may only be a brief overview during your pitch to demonstrate you understand the necessary requirements to make your enterprise a success.
- **Finances** A key part of any pitch is knowing the figures that will make your enterprise work. This should include all costs in setting up and running your enterprise, forecasts for sales figures and pricing and targets.

◼ What makes a good business plan?

DID YOU KNOW?

A business plan has several purposes. It is often used to convince potential lenders or investors that the business will be successful or generate a good return on their investment. Business plans are also used as a working document to help guide decision-making and to review the performance of a business.

KEY TERM

Business plan – a formal document used to outline the details of a business start-up. Your micro enterprise pitch will include much of the information found in a business plan

ACTIVITY

Now that you have a mind map for the contents of your pitch, you will need to decide on the order. The order of the contents of your pitch is important as it ensures that your pitch flows in a logical way. Using your mind map, discuss with your peers the most logical order, and decide what should come first, second, last, etc. Create a table like the one below to show the order.

Order	Topic	Notes	Timings
1			
2			

CHECK MY LEARNING

Rank in order of importance this list of things that could be included in a pitch, and explain why each is important to a successful pitch.

1 Information about the target market

2 Information about the competition

3 Information about pricing

4 Information about the resources required to set up the enterprise

Presentation skills: delivering a professional pitch

GETTING STARTED

What does the term professional mean?

- Write down a sentence using the term professional.
- Think of a person you would describe as being professional. Why do you associate professionalism with them?
- What are three things that make someone act or be professional?

You'll need to be professional when you present your pitch – and to maintain professional standards of behaviour and appearance when you are running your own enterprise.

Professional pitches

Professionalism involves acting in a way that is appropriate for a professional in a certain occupation. For example, a doctor is expected to be courteous and respectful to people's illnesses; a teacher is expected to treat their pupils fairly and make provision for their particular learning needs; anyone who works in a customer service industry is expected to respond to customer queries or complaints promptly. Although you are not yet a professional in a particular trade or profession it is important that you practise appropriate professionalism during your micro enterprise pitch.

KEY TERM

Professionalism – the competency, skill and behaviours expected of someone who is a professional.

Dress

In most business scenarios in most cultures it is traditional for a business person to wear a suit. For a woman this could be a suit with matching trousers or a skirt. A man may also be expected to wear a neck tie in certain industries. A suit may not be necessary in all circumstances and smart dress may suffice. Although suits are associated with the business world, many companies have less formal cultures where employees are encouraged to wear what they like. Steve Jobs was a famous CEO of Apple. He regularly gave promotional pitches for new Apple products, such as the iPad and iPhone. During his pitches, Steve Jobs was known for wearing a long sleeve black polo neck and jeans.

◻ Why is it important to dress in a professional way?

DID YOU KNOW?

The necktie originated in the 17th century, during the 30-year war in France. King Louis XIII hired Croatian mercenaries who wore a piece of cloth around their neck as part of their uniform.

ACTIVITY

Discuss with your teacher the most appropriate dress code for your enterprise pitch. This might include wearing a suit if you have one, a shirt and tie, or smart trousers/dress and a shirt or jumper. Make a plan for the outfit you intend to wear for your pitch.

Greetings

Greetings are an important part of giving a professional pitch. In the UK and Europe most cultures greet formally with a hand shake and a greeting such as 'Hello, pleased to meet you' or 'Good morning, my name is _____'. Professionalism involves being polite and courteous at all times during your pitch. How you start and end your pitch is very important. Table 2.2 gives a few suggestions that you should consider using.

Table 2.2: Tips for greetings and goodbyes

Greeting and goodbye	Examples
Introduce yourself	'Good morning/afternoon my name is _____'
Shake hands	Make sure your handshake is not too limp or too tight.
Introduce your pitch	'Today I would like to pitch to you my micro enterprise [insert enterprise name].'
Closing the pitch after questioning	'Thank you for your time today and the opportunity to share my idea with you all.'

Positive attitude

Remember that you are trying to persuade your audience that your idea is a good one. Positivity is infectious. If you are enthusiastic, excited and smile, then your audience will be positive too. After your pitch, your audience are likely to ask you questions. It is important that you welcome these questions and see them as an opportunity to clarify your idea and give your audience further details.

Rehearsing your pitch

It is important to you are fully prepared and rehearsed before giving your pitch. It is natural for you to have a few nerves before giving a presentation, but rehearsing is the best way to build your confidence. It is not necessary to know a speech word-for-word. Instead, it is better to know the order and the key points you need to get across. Many people rehearse in front of a mirror or privately in front of friends. Take as many opportunities as you can to practise your pitch.

ACTIVITY

Now you have a general plan for the contents and the order of your pitch, it is time to prepare a script for your pitch. Write down everything you want to say. When you give your pitch do not read from your script; instead condense your script into a set of notes that you can use (if you want to) during your pitch.

CHECK MY LEARNING

What are the three most important things you will do during your pitch to ensure you come across as a professional?

Presentation skills: the needs of your audience

GETTING STARTED

What makes for an engaging school lesson? What sort of things do your teachers do that make lessons interesting, engaging and make you want to listen?

When you make your pitch, it's essential that you consider carefully what your audience need to see and hear in order to make them feel involved.

Engaging your audience

During your pitch you should consider the interests and needs of your audience. To engage your audience your pitch must relate to them in some way – perhaps through personal experience or a solution to a problem they have. We have already considered some of the techniques that can be used to ensure your pitch is engaging and memorable (page 93). Below are other factors you need to consider so the needs of your audience are met.

Involving your audience

People are more engaged in something if they are involved, so one option is to involve your audience during your pitch. For example, your audience could be involved in a demonstration of your product or service. You might have the opportunity to pass around a sample of your product or you could simply involve your audience by asking them questions about their own experiences. If you intend to involve your audience, you will need to plan this so carefully that it does not disrupt the flow of your pitch or take too long.

At the end of your pitch, it is appropriate to give your audience the opportunity to ask questions. Generally, the questions will involve clarifying something you said during your pitch or seeking more information about a particular aspect of your idea. Questions are an important part of any pitch as they provide you with useful feedback and allow your audience to find out exactly what they need to know. (You can learn more about dealing with questions on pages 104–105.)

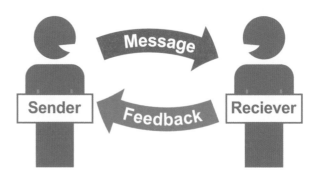

◼ Figure 2.1: Involving your audience through questioning is an important part of the feedback loop. The questions your audience ask will help you evaluate your pitch

LINK IT UP

Your audience may well be your target market. Look back over Learning aim A to review what you learned about understanding your customers.

ACTIVITY

At the end of your pitch you will give your audience the opportunity to ask questions. As a class, watch a past episode of *Dragons' Den*. Following one entrepreneur's pitch, pause the video before the *Dragons* begin their questioning.

In small groups, come up with ten questions you would ask the entrepreneur about their business idea. Play the rest of the episode and see if you and the *Dragons* asked similar questions.

Ways to engage your audience

The following techniques might be appropriate to ensure your audience are engaged from the outset.

- **Ask a yes/no question.** Straight away this will require your audience to think and act. For example, 'Raise your hand if you have ever...'.

- **Ask your audience to imagine something.** Another way to get your audience thinking is to ask them to imagine something and then pause for five seconds before continuing. For example, 'Imagine how you might feel if...'. What you ask them to imagine should link to your product or service.

- **Use humour.** Most advertisements use humour to generate positive associations. If you laugh when watching an advertisement you are likely to have a positive association with the product being advertised. Humour is an effective way to relax your audience and make them feel comfortable.

- **Give your audience a task or exercise to complete.** This might involve a product demonstration, tasting food or taking part in a short quiz.

▣ **What can you do to keep the attention of your audience?**

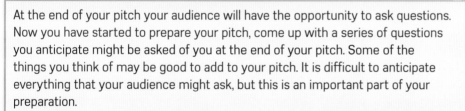

ACTIVITY

At the end of your pitch your audience will have the opportunity to ask questions. Now you have started to prepare your pitch, come up with a series of questions you anticipate might be asked of you at the end of your pitch. Some of the things you think of may be good to add to your pitch. It is difficult to anticipate everything that your audience might ask, but this is an important part of your preparation.

Potential questions	Response

Watching your peers practise their pitches will help you formulate questions and reflect on your own pitch.

CHECK MY LEARNING

Summarise how your pitch will achieve the following:

- Engage your audience
- Keep your audience interested
- Involve your audience

Presentation skills: using visual aids

Using visual aids, for example a slideshow, in your pitch will help to engage your audience. It also makes it easier for them to understand and remember the important points you want to make.

Visual aids (Computer projections)

In a formal pitch most presenters will use some form of visual aid. Most commonly, presenters may choose to use ICT presentation software such as PowerPoint®, Keynote or Prezi. Most have a built-in tool for creating speaker notes, so that the presenter can view a separate set of notes. Visual aids allow a presenter to communicate far more information than if they were simply talking. Diagrams can be used to explain complicated concepts or processes, and images can be used to interest the audience or grab their attention. A **slideshow** or **slide deck** is very useful because it helps a presenter keep track of their pitch and stick to a plan.

KEY TERMS

Slideshow/Slide deck – a presentation of a series of still images and text on a projection screen or electronic display to help a presenter to communicate information to an audience.
Legibility – the quality of handwriting. Being clear and easy to read.

DID YOU KNOW?

Dual-coding is the process of using verbal explanations (words) and imagery (pictures and diagrams) to explain something. Visual and verbal information are organised differently in the human brain, so your brain can organise and understand verbal and visual information at the same time. When explaining something to an audience the most effective way is to use verbal and visual methods together. This is why visual aids are effective when giving a pitch.

Text and graphics

A slideshow will usually combine text and graphics. The key to a good slideshow is to ensure each slide does not contain too much information. If it does, your audience will be spending too much time trying to understand a diagram or graph, or reading text. While they are doing this, they are not focused on your pitch. Your slideshow should be clear and use a clear font at a large size. You may also use some handwritten notes or diagrams in your presentation. It is very important that these are easy for your audience to read. You should also check your slides for spelling, punctuation and grammar.

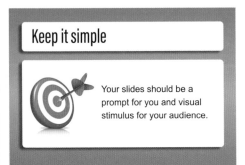

□ **Figure 2.2: Which of these slides looks better to you?**

Use the ideas and information you have for your pitch to create a slideshow to accompany your presentation.

1 Take two pieces of A4 paper and fold each into six sections.

2 Unfold the paper and number the sections 1–12. Each box will represent one slide of your slideshow.

3 In each box make a rough plan for the contents of that slide. What text will it include, what images, diagrams or graphs will it feature? Use the plan of your pitch to do this.

4 Using slideshow software, such as PowerPoint®, create a template for your presentation. Your template should include the colours, styles and fonts you will use in your slideshow. You could use one of the many template features in the software or create your own.

Handouts

One way to provide your audience with information is to provide handouts. Handouts can take many forms: for example, a simple brochure featuring product details, financial information and forecasts for the business, or simply a paper copy of your slideshow. Table 2.3 lists a number of benefits and drawbacks of using handouts in a pitch.

◻ **Table 2.3: The pros and cons of handouts**

Benefits	Drawbacks
• Handouts provide the audience with additional information that might not fit into the pitch. • The audience can go back over information and absorb it at their own pace. • Your audience can take notes as you give your pitch.	• Handouts can be a distraction from what you're saying during your pitch. • Your audience can read ahead. (You might not want your audience to know what's coming).

1 Why are visual aids important during a presentation or pitch?

2 Identify three characteristics of a good slideshow.

3 How can handouts support a presentation or pitch?

Communication skills

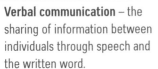

In a small group, consider how a person can use the following to communicate with other people. For each, give specific examples of how they communicate meaning without using words.

- Facial expressions
- Body language (e.g. the way you stand)
- Eye contact
- Tone of voice

KEY TERMS

Verbal communication – the sharing of information between individuals through speech and the written word.

Non-verbal communication – communicating with individuals without speaking. Non-verbal communication includes body language, gestures, facial expressions, proximity and touch.

Communication is about much more than just speaking – the way in which you say something is just as important as what you are saying.

Verbal and non-verbal communication

The communication of messages or information through words is called verbal communication. Verbal communication may be two types: written and oral. Verbal communication takes place through face-to-face conversations, group discussions, counselling, interview, emails or letters. When messages or information are exchanged or communicated without using any spoken or written words it is known as non-verbal communication. Non-verbal communication takes place though gestures, facial expressions, eye contact, physical proximity, touching, etc.

Non-verbal communication is a powerful means of communicating in face-to-face encounters, and can be expressed and perceived consciously or unconsciously. Much of non-verbal communication is unintentional, and people are often unaware that they are sending messages.

It is important to appear confident when you are communicating, especially if you are delivering a presentation to an audience. It's normal to feel nervous but you need to make sure your nerves don't get the better of you and spoil your pitch. Be confident about what you are saying and be sure to prepare and practise beforehand.

Table 2.4 outlines some forms of communication which are important for a presenter.

▣ **Table 2.4: Forms of communication and what they can mean**

Form of Communication	Explanation
Body language and gestures	There are many forms of body language including the way a person stands, the way they sit, how they walk and the way they use their hands. For example: • crossing your arms can be a sign of defensiveness • nail biting can be a sign of stress • tapping/drumming your fingers can be a sign of impatience • standing up straight with your shoulders back may show confidence • placing tips of fingers together when talking (steepling of the fingers) is a demonstration of control and authority • palms open, facing upwards is a sign of openness and honesty.
Eye contact	Eye contact is important in most forms of communication. Maintaining eye contact shows that you are paying attention and are interested. Lots of eye contact with your audience will help build trust and show you are confident. Be careful to look around the room, to the back and front of your audience. Make eye contact with lots of people and do not keep looking at the same part of the room or holding one person's eye.

Tone, pace and volume

The tone and volume of your voice will influence the atmosphere and nature of your pitch. Tone refers to how your message comes across. For example, saying 'Hi' instead of 'Good morning' at the start of your pitch may come across more informal and friendly. Pace refers to the speed that you move through your pitch and volume refers to how loud your voice is. It is important that all members of your audience can hear you. If you speak too quietly and at a slow pace, your audience could easily get bored. However, speak too fast or loud and you will come across as nervous or aggressive.

TIPS

Nervous presenters have a tendency to speak fast. Make a conscious effort to slow down your pace and take short pauses after key bits of information (perhaps even write 'pause' on your notes as a reminder) to help your audience absorb what you're saying.

DID YOU KNOW?

Some studies have found that that 7 per cent of any message is conveyed through words, 38 per cent through certain vocal elements (such as the tone of voice), and 55 per cent through non-verbal elements (facial expressions, gestures, posture, etc.). So, non-verbal communication (how we say it) might be more important that verbal communication (what we say) when communicating with others.

ACTIVITY

Consider the following non-verbal forms of communication during your pitch. For each, explain what it will communicate to your audience and why it is part of a professional pitch.

Non-verbal communication	Explanation
Standing up straight during your pitch	
Looking each member of your audience in the eye while giving your pitch	
Smiling during your pitch	
Speaking clearly and at a moderate pace (not too fast or too slow)	

CHECK MY LEARNING

1 Why is eye contact important when communicating with someone?
2 Why is it important to speak at a regulated pace when giving your pitch?
3 Identify three gestures a person might make with their hands or arms and explain what they might mean.

Responding to questions

If you can anticipate the kinds of questions your audience might ask you about your pitch, you will find it a lot easier to answer them!

Component 1	Component 2	Component 3
Creativity and innovation	Financial forecasts	Marketing mix
Customer loyalty	Break-even	Market segmentation
Sole trader	Target market	Invoice
Qualitative research	Start-up costs	Current liability
Recession	Quality control	Liquidity

Using business terminology

During this course you have learned about a wide range of important business and enterprise concepts and aspects of running an enterprise such as market research, marketing, finance, human resources, production and planning. Your pitch is an opportunity to demonstrate your understanding by appropriately using business terminology accurately during your pitch. Appropriate and accurate use of key terminology will help you deliver a professional and convincing pitch.

ACTIVITY

Review the current plans you have in place for your micro enterprise pitch along with your notes and work from the course. Use a table like the one below to highlight all of the business terminology that you will need to use during your pitch. When you have created your list, check your understanding with your teacher and ensure you understand why and how you can use this terminology in your pitch. During rehearsal for your pitch, you can practise using the terminology confidently.

Key terminology	Check understanding and appropriate use

Listening and responding to questions

At the end of your pitch you should offer your audience the opportunity to ask you any questions about your micro enterprise activity. You should end your pitch by asking this question. Although you have carried out an activity to help you prepare for these questions, it is very difficult to anticipate what your audience may ask.

It may seem obvious, but to answer your audience's questions well you must understand what they are asking. Listen carefully to every question and ask the person to repeat it or clarify what they mean if needed. A question may have a number of parts, for example, 'Can you tell me your average selling price, how you arrived at this price and your estimated sales revenue for the first month?' There are three questions here. Take each question in turn and check with the audience member that they are happy with your response to each one. Typically, your audience may ask you a question you don't know the answer to or something you haven't thought about before – don't worry. It is fine not to know the answer to everything, but make sure you know what you will say when either you don't know the answer, or the question raises something about your idea you hadn't thought of before.

ACTIVITY

To answer the questions from your audience well and respond appropriately if you do not know the answer, prepare a range of statements you could use during this part of the pitch. The first column of the table below outlines a potential situation. In the second column, prepare a question, statement or response you could use.

Potential situation/question	Your response
Offer your audience the opportunity to ask you any questions at the end of your pitch.	
You don't understand the question from an audience member.	
An audience member asks a multi-step question.	
An audience member asks you a question you don't know the answer to.	
An audience member brings up an issue about your micro enterprise activity that you have not thought of.	

TIPS

When being asked a question it is sometimes useful to repeat the question as a way of seeking clarity. Not only will this help you understand the question better, it will also give the audience member the opportunity to clarify that you have understood the purpose of their question. This will also give you valuable thinking time to compose your response.

◘ **You should listen and respond to your audience's questions carefully**

CHECK MY LEARNING

Identify three things you will do to effectively answer your audience's questions.

Learning aim B: assessment practice

How you will be assessed

Now that you have studied the topics in Learning aim B, you will need to prepare a short pitch of your micro enterprise activity and present it to an audience. The pitch will show the audience your idea in summary format. The audience may include teachers and/or peers. You need to demonstrate the presentation and communication skills outlined in Learning aim B when pitching the plan.

To achieve the highest standards, you should summarise the key elements of your plan to an audience logically. You should fluently use a range of appropriate presentation and communication skills. You should discuss and agree with your teacher how long your pitch should last. As part of your discussion with your teacher you should also include:

- a summary of the final plan
- speaker notes
- handouts for the audience (if you are using them)
- rehearsal of the pitch
- anticipating potential questions and preparing potential replies.

TIPS

Use tracking documents and keep them up to date on a daily basis, recording all actions, contributions, successes, problems and solutions. This will help you when you come to review your performance.

CHECKPOINT

Strengthen

- What factors contribute to a professional pitch?

- What are three rules for effective slideshows and visual aids when giving a presentation?

- Why is body language (non-verbal communication) important when communicating with an audience?

Challenge

- List three key messages you want to get across to your audience during your micro enterprise pitch.

- What is the best way to make a pitch memorable?

- What are the three most common lines of questioning from an audience following a business pitch?

To complete this task you must bring together the preparations you have made for your plan of a micro enterprise activity and deliver your pitch to an audience. Your audience could include teachers and peers. Your evidence for Learning aim B could include:

- a summary of the final plan
- rough notes you have used to prepare for your pitch
- draft plans for your slideshow presentation
- a set of speaker notes
- a set of handouts you have prepared for your audience
- a record of rehearsals you have completed and accompanying notes on changes you have made leading up to your pitch
- a set of questions you have prepared in anticipation for the questions your audience might ask
- a recording of your final pitch and audience Q&A.

TAKE IT FURTHER

When preparing for your micro enterprise activity pitch, keep a detailed record of all decisions, supported with a portfolio of evidence, for example, draft speaker notes, draft designs of slides, photos, letters and testimonials. To achieve higher criteria you need to be able to demonstrate the development of your pitch and how you have prepared to demonstrate excellent presentation and communication skills. Evidence could also include teacher feedback and recordings of rehearsals. You could also review your understanding of presentation and communication skills by producing a checklist for what excellent presentation and communications skills would look like in your final pitch.

Giving feedback

We give feedback all of the time, usually to our friends, family, and to ourselves through self-reflection.

Giving good feedback

Feedback is the reaction to a product or a person's performance of a task, which can be used to inform improvements. As part of the process, it is likely that you will need to give feedback to your peers too. Giving feedback to your peers will be really useful because you are going through the same process yourself. Indeed, by giving and receiving feedback in this way, you will be able to compare the similarities and differences between your pitches and collaboratively learn from this process. Giving feedback is a personal communication skill that professionals such as teachers, trainers, artists, consultants and inspectors develop over years of experience and practice.

Models for giving feedback

There are a wide variety of models that can be used within business to support the process of giving effective feedback. Most of these models focus on ensuring the process of giving and receiving feedback is positive.

ACTIVITY

To help you formulate and give effective feedback to your peers, create your own feedback crib sheet. This crib sheet could be a form that you design which you can fill in before giving your feedback. You can work in a small group on this activity. Use ideas from the feedback models below to help you design your crib sheet.

THE BOOST MODEL

Using an acronym, the BOOST model suggests five things to remember when giving feedback.

Balanced: the focus during feedback sessions should be on the areas of the receiver's development and strengths, with a focus on how the strengths can be further developed or used to good effect. When giving 'negative feedback' be sure to include good and constructive points too.

Observed: you must always base your feedback on what you have observed, rather than on what you think about it or your feelings about an issue.

Objective: when giving feedback, don't refer to the personality of the receiver but only on the actions and outcomes. Be descriptive, not evaluative.

Specific: make sure that you back up your comments with specific examples of the observed behaviour. For example, when giving feedback explain exactly what he/she did well.

Timely: always endeavour to give your feedback as soon as possible, after the activity. Doing this ensures that you capture the observed action(s) as accurately as possible.

THE SKS MODEL

The SKS requires the person giving feedback to focus on three main questions:

- What should the person **Stop** doing?
- What should the person **Keep** doing?
- What should the person **Start** doing?

WHAT WENT WELL AND EVEN BETTER IF...

Perhaps the simplest model of feedback is to use 'What went well' (WWW) and 'Even better if' (EBI). This model is simple and useful as the giver of feedback will start by focusing on the positives (WWW) and they can then go on to explore ideas for improvement through EBI. The benefits of using EBI is that it frames the feedback positively.

ACTIVITY

To support your peers in making improvements to the micro enterprise idea and pitch, provide them with some feedback they can use to make the necessary improvements. For this activity you can use the feedback crib sheet you created above or use the template below.

Try to give your peers feedback on the following areas of their project (making sure you are as specific as possible):

- the micro enterprise idea
- the contents of the pitch
- presentation skills
- communication skills.

Name:	Idea:
WWW	EBI

CHECK MY LEARNING

1 What does WWW and EBI stand for?
2 What three pieces of advice would you give to someone who is about to give someone feedback?

Receiving feedback

Think of a time when you received some **positive feedback**. How did it make you feel? How did you respond?

Now, think of a time when you received some **negative feedback**. How did it make you feel? How did you respond?

It isn't always easy or comfortable to receive feedback but you can learn from it – and it can help you to improve your performance and your pitch.

The benefits of feedback

Effective feedback, both positive and negative, is very helpful. Feedback is valuable information that will be used to make important decisions. Top performing companies are top performing companies because they consistently search for ways to be even better. In a business context, feedback can come from a number of sources – customers, clients, employees, suppliers and stakeholders. Top performing companies are not only good at accepting feedback, they deliberately ask for feedback. And they know that feedback is helpful only when it highlights weaknesses as well as strengths. Following your pitch it is important that you receive and act on feedback. Feedback is not criticism, it is the best way to learn and improve. Effective feedback:

- has the ability to motivate (whether the feedback is good or bad)
- helps people understand one another
- is a process for learning
- leads to improved performance (an important part of your assessment is making recommendations on how you could improve your plan and pitch).

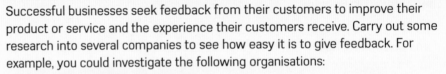

ACTIVITY

Successful businesses seek feedback from their customers to improve their product or service and the experience their customers receive. Carry out some research into several companies to see how easy it is to give feedback. For example, you could investigate the following organisations:

1 a public service, such as the NHS

2 a multinational corporation, such as Nestlé or BMW

3 a local high street independent retailer

4 a charity, such as Oxfam.

TIPS

Sometimes when receiving feedback, it is easier to focus on the negatives and overlook the positives – this is natural human behaviour. Straight after receiving feedback, start by reflecting on the positives and making a note of everything that went well before thinking about how you can improve next time.

DID YOU KNOW?

The most commonly used form of gathering feedback in a simple quantifiable (measurable) way is using a Likert scale. A Likert scale allows customers to choose an option from a range of scaled options. For example, a typical five-level Likert scale could be 1. Strongly agree, 2. Agree, 3. Neither agree nor disagree, 4. Disagree, 5. Strongly disagree.

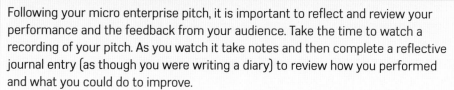

◨ Figure 2.3: Many companies allow customers to complete short surveys where they can rate their products and services using a simple Likert scale.

ACTIVITY

Following your micro enterprise pitch, it is important to reflect and review your performance and the feedback from your audience. Take the time to watch a recording of your pitch. As you watch it take notes and then complete a reflective journal entry (as though you were writing a diary) to review how you performed and what you could do to improve.

Content Did you get across everything you intended? Did your pitch flow in a logical way and did it make sense? Were you able to answer the audience's questions?

Presentation skills Was your pitch professional? Did your slideshow and handouts communicate what you intended? Did your presentation engage your audience?

Communication skills Were you clear? Did you come across as being confident? Were you enthusiastic and positive about your idea?

My pitch review
The content of my pitch
My presentation skills
My communication skills

To summarise your strengths and areas for development, you could use one of the feedback models discussed on page 108.

CHECK MY LEARNING

1 What is the purpose of feedback?

2 What is a Likert scale?

3 What are two benefits of receiving feedback?

4 Why might someone feel nervous about giving or receiving feedback?

Learning aim C: assessment preparation

How you will be assessed

Now that you have studied the topics in Learning aim C by giving and receiving feedback on your idea and pitch, you will need to produce a full written review of your plan and pitch. The review will be based on your personal reflections and the opinions and advice from your peers and teacher. Your review should include the strengths of your plan and pitch and areas for development. You should refer to the evidence collected throughout Learning aim C in your review.

To achieve the highest standards, you should consider in detail and reach a conclusion about how your use of presentation and communication skills contributed to the success of your pitch. You must reach a reasoned conclusion on the success of your pitch and give reasons for any recommendations. You should refer to your strengths and development needs by drawing on evidence from audience feedback. Finally, you should reach a justified conclusion on your plan and propose logical and feasible amendments that will add to its potential success.

TIPS

When identifying areas for improvement you should be as specific as possible and use examples to illustrate your point. Throughout your review refer to the evidence and feedback you have collected.

CHECKPOINT

Strengthen

1. What have you learned about giving feedback to other people?
2. Explain one model you could use to give feedback to your peers or colleagues in the future.
3. Why is the process of giving and receiving feedback important in a business context?

Challenge

1. What improvements would you make to your micro enterprise idea/activity?
2. What have you learned about your own strengths?
3. Summarise your performance of your pitch in a few sentences.

ASSESSMENT ACTIVITY   LEARNING AIM   C

To complete this task, you must bring together the feedback you have received and your personal reflections of your plan for a micro enterprise activity and pitch to complete a comprehensive review and recommendations for improvement. Your evidence for Learning aim C could include:

- records of feedback from your audience (peers and teachers)
- records of your personal reflections following your pitch
- a review of your pitch after you have watched the video recording
- a final document that evaluates the success of your plan and pitch, and recommends how improvements to the plan and pitch could be made.

TAKE IT FURTHER

The review of your plan could go a step further and lead to a revised plan being produced. This could include producing new materials for your pitch, such as slideshows, speaker notes and handouts. Finally, following your feedback you could deliver your improved pitch in front of an audience.

03 Promotion and Finance for Enterprise

Introduction

Once you have an idea for an enterprise, the next thing you will have to do is promote it. In other words, you will need to think about how to make sure all your potential customers know about your goods and services. You will also need to plan the finances of your enterprise carefully – where would you start with this? What help is there for enterprises to guide them through this process?

In this component, you will learn about how an enterprise can use the promotional mix to communicate its goods and services effectively to its customers. You will learn about the characteristics and relative benefits and drawbacks of different promotional methods such as advertising, sales promotions, personal selling, public relations and direct marketing. You will also explore how successful enterprises combine a range of strategies to create awareness and a strong brand image, and reach specific customers through targeting and market segmentation.

Additionally, you will look at the financial management of enterprises. This will include the day-to-day processing of sales and purchases, and the financial documents an enterprise will use to manage and record this process effectively. You will learn about financial planning, including a number of management tools such as cash flow forecasts and break-even analysis, which allow managers and owners of enterprises to ensure they have enough cash to operate and can make a profit. You will also learn the range of sources an enterprise may use to finance its operations, expand and grow.

LEARNING AIMS

In this component you will learn about:

A	Promotion
B	Financial records
C	Financial planning and forecasting

The promotional mix: methods and message

KEY TERMS

Media is the general term used to describe all of the following collectively: newspapers, magazines, books, television, radio, websites and the internet. The media is a form of mass communication, which can be used to reach large amounts of people.
A **medium** is how an enterprise chooses to communicate with and advertise to its market.
The **promotional mix** is the range of techniques and mediums an enterprise could use to communicate with potential and current customers. It uses the mix to inform and persuade people to buy its goods and services.

Enterprises use promotion to communicate with their current and potential customers. This is an important part of how they attract business.

Promotion

The main aim of any promotion is to:

- build positive associations with the enterprise
- encourage customers to purchase products (goods or services).

There are many ways that an enterprise might be promoted and the combination of methods and **mediums** an enterprise might use are referred to as the **promotional mix**. Over the coming lessons, you will learn about each of these methods and how an enterprise can use them.

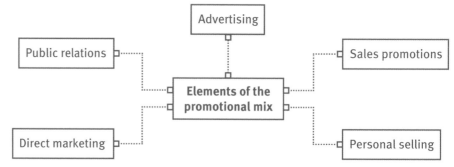

■ Figure 3.1: The promotional mix

The message

The message of a promotion means *what* it needs to say. Any form of promotion has the aim of communicating one of two things:

1 the features and benefits of an enterprise

2 the products offered by an enterprise.

Forms of promotion might achieve this in a variety of ways. Some might display images of goods. Some may include a video of the product or service being used. Some may use text to provide detailed information about specific features and benefits.

Features and benefits

By communicating features and benefits a promotion can:

- inform customers
- remind customers
- persuade customers.

For example, some companies will show a ten-second advert on TV. Ten seconds might be too short a time to communicate a lot of information to customers, but might be long enough to remind customers of a product they like and are familiar with.

Finding the right medium

Often, a promotion might inform, persuade and remind all at once, depending on the medium the enterprise has chosen. An advert placed in a local newspaper or national magazine can often communicate quite detailed information, as the example on the right shows.

Successful promotion

The purpose of promoting an enterprise is to create positive associations with it and persuade customers to take an interest in it. Interacting with the enterprise might mean visiting it, getting involved in a good cause or buying its goods and services.

Analysing impact

It is not always easy to identify which element of the promotional mix had the greatest impact. Often, businesses will use a variety of methods at the same time. For example, they may:

- set up an Instagram account
- send out flyers in the local press
- hand out free samples of their goods.

Using more than one method means it is sometimes difficult for an enterprise to work out which ones led to the highest number of sales. Therefore, it can be challenging to decide on the type of promotion it would be best to continue with.

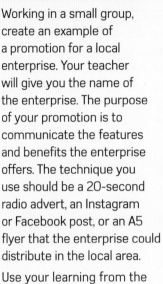

EMPRO+ECT

Why wait for scientists to prove that mobile phones are dangerous?

Buy EMPRO+ECT now!

Emprotect is a small lapel badge that contains special crystals that provide biofeedback resonance to protect your brain cells.

For only £100 you can protect yourself today!

- Do you think this advert has more information in it than you could fit in a ten-second video?

DID YOU KNOW?

A flyer is a small printed handout giving details about something. It can also be called a 'pamphlet', 'leaflet' or 'circular'. Advertising in this way has been around since printing presses were invented more than 500 years ago.

CHECK MY LEARNING

1 In a small group, create a list of five criteria you could use to evaluate the promotion methods of an enterprise. Once you have created your list, turn it into a table (like Table 3.1 below). Then use your table to evaluate the promotions your class produced in the previous activity.

- Table 3.1: Evaluating promotions

	Criteria 1	Criteria 2	Criteria 3	Criteria 4	Criteria 5
Method 1	Score 1–5				
Method 2					

2 Once you have completed your table, discuss with your group what you think makes a good promotional mix for a business enterprise.

Advertising

Advertising is widely used by enterprises that wish to make more customers aware of the products that they offer. Next time you open a magazine or a newspaper, see how many adverts you can spot.

What is advertising?

Advertising entails an enterprise paying for space in the media to communicate with the public about its goods and services. Advertising can be expensive, so enterprises must ensure they spend their advertising budgets carefully. Some businesses choose to use a **digital advertising** format, as the cost of this is often considerably less.

KEY TERM

Digital advertising is done online or using a device such as a mobile phone.

The purpose of advertising

As we have discovered, there are two main purposes of advertising.

1 To inform people: an enterprise needs to make potential customers aware of a new product and its benefits.

2 To persuade people to make a purchase: an enterprise might tell people about the benefits its products offer or their value for money.

Different companies use adverts according to their individual needs, with one or both of these purposes in mind. For example, in the UK, Weight Watchers UK might use adverts to:

- *inform* people (purpose 1) about the dangers of obesity
- *persuade* people (purpose 2) to lose weight using their service.

ACTIVITY

1 Collect six different adverts from newspapers and magazines. Then take photos of six adverts in public spaces, such as billboards and posters.

2 Divide the adverts you have collected according to whether they are trying to inform, persuade or both. For each one, write a short explanation of how it uses words and pictures to achieve these purposes.

DID YOU KNOW?

Adverts printed on odd-numbered pages of a magazine or newspaper (the right-hand side) can cost more than those printed on even-numbered pages (the left-hand side). This is because people see the right-hand side of the magazine or newspaper first when they are turning pages and are more likely to pay attention.

Methods of advertising

An enterprise can choose from several methods of advertising. Look at the options in Table 3.2.

◘ Table 3.2: Methods of advertising

Method of advertising	Where this type of advertising is used	Why this type of advertising is used
Moving images and videos	On television, in a cinema or posted on a video streaming site, such as YouTube	These would be suitable for goods that have several features or moving parts because the images can show demonstrations of goods being used.
Print	In newspapers and magazines, or on billboards	These will generally be seen by large numbers of people. For example, eye-catching billboards can be placed beside busy roads. Modern technology means that digital adverts can be changed at different times of the day to target a particular audience – for example, an advert for a new type of laptop could be programmed to be displayed during rush hour, when commuters and businesspeople are more likely to see it.
Ambient	Public spaces, such as the sides of buses	Ambient advertising can be effective at catching the attention of potential customers who are passing by or waiting.
Digital	Websites, or sent to customers via text message or email	Digital advertising reaches large numbers of people very quickly. Companies such as Google and Facebook have developed technology that makes adverts appear when people type in certain key words in their website browser.
Audio	Radio adverts, and adverts on music streaming platforms such as Spotify	They allow enterprises to talk to customers about their products. For a relatively low cost, an enterprise can tell people about the features of their product and where it can be bought. Sometimes these adverts feature famous voices to give them extra credibility.

◘ **Why are escalators an effective place for an ambient advert?**

Sales promotions

GETTING STARTED

Think about a time when you felt you had bought a bargain. What did you buy? Why did you think it was a bargain? Why do you think the business made you this offer?

Enterprises are always thinking of ways to attract customers. This is often achieved through sales promotions. When did you last see a promotion that said something like 'ten per cent off your next purchase', or 'buy one get one free'? Did it persuade you to buy something?

The purpose of sales promotions

A sales promotion gives customers an incentive (often limited to a period of time) to buy an enterprise's products. For example, a sales promotion might offer you a discount on the price of a product if you buy it within a certain period of time.

Enterprises use sales promotions in a number of ways.

1 To entice people in – an enterprise might use special offers and promote them in a shop window to attract customers into its shop. Customers may then be encouraged to purchase other products in the shop that are not part of a sales promotion.

2 To boost sales figures – some enterprises, such as a local car dealership, will be judged on the number of sales they make. Sales promotions help to boost sales figures near a month's end, for example.

3 To attract first-time buyers – special offers might encourage customers unfamiliar with a brand to try it for the first time, for example by giving away free samples. If they enjoy the product, these customers may then become loyal to the enterprise and buy from it in the future.

4 To clear old stock – sometimes enterprises have excess stock they want to sell off. This is could be because they produce food that has a sell-by date, or clothes that may go out of fashion. A sales promotion on the stock they wish to clear will help a business to make room for new items.

ACTIVITY

Select five products you are familiar with – one from each of the following categories:
- food
- clothing
- a smartphone
- a service
- a car.

For each product you choose, identify a sales promotion technique that you think would be effective at boosting its sales. Make sure each technique you identify is different.

□ **Why might someone be attracted by these sales promotions?**

Methods of sales promotion

Table 3.3 shows some methods of sales promotions and how they work.

◻ **Table 3.3: Methods of sales promotion**

Method of promotion	How it works
Coupons	A small paper or card token offering a discount or free gift is given to a customer. Coupons are often used to encourage customers to buy again from the enterprise at a later date.
Competitions	Customers have the chance of winning prizes when they buy a product. A competition might include: • an 'instant win', such as a prize within the product itself • entering the customer into a prize draw when they make a purchase.
Money off/discount	A business gives customers a discounted price – for example, ten per cent, 20 per cent or 33 per cent off the original price.
Loyalty schemes/ incentives	Regular customers are rewarded for their loyalty. Customers can build up points that have a monetary value. They can then use these points: • in exchange for goods • to collect something free, such as a cup of coffee. Loyal customers also gain access to special offers at certain times.
Free samples	Customers get to try something without having to buy it first. Enterprises often give away small free samples hoping a customer will like the product and buy it in the future.
Buy one get one free	Buy one get one free (BoGoF) is exactly that – customers get one free product when they buy something. This is effectively a 50 per cent discount, which makes it similar to 'money off' offers.

Sales promotions can be an effective way to boost sales. However, when an enterprise uses sales promotions, such as lower prices or free gifts, its profit margins are reduced. This is because revenue per unit is lower when using a sales promotion. For this reason, most businesses will only use sales promotions at certain times.

ACTIVITY

Take a look at this graph, which represents the sale of a product over time.

1 Identify two or three points on the curve where you might choose to use a sales promotion.

2 For each point, explain why you would use a sales promotion at that time.

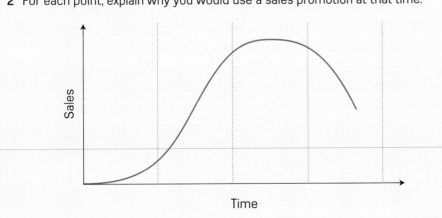

Personal selling

Personal selling is where a representative of an enterprise contacts potential customers directly. The salesperson uses their interpersonal skills and knowledge of the product to try to persuade potential customers to make a purchase.

The purpose of personal selling

Personal selling has a range of benefits that other forms of promotion, such as advertising, do not have. The main benefit is that personal selling is a two-way process. This means:

- the customer can ask questions and give feedback
- the salesperson can adapt their sales message to target and meet the needs of customers.

Because it allows detailed explanation and can be tailored to each individual customer, personal selling is very useful for promoting products that can be complicated or have many different features – for example, home insurance or a new car. Can you think of any other examples of goods or services that might benefit from personal selling?

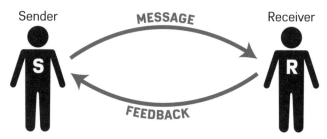

□ Figure 3.2: Can you think of an example of how a salesperson can adapt their message to meet a customer's needs?

The salesperson may also:

- be an expert in the product they are selling
- demonstrate a product, giving detailed information about its features and benefits
- provide the customer with advice specific to their wants and needs.

ACTIVITY

Keep the right-hand page of this lesson covered up as you complete the task below.

There are many models for how the personal selling process works.

The sales process involves a number of stages that the salesperson will work through in order to encourage a customer to purchase a product.

Listed below are the five stages a salesperson should use when they are selling something. However, they are not currently in the correct order.

- Demonstrate solutions and value
- Generate leads (potential customers)
- Deliver and support.
- Qualify (further research) leads
- Manage objections

1 Put these stages in the correct order.

2 Explain what you think each stage might involve.

Methods of personal selling

There are several different methods of personal selling, as Table 3.4 shows.

◻ **Table 3.4: Methods of personal selling**

Method of selling	How the method works
Face to face	The salesperson is able to: • listen to the customer • watch the customer's body language and signals • adjust their message to demonstrate how the product solves a problem and meets the customer's needs. Personal selling requires interpersonal skills and the salesperson may sometimes deliver a prepared pitch.
Telephone	• Some enterprises use sales teams who make phone calls from a call centre to potential customers. • Customers may also phone a call centre with an enquiry. • This method does not allow the salesperson to 'read' (see) the customer's body language. However, a good salesperson will be able to interpret a customer's interest from the tone of their voice.
Email	• Customers receive emails trying to sell them products. • This type of personal selling may take longer than face-to-face conversations, but can also give a customer greater detail. • The salesperson can send potential customers attachments with the email, such as guides and brochures. • The salesperson can also include links to relevant websites and video demonstrations.
Video or web conferencing	• The salesperson can see the customer, wherever they are in the world. • The salesperson can demonstrate goods, via the camera. • The salesperson can also send files and links to relevant websites.

◻ Some enterprises use call centres like these for personal selling. Can you explain, in your own words, how call centres work?

Public relations

GETTING STARTED

Some medium to large enterprises employ a public relations manager/officer. Their responsibilities might include dealing with enquiries from the media, the general public or other organisations. What other responsibilities might be associated with this job?

Public relations (or PR, as it is sometimes known) involves promoting an enterprise, a brand, a product or a service by placing information about it in the media. Unlike advertising, the time or media space gained from PR is not paid for directly. PR relates to how an enterprise manages its **image** through the media. Look at some expensive sportswear or perfume, for example. The opinion you form about these products is probably influenced by whether or not you like the image they present.

The purpose of public relations

Public relations can be used at any time during a promotion to sell a product. Enterprises often employ PR specialists to:

- help manage their brand image
- encourage positive publicity through the media
- encourage positive views from the general public and other organisations.

Protecting the brand image

KEY TERM

Image is people's opinions of goods or a service and what they associate it with.

PR can sometimes be interpreted negatively by the media and, as a result, the general public. This means people may not want to be associated with the 'brand image' that has been created.

Table 3.5 shows the benefits and the drawbacks of PR. Notice that it does not take much for a benefit to become a drawback.

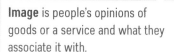 **Table 3.5: Benefits and drawbacks of PR**

Benefits of PR	Drawbacks of PR
It is free.	It is hard to control what is said by a third party (the public, the media and other organisations).
A good PR 'story' can reach a wide audience.	There is no guarantee that a PR 'story' will be picked up by the media.
It can improve a business's reputation and sales.	It is difficult to measure the impact on reputation and sales.
When it is *positive*, people tend to pay more attention because it comes from an impartial (neutral) source.	A *positive* story passed to the press could be turned into a *negative* one by a journalist.

Methods of public relations

Enterprises use many different methods of PR, depending on their individual needs, business aims and targets.

Press releases

A press release is an article that is produced by an enterprise to share interesting stories, news and information. A press release will include:

- positive information – often about a new product, an event or an activity
- at least one photograph.

Press releases vs. adverts

An enterprise will often send a press release to newspapers in the hope they will publish it (in print or online). Press releases are free, whereas advertisements are usually paid for. Unlike advertisements, the agency that receives a press release can choose whether or not to publish it, and is also able to edit it if it chooses. This means the enterprise does not have control over the final content.

Sometimes the media may contact the enterprise first, if they think the general public might be interested in its news.

Exhibitions

An exhibition is when companies display their goods or services in the same venue. These are often large events, such as Clothes Show Live, where many different stalls are set up to highlight the latest and most exciting new products on offer.

Promotional stunts

A stunt will often catch people's attention and encourage the media to write about it. Often, a stunt is something that people will find amusing and interesting, or is done to promote a good cause. A stunt is generally a unique, one-time event, as otherwise it would stop attracting attention.

Sponsorship

Sponsorship is where a business pays to have its brand or goods displayed at an event or on something that could be associated with the enterprise. For example:

- a car company, like Volvo, might sponsor television programmes that feature cars
- a watch company, like Omega, might sponsor international sporting events such as the Olympics, and have its name on timekeeping boards.

Large companies often sponsor celebrities to use, drink or wear their goods. Sponsorship allows a business to associate its brand with a good cause or even the personality of a celebrity. People who support the cause, or like the celebrity, may be encouraged to purchase from that enterprise if someone they admire and respect is seen to be endorsing it.

ACTIVITY

Review four different examples of PR. Use two positive examples and two negative ones.

1 For each example, explain the impact you think the PR will have on the organisation (or person) it is associated with.

2 In each case, consider the level of control the organisation or individual has over it.

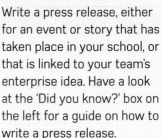

CHECK MY LEARNING

Answer the following questions to review your understanding of PR.

1 What is the difference between public relations and a sales promotion?

2 Why do people often pay more attention to PR than they would an advert?

3 Why are publicity stunts an effective way to generate media attention?

Direct marketing

Direct marketing is exactly that: it is when an enterprise communicates with a customer directly to try to sell them something. It involves any communication that is directly targeted at customers. When was the last time you, as a customer, received any direct marketing?

The purpose of direct marketing

Direct marketing allows an enterprise to establish and build a relationship with its customers. In order for it to take place, a business must have the contact details of its customers, such as their:

- postal address
- telephone number
- email address.

As the business already knows its customer, it is able to tailor the message being sent to their needs.

Building positive associations

Direct marketing can be very effective at encouraging repeat purchases, by:

- building positive associations with a brand
- introducing customers to new products.

Businesses can also acquire contact information on potential customers without them having purchased products from the business in the past. This means some businesses can send marketing material to people without prior permission.

Methods of direct marketing

Direct mail

Leaflets, letters and brochures about new products or special offers are posted directly to both customers and non-customers. These are sometimes called '**junk mail**'.

DID YOU KNOW?

In 2016, the positive response rate to direct mail was 2.9 per cent, meaning that out of every 100 households sent direct mail, almost three had a positive response. This is a considerable improvement on previous years, because businesses have improved ways of gathering information about customers and are better able to tailor their marketing to their audience.

Mail order catalogues

Catalogues, which show photographs and give details of different goods and services, allow customers to look at them whenever they want to, and for as long as they want to. Sometimes these catalogues are delivered by agents working for the business, which gives agents the opportunity to communicate directly with potential customers.

Magazines

Some companies produce magazines that are then sent to the people on their mailing list. These will contain pictures, articles and stories relating to the products and brands of the business, and allow customers to keep up to date with its news, developments and any special offers it might be running.

◻ **Why do you think some types of special offers are known as 'junk mail'?**

Telemarketing

Customers are telephoned and told about a company's latest products or offers, and invited to make a purchase. Telemarketers sometimes make uninvited calls to customers. As mentioned in a previous lesson, this is known as 'cold calling'.

Digital mail

As well as using the post, businesses can send direct marketing to people via email and text messaging. This can be effective, as modern technology means people are able to check their email frequently and can easily follow links included in the messages they receive.

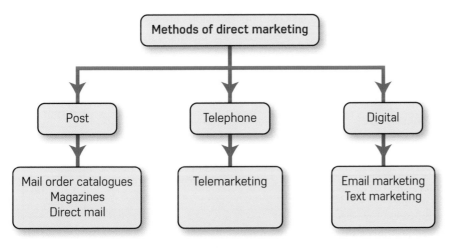

■ Figure 3.3: Try to think of a sentence that describes methods of direct marketing

Types of market

GETTING STARTED

Consider the following two scenarios.

1   You are going out for a meal with friends and have decided to eat at a burger restaurant.

2   You are the owner of a burger restaurant.

In each scenario, you will make a purchase from a business. In the first scenario, you are buying a meal. In the second scenario, you are buying the ingredients to make your burgers.

In each scenario, what factors are important to you when making a purchase?

Have you ever come across the terms B2C and B2B when reading about enterprises and businesses? They are shorthand for '**business to consumer**' **(B2C)** and 'business to business' (B2B). Each of these is a different type of market, which you will learn about in this lesson.

Targeting the right market

To create an effective promotional campaign, an enterprise must consider:

- the needs of its customers
- suitable promotional techniques that allow it to communicate with the correct target market effectively.

When **consumers** buy a product, they are buying in a business to consumer (B2C) market. However, businesses often sell to other businesses (B2B) when markets are very large.

Business to consumer (B2C) markets

Anything you buy for yourself – for example, clothes, toys, electronics, food and leisure activities – is a transaction taking place in a B2C market.

In a B2C market, the purpose of promotion is to gain sales from the public. Unlike businesses, consumers will often want to purchase a product through a variety of different channels, depending on:

- what is most convenient to them
- their emotional response to the product and promotion.

Customer decisions

Promotional strategies, using images and emotive language, can be very effective when selling in B2C markets, as customer decisions are so often influenced by their individual needs and feelings. As well as these factors, decisions in B2C markets might be based on a number of other things, as shown in Figure 3.4.

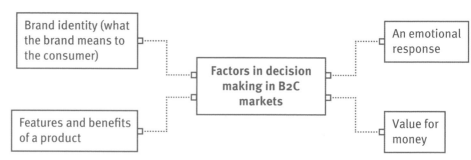

◻ Figure 3.4: How B2C markets are driven

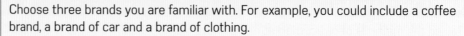

ACTIVITY

Choose three brands you are familiar with. For example, you could include a coffee brand, a brand of car and a brand of clothing.

For each brand, discuss the factors that have contributed to its brand identity. You could start by writing down a list of words you associate with each brand. What promotional strategies might the companies have used to create their brand identities?

Business to business (B2B) markets

When an enterprise sells goods or services to other enterprises, it is targeting a business to business (B2B) market. Often, it is large companies that are part of these markets. Consider the company Kellogg's, for example – its customers include large supermarket chains, such as Tesco and Sainsbury's, that will:

- purchase Kellogg's breakfast cereals from the company
- sell them to customers in their stores.

Businesses in B2B markets will use a combination of **push** and **pull strategies** to sell their products.

Creating demand

Kellogg's uses a pull strategy to create demand for its products. To do this, it uses marketing such as TV adverts to target the end customer – the consumer of the product. If there is demand for a product, then supermarket chains will buy it from Kellogg's, because they know it will sell in their stores.

Kellogg's uses a push strategy to promote its brand to supermarket chains, encouraging them to stock its goods. This could be a promotional campaign, such as giving supermarkets a discount for buying large quantities.

Decision-making in B2B markets is driven by several different factors, such as those shown in Figure 3.5.

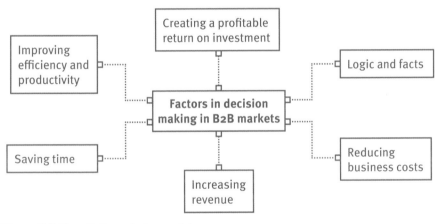

Figure 3.5: How B2B markets are driven

ACTIVITY

1 Consider the following products:
- laptop computer
- microwave pizzas
- package holiday to Spain
- flat pack dining room table and chairs.

For each one, suggest which promotional methods you would use to sell it in:
a) a B2B market
b) a B2C market.

2 Give a reason for each of your choices.

CHECK MY LEARNING

Answer the following questions to review your understanding of B2B and B2C markets.

1 Why do companies in a B2B market require more information from promotions?

2 Why are decisions in a B2C market based more on emotions?

3 How might promotion in a B2B market be different from a B2C market?

Market segmentation: demographic and geographic

No two people are the same – everybody has different needs, wants, characteristics and personal preferences. Because of these individual differences, very few products are able to meet the needs of everyone. Even a product like milk is available as a variety of different types for different people.

Why markets are divided

Markets can be divided into different sections or market segments (see Figures 3.6a and 3.6b). Each segment is made up of customers who have similar characteristics and needs. The process of analysing a market and identifying the different segments is known as 'market segmentation'.

There are several benefits of segmenting a market for enterprises.

- They are able to understand the characteristics and needs of their customers better.
- They can develop goods and services for a specific market segment, so that the product or service is better suited to that segment.
- They can identify and choose a target market to specialise in.
- They can choose promotional strategies that are better suited to their target market.

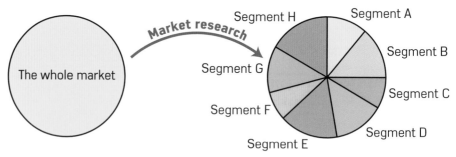

◻ Figure 3.6a: All customers who buy a product/service (the market)

◻ Figure 3.6b: Market broken down into eight segments (categories); each category contains a group of customers with similar characteristics and needs

A market can be segmented using a range of approaches. Often, several factors are considered at the same time.

ACTIVITY

Below are examples of three different families.

Family 1: Two parents with three children aged three, five and eight.

Family 2: A newly-wed couple (both aged 29).

Family 3: A couple married for 35 years with two children who have left home.

For each family, identify a suitable choice if they were to buy:

a)   a car

b)   a holiday.

Demographic segmentation

Demographic information refers to the key characteristics of a population. The full range of factors contributing to demographic segmentation is explored in Table 3.6.

◼ Table 3.6: Factors contributing to demographic segmentation

Demographic factor	Example
Age	Infants, teenagers, young adults and over 65s all have different tastes and interests. Clothes are typically targeted at different age groups.
Gender	Men and women have different tastes and needs. Toiletries are an example of a product segmented by gender.
Income	People with higher income have more disposable income (spending money) to spend on luxury goods, such as designer watches and clothing brands.
Social class	Socio-economic groups are based on income and the types of occupation a person has. For example, Social Grade B is middle class and covers people employed as intermediate managers, teachers and nurses.
Ethnicity	Many different ethnic groups live in the UK. Increasingly, businesses are taking cultural preferences into account.
Religion	People of different religions have different tastes. Muslims and Jews, for example, do not eat pork.
Family size	Larger families will buy in bulk. Some goods sell in 'family size' amounts, such as breakfast cereal or washing powder.

LINK IT UP

To remind yourself how to identify a target market, look back at Learning aim A of Component 2.

Geographic segmentation

Different customer types are likely to have different needs, depending on where they live. For example:

- people living in hot climates will have different needs from people living in countries such as the UK
- there may be greater demand for convertible cars in warmer climates, but greater demand for four-by-four vehicles in countries with rocky terrain
- countries have different cuisines, so types of food will vary from place to place.

Geographic segmentation across a town or city may simply involve how far away customers live from the business. For example, a local fish and chip shop will target people living close by, because:

- they can provide a more convenient service
- customers are likely to travel to the nearest place.

CHECK MY LEARNING

Choose a service or goods you are familiar with. Then consider how the areas of segmentation apply to it. Which factors are most relevant and why? For example, is gender more important than income?

Market segmentation: psychographic and behavioural

Remember that the purpose of segmentation is for an enterprise to find the right customers for its products. As we know, there are different ways in which markets can be segmented. Here, you will look at psychographic segmentation and behavioural segmentation.

Psychographic segmentation

Grouping customers according to their social class, attitudes, lifestyles and personality characteristics is called psychographic segmentation. However, as enterprises may not have this information about their customers, it can be very difficult to categorise people on this basis. Here are some examples of products and segments based on this process.

- Sports equipment and clothing may be aimed at those interested in extreme sports, such as snowboarding or mountain climbing.
- Some newspapers may be targeted towards Labour voters while others may be targeted at Conservative voters.
- Some brands that include recycled goods, Fairtrade goods and sustainably sourced ingredients may be aimed at environmentally conscious customers.
- Certain brands create an 'exclusive' to appeal to customers who care about status. This might include a high price tag or a membership where customers have to go through an application process before being granted access (for example, clubs or events such as music festivals and shows).
- Chocolate manufacturers have segmented the market based on the reason people eat chocolate. For example, some people eat chocolate to de-stress or as a treat, while others eat it as a snack during the day.

ACTIVITY

Below are lifestyle profiles for two people.

Profile 1: Rivkah loves spending time with her family; her children are her priority. She cares deeply about their education and is extremely 'hands on' in how they are brought up. When Rivkah is not with her family, she enjoys relaxing with peaceful music or a good book.

Profile 2: Terry enjoys the outdoors and loves nature. He is a member of a running club, a cycling club and a local conservation society. Terry is not interested in possessions and considers his best friends to be his two dogs – Brook and Sandy.

For each person, identify a range of goods or services that could be aimed at them, giving reasons for your answers. How could enterprises market these goods or services in a way that would promote customer loyalty from Rivkah and Terry?

Behavioural segmentation

Segmentation according to behaviour attempts to segment markets based on how people relate to a product. As Table 3.7 explains, behavioural segmentation may include:

- usage rate
- loyalty
- desired benefits.

◘ Table 3.7: Definitions and examples of behavioural segmentation

Segment	Definition	Examples
Usage rate	Customers are categorised by how often they purchase a product.	Many airlines and hotel chains set up special membership clubs for customers who have a high frequency of purchase. These customers may receive special deals and have the opportunity to collect rewards.
Loyalty	The level of loyalty customers show to a brand (high and low).	• Some customers are very loyal because they seek familiarity and consistency, and the brand meets those needs. Where this is the case, a business will aim to build close relationships through regular communication. • Other customers have no loyalties to any brands and will choose a product in the moment. How enterprises target these customers will be very different from their interactions with regular customers.
Desired benefits	Most products have a range of features that provide customers with several benefits or solve a range of needs.	• Some customers may purchase a smartphone in order to connect with people through social media. • Other customers may purchase the same smartphone and use it primarily as a phone. A manufacturer of smartphones may target these two types of customer differently.

LINK IT UP

To remind yourself about carrying out market research in order to understand the customer, go back to Learning aim B of Component 1.

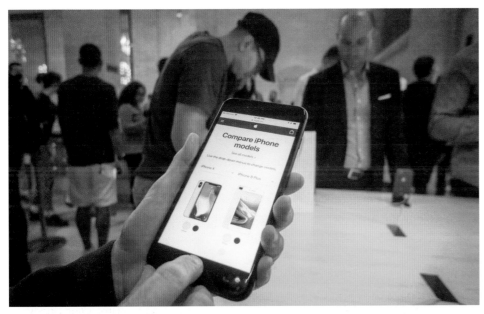

◘ What features would you prioritise when choosing a smartphone?

DID YOU KNOW?

An enterprise must fully understand its customers before it is able to do psychographic or behavioural segmentation. These days, an enterprise can use 'business intelligence' to help them do this – for example, technologies that allow this kind of data to be analysed.

ACTIVITY

1 Make a list of all the features of a popular smartphone.

2 Explain, using examples, how the smartphone might be aimed at three customers with different lifestyles and interests.

3 How might a smartphone manufacturer target these different customers?

CHECK MY LEARNING

To review your understanding of market segmentation, answer the following questions.

1 Identify one benefit of market segmentation.

2 What sort of products might be segmented based on age?

3 Why would an enterprise choose a target market?

4 State two factors that are involved in psychographic segmentation.

5 Give an example of how product loyalty might be used to segment a market.

Factors influencing the choice of promotion

GETTING STARTED

Think about these two businesses.

- McDonald's, a fast food chain selling burgers worldwide.
- Greenpeace, an environmental organisation that strives to defend the natural world and promote peace.

How might the promotional activities between the two companies differ? Think about which methods of promotion each business is most likely to use. Try to identify benefits and drawbacks of each method of promotion you have identified.

As you know, enterprises often use promotions to encourage customers to buy their products. However, this is not a straightforward process, and there are a number of factors to consider when planning what to promote and how.

Size of enterprise

A large enterprise will often use different promotional tools from a small one, as Table 3.8 shows.

◻ Table 3.8: How enterprises choose promotional techniques

Large enterprises	Small enterprises
• Large enterprises are likely to use all of the promotion strategies you have been learning about. • They may employ specially trained workers to be responsible for each strategy. For example, a large enterprise may employ a team of trained salespeople led by a sales manager. • They may also employ public relations managers or brand specialists who are each responsible for the promotion of one of the company's many brands or product ranges.	• Small enterprises are likely to have a narrower range of promotions. • They are unlikely to employ specialists. • Their promotions may be linked to the skills of their employees (perhaps just the entrepreneur and owner), their budget and the nature of the goods/service. • They may only run promotions at certain times, in order to minimise costs.

Budgetary constraints

KEY TERM

Budget is the amount of money designated for a specific activity or period of time.

An enterprise's **budget** (the amount of money available to it) for a promotion will often depend on its size. At different stages of growth, a business may decide to allocate different sums of money to promotional activity. For example:

- when a business first opens or launches a new product, it will often budget more money for its promotional activity
- if it is struggling financially, a business may have to make difficult decisions on what spending will lead to the greatest growth in sales. It may have to spend less in some areas in order to prioritise others.

ACTIVITY

Research the costs of the following promotional mediums. Compare the prices and explain why you think some are more expensive than others:
- 500 full-colour A5 leaflets (distributed in store)
- an advert of half a page in a local newspaper
- a 20-second advert on local radio
- a 30-second advert on national TV
- the average salary for a sales executive.

DID YOU KNOW?

In 2015, it was estimated that a 30-second advert during a commercial interval of the Super Bowl, America's most watched sporting event, cost US$4.5 million.

Appropriateness for product/service

Enterprises are unlikely to use all methods of promotion and will instead choose those that are most appropriate for their products. For example, national fast food chains will rarely employ a sales force to promote and sell burgers or pizza, but may use TV adverts to promote their latest deals. Similarly, enterprises that work to support the local community might use PR to attract positive attention.

Where enterprises are able to collect information on their customers, they may use market segmentation to target specific groups of people, and forms of direct marketing to build relationships and encourage loyalty.

ACTIVITY

In a small group, using the matrix diagram below as an example, discuss where each promotion method mentioned in the previous activity should be positioned. When you have agreed, add them using a dot with a label to show the position.

Y = the overall cost of using the promotion (the overall total or cost per contact)

X = the reach of the promotion (how many relevant people will see/read/hear it)

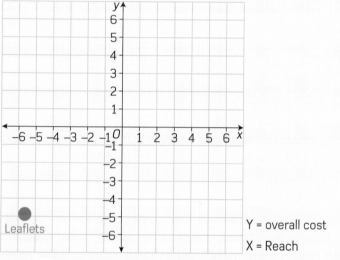

Y = overall cost

X = Reach

Leaflets distributed in store would be relatively cheap to produce amd would only reach currecnt customers who visit the store.

Target market

Promotion will not work if it does not reach and connect with the target market. An enterprise must always carefully consider the characteristics of its target market, such as:

- what sort of mediums individuals engage with
- what newspaper individuals read
- where individuals spend their work and leisure time
- the types of events that individuals attend.

For example, an enterprise wishing to promote any products associated with motorcycles might choose to place an advert in a motorcycle magazine or set up a trade stand at a motorcycle show. Similarly, a toy manufacturer might pay for a TV advert during breakfast time or at 3–4pm when children return from school.

LINK IT UP

To learn about the costs of running an enterprise (and how these are categorised), go to Learning aim B of this component.

CHECK MY LEARNING

You will find a scenario at the end of each learning aim in Component 3 of this book. They are:

Learning aim A: Brocco on the Park

Learning aim B: The Custom Bear Company

Learning aim C: The Portable Pizza Company

For the enterprise in each case study, choose the promotion methods that you think would be the most appropriate. Clearly justify your choices.

Learning aim A: assessment practice

How you will be assessed

You will be assessed on Component 3 of your course by a written externally assessed task. This component builds on the knowledge, understanding and skills that you have acquired and developed in Components 1 and 2. In your assessed task, you will be presented with a short case study of a small to medium enterprise (SME), and a series of activities to complete. These tasks will relate to the nature of the enterprise in the case study and the products or services it sells. The externally assessed task will be worth a total of 60 marks and will be completed under supervised conditions.

This assessment practice gives you an opportunity to practise part of what you will encounter in the assessed task.

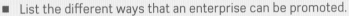

TAKE IT FURTHER

The best way to develop your understanding of promotion and marketing is to apply these concepts to real enterprises. Look at a range of promotional tools and evaluate their effectiveness for different businesses. Think about who the target market is and the purpose of the promotion. Consider how real enterprises could improve the way they use promotion.

CHECKPOINT

Strengthen
- List the different ways that an enterprise can be promoted.
- Explain the promotion methods that are best at developing good customer relationships.
- Outline why market segmentation is important.

Challenge
- State the promotional tool that you think has the greatest impact.
- Explain why it is important for an enterprise to use a variety of promotional tools.
- Explain why some market segments might be more profitable than others.

The activities in this assessment practice are based on the following scenario. You should read the scenario carefully before you begin. Make sure you complete all the activities.

SCENARIO: BROCCO ON THE PARK

Brocco on the Park (www.brocco.co.uk) is a luxury boutique hotel and restaurant in the heart of Sheffield. Brocco prides itself on the finest details and ensuring its unique and luxurious rooms feel like a home from home, where guests can sleep soundly and dine in style.

The boutique hotel features eight individual rooms named after birds, each with a unique design and feel. Brocco refers to its restaurant as a neighbourhood kitchen and sources the best local ingredients to serve high-quality healthy food, catering for vegetarian, vegan, wheat intolerant or gluten-free requirements.

Brocco has its own social club and invites its customers to take part in a variety of events throughout the year, including wreath-making, drawing classes and heirloom restoration. In 2017, *The Good Hotel Guide* awarded Brocco the Best City Hotel of the Year.

Activity 1

Brocco's target market includes middle-class professional couples who enjoy fine dining and home comforts. Many of its customers enjoy meeting new people and learning new crafts and hobbies. Most customers come from the region and appreciate the best ingredients, culture and events that Sheffield has to offer.

Based on the information above, what methods do you think Brocco uses to segment its market? Select three more options from the choices below.

Gender	Age	Lifestyle
Income ✓	Geographic	Ethnicity

(3 marks)

The owner of Brocco is reviewing the hotel's promotional mix for the autumn season. She has chosen two promotional methods that could be used, and has asked you to produce a summary of the advantages and disadvantages of both.

Identify one advantage and one disadvantage for each of the promotional methods in the table below.

Money-off coupons	Advantage	Will attract customers to the restaurant because they get a reduced price when buying food or booking a hotel room.
	Disadvantage	
An advert in a local lifestyle magazine	Advantage	
	Disadvantage	

(4 marks)

Activity 2

Brocco collects information on its customers when they visit the restaurant or the hotel. This information includes the customer's:

- name
- address
- email address
- birthday and anniversaries.

How could this information help the owner of Brocco promote her business?

(3 marks)

Recently the owner of Brocco posted an image and a message on Brocco's Instagram feed. The message reads:

'Our talented chef, Marcus, has come up with a range of fantastic dishes ready for our new autumn menu. #WildBoarMeatballs.'	Posting a tweet is an example of
The image is of the meatballs.	Enterprises use this to
Explain the benefits to the restaurant of the owner posting the message on social media.	The benefits for Brocco are

Complete the sentences in the second column of the table. **(3 marks)**

Financial records

GETTING STARTED

A financial transaction occurs when a buyer purchases goods or services from a seller. What types of information do you think an enterprise would collect and record about its transactions with customers and other businesses? What types of documents record this information?

How do you manage your money? Do you keep records of how much you are spending and how much you have left? As a young student, you might not need to keep financial records, but all enterprises need to keep these records. Over the next few lessons, you will learn how businesses keep track of their money.

Financial documents

Enterprises of all sizes use and fill in a range of documents when completing financial transactions. The purpose of these documents is to ensure that the business, its customers and its suppliers have an accurate record of all trading that has taken place. These financial documents contain a range of information. They might be a physical paper document or an electronic file, sent via email.

Enterprises keep financial documents so that:

- managers and owners are able to calculate revenues, costs and profit/loss
- they have records of all customers and suppliers for future business and marketing
- faulty goods can be tracked, mistakes put right or refunds sent to customers.

Taxation

One important reason why enterprises keep financial records and documents is because they are required by law to do so. These records are used to calculate the tax an enterprise must pay to Her Majesty's Revenue and Customs (HMRC).

Figure 3.7 shows a flow of financial documents, which explains how they connect with each other. Table 3.9 explains some of these documents in more detail.

KEY TERM

Assets are items that an enterprise owns – including property, machinery and cash. Assets can also be conceptual things that have a value, such as a brand.

DID YOU KNOW?

It is a legal requirement for limited companies to keep financial records of:

- all the money they receive and spend
- their **assets** (things they own)
- their debts (money they owe to others)
- all goods bought and sold (and to whom).

ACTIVITY

In the following examples, identify the relevant financial document that should be used when:

- goods are sent to a customer
- a customer makes payment
- the customer returns their goods because they are faulty
- a customer requests goods or services
- a seller requests payment.

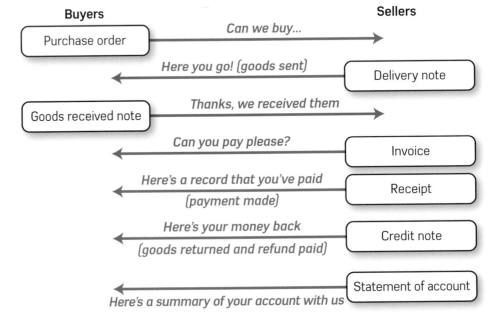

■ Figure 3.7: How financial documents flow between buyers and sellers

◻ Table 3.9: When financial documents are used and why

Financial document	When they are used	Why they are used
Purchase order	When a buyer orders goods or services from a seller	• Lists types, quantities and agreed prices for goods or services seller will provide to buyer • Constitutes a legal offer to buy goods or services (that is, a request to purchase goods or services)
Delivery note	When goods are delivered to the buyer	• Lists details about the order • Explains the contents of a package • States anything ordered that is *not* in the package (due to lack of stock, unavailability, etc.) • Used by customers to check-off goods and ensure they match the purchase order
Goods received note	When goods are received	• Confirms all goods have been received • Can be compared against purchase order before payment is made
Credit note	If a customer returns their goods to the seller	• Acts as a record that goods have been returned and the customer has received a refund • May be issued so that the sum of money owed can be used later to buy goods or be discounted against another purchase from the same seller
Invoice	Details money owed, usually after goods have been received	• Details the amount owed • Gives date by which money must be paid • Explains how to pay (cash, bank transfer, etc).
Receipts	A document acknowledging and providing proof of the purchase of a good or service	• Used as proof of purchase should a product need to be returned to the seller for a refund. • Provides details of the item, price paid and date of purchase.
Statement of account	A summary of these recent transactions between a company and a customer including the total of any outstanding invoices or reimbursements to the customer.	• Used with customers who have a large account and regularly purchase goods / services.

The importance of accuracy

It is very important that financial documents are detailed and accurate. If financial documents are inaccurate it can lead to significant mistakes being made. For example, a business might:

• send the wrong goods to a customer – which could cause a business to lose money
• request that an incorrect amount is paid – which could cause disputes between suppliers and customers.

If financial documents are not kept or contain mistakes, then the calculations for revenue, profit and tax will be incorrect and could lead to business failure. For examples of all the financial records explained on these pages, go to Appendix 2.

ACTIVITY

Choose one of the financial documents you have learned about in this lesson.

1 Make a list of the key information the document should contain.

2 Now draft an example template including all the relevant information. Think carefully about how the document should be presented. Remember, financial documents should be clear and easy to follow.

LINK IT UP

To find out more about assets, go to the lesson 'Financial terminology: assets and liabilities' later in this learning aim.

CHECK MY LEARNING

1 Close your text book and try to identify all the financial documents that might be included in a business transaction. List them in the order they would be sent.

2 For each document, identify three pieces of information that might be included.

Methods of payment

GETTING STARTED

What are the differences between the following methods of payment?

1 Cheque

2 Debit card

3 Store card

4 Online payment technology such as PayPal

How do you pay for the things you buy? Cash? Debit card? Do you use different methods depending on where you buy from? Businesses and customers alike have a variety of options these days. Improvements in technology have made payments faster and easier.

Payment methods

Common methods of payment include:

- cash
- credit cards
- debit cards
- direct debit
- a range of payment technologies.

In this lesson, each of these methods will be examined more closely.

Cash

The most traditional form of payment is cash. However, there can be problems with cash transactions such as:

- money being lost or stolen
- mistakes being made during transactions, such as the wrong change being given.

For some transactions, cash is still the most appropriate method. This can be because:

- technology is not available (to either the buyer or seller)
- the sums being dealt with are too small to justify electronic (online) money transfer.

Credit cards

Credit is where payment is deferred (put off until later). A credit card acts as an agreed sum of credit or loan from the credit card company. Customers can then spend up to the credit limit (the agreed sum) and make monthly repayments to pay it back.

Credit cards:

- are similar to short-term loans – that is, they allow customers to 'borrow' money and pay off the debt at a later point
- can be a flexible way of borrowing – you can use them when you need to
- charge interest on the outstanding balance (the amount of money you owe) – but sometimes the interest can be very high, which makes credit cards an expensive way to borrow money.

Surcharges

There is another cost associated with credit card transactions, known as a surcharge. Businesses have to pay this cost, and sometimes the charge is passed on to the customer by being added to the cost of their purchase. A credit card transaction can range from 0.3 per cent to 20 per cent.

Debit cards

Debit cards work in the same way as credit cards, but are directly linked to your bank account. When a transaction is processed, a message is sent to your bank account informing the bank that a payment should be transferred to the business's bank account.

DID YOU KNOW?

If you buy cinema or concert tickets from a booking office with your credit card, you will often have to pay a surcharge in addition to the ticket price.

Direct debit

A direct debit is an agreement made with a bank that allows you to transfer money to someone else, usually a business, on an agreed date. Direct debits can be:

- set up for regular payments
- most effective when paying bills such as utility bills (gas, electricity, water)
- used to pay off loans from a bank.

The amount of money transferred each time may vary depending on how much is owed. An example of this would be the amount of data used on a smartphone contract, as this could be different each month.

Payment technologies

Many transactions now take place online using ecommerce, as these examples show.

- Companies such as PayPal allow the general public and businesses to transfer money between buyers and sellers.
- Online payment services can be directly linked to a bank account, which means funds are transferred from one party's bank account straight into another.
- Online customer accounts linked to an ecommerce website allow returning customers to buy things easily at online checkouts because their payment details are already stored.
- Apps such as Deliveroo (the fast food delivery company) and Uber (the taxi hailing company) mean customers can complete transactions using a smartphone.

Impact of payment methods on enterprises and customers

You have explored the benefits and drawbacks of the different payment methods for enterprises and customers in this topic. New technologies have opened new channels of payment making transactions between enterprises and customers more accessible and simple. The technology is also more accessible for small enterprises, such as a self-employed business owner. Although some new payment methods incurred a cost for both customers and enterprises (such as PayPal) payment transactions can be fast, safe and made without customers and enterprises actually meeting in person. These methods also reduce the need for customers and enterprises to deal in cash.

■ Did you know that modern card readers can be linked to smartphones to process payment transactions?

DID YOU KNOW?

Generally, debit and credit cards require a four-digit pin code to operate. However, technology also allows contactless payment, where transactions are made by swiping your card over a scanner.

ACTIVITY

Go to a website that allows you to purchase goods such as clothing. Place items in your online basket and proceed to the checkout, but *do not enter any payment details*. Now complete the following tasks.

1 a) Produce a flow chart of the steps required to purchase a product using an ecommerce website.

   b) List the features the website uses to make purchasing products easy.

   c) List the financial documents (electronic versions) required to complete online transactions.

2 Discuss, and make a note of, the benefits and drawbacks of purchasing products online, rather than going to a retail store.

CHECK MY LEARNING

For each of the following payment methods – debit card, credit card, direct debit, cash, payment technology – identify the following:

- an example of when it would be the best way for a customer to pay
- a business that mainly uses that form of payment method.

Sources of revenue and costs

All businesses have costs, and hopefully they have revenue too! In this lesson you will consider how these two things are broken down.

Revenue

Revenue is the income an enterprise receives through various activities. The most common form of revenue is the income a business receives from selling goods and services. The formula to calculate revenue earned for each of the goods or services a business sells is:

$$Revenue = Number\ of\ sales \times Price\ per\ unit$$

An enterprise may also receive income through servicing products it has already sold. For example, a motorcycle retailer may receive additional income from repairing or servicing the bikes of its customers. Enterprises can also receive revenue from other sources too, for example:

- interest paid on money in a bank savings account
- investment income from putting money into other enterprises and receiving a share of the profits
- leasing or rental income from renting out property or equipment to another enterprise
- selling assets – raising money by selling items, such as vehicles and machinery, that are no longer required.

DID YOU KNOW?

The amount of money used to start up a business is also referred to as start-up **capital**.

LINK IT UP

To find out more about capital, go to 'Financial terminology: assets and liabilities' later in this component.

KEY TERMS

Capital is the money, buildings and equipment that an enterprise uses in order to trade.

Start-up costs are the amount of money spent setting up a business before it starts trading.

Running costs are the fixed costs and variable costs that have to be paid to keep a business trading.

ACTIVITY

Think back to the 'Getting started' activity on running a sandwich shop.

1 Estimate the amount of revenue the shop might make on a typical day of the week. To do this you will need to use the calculation for revenue.

2 Estimate the average price of a meal sold at the shop. Will people just buy a sandwich or will they buy a drink and a cake too? Then estimate the number of customers the shop might serve on a typical day. Compare your estimate with others in your class.

Costs

The costs incurred in running an enterprise can be split into two main categories: **start-up costs** and **running costs**.

Start-up costs

When people start a new enterprise, they will need various items before they can start trading. For example:

- a driving instructor needs a car
- a print shop needs a computer and a photocopier.

Both of these businesses will need to advertise their enterprises to attract customers.

Savings and loans

It is important to remember that start-up costs are incurred before any income is received, which means the owner has to find the money to pay for them. This might come from savings, but the majority of enterprises are formed using money obtained from a loan – usually from a bank or, perhaps, from family members.

Running costs

These are the day-to-day costs incurred in the running of a business. For example, a driving instructor must buy fuel for their vehicle, and a print shop has to buy paper and pay for electricity.

The running costs of a business can be split into fixed and variable costs.

Fixed costs

Some bills have to be paid no matter how many products the business provides or sells or how many customers it has. Driving instructors must tax and insure their cars, whether they have one client or 50. The print shop must pay for heating and lighting even if no customers visit that week.

Variable costs

Some costs are directly related to the number of items sold or produced. Driving instructors use more fuel if they have more clients, because they are on the road more often. Print shops use more paper and ink if they are producing more posters or documents.

Figure 3.8 provides an easy-to-remember summary of these types of costs.

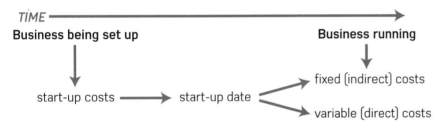

◻ Figure 3.8: Try to remember these types of business costs and what they cover

Total costs

The total costs of running a business are found by adding the fixed costs and the variable costs using this formula:

Total costs = Fixed costs + Variable costs

ACTIVITY

Think back again to the 'Getting started' activity on running a sandwich shop.

1 Separate your list of running costs for the sandwich shop into fixed and variable costs.

2 Use the formula to calculate the total costs of the business for a year if the fixed costs per month are £1000 and the total variable costs per month are £2300.

3 List the things that the owners of a sandwich shop could do to reduce the running costs.

CHECK MY LEARNING

Create a flow chart demonstrating the costs and revenues of a business. Your flow chart should begin with start-up costs and end with profit/loss.

Financial terminology: turnover and profit

Enterprises use a wide range of financial terms in order to understand financial performance. The basic concept of how finance in an enterprise works is:

Money in – Money out = The reward for running an enterprise

or

Profit = Total revenue – Total costs

Understanding financial performance

To fully understand the financial performance of an enterprise, owners and managers will categorise different incomes, expenses and profits so they can have a greater understanding. The financial terms and figures they use – such as 'turnover' and 'cost of sales' – are recorded in financial documents.

Understanding terminology

Here are some key financial terms that enterprises use:

- turnover
- gross profit
- net profit.

- **cost of sales**
- expenses

Try to memorise what each of them means.

Turnover

Turnover (also referred to as net sales) is the total revenue an enterprise receives in a given financial period.

- Turnover might come from a range of different products.
- Revenue is calculated as: *price × quantity sold*.

Cost of sales

It costs money to make or produce any product. This is called the cost of sales, or cost of goods sold. Imagine you are making teddy bears and the raw materials for each one cost £10; this would be your cost of sales. You would then deduct the total cost of sales from turnover to calculate your gross profit.

Gross profit

Gross profit is the profit a business makes on selling its products. It considers the direct costs of producing or supplying products, but does not take into account indirect costs, also known as expenses.

The formula for gross profit is:

Gross profit = Turnover – Cost of sales

Table 3.10 lists the effects of gross profit on an enterprise.

Expenses

Expenses include all of the indirect costs of an enterprise. These are the costs not associated with products the enterprise sells (cost of sales). Examples of costs that are included in expenses are:

- administration
- the salaries of managers
- utility bills (gas and electricity)
- advertising.

Expenses are deducted from gross profit to give **net profit.**

■ Why do the costs of running an office impact on the net profit of an enterprise?

> **KEY TERM**
>
> **Net profit** is the money made from selling a product after all costs have been deducted from gross profit.

> **ACTIVITY**
>
> List all the costs that could be included in expenses. Remember, these should not be the direct costs associated with selling products. Try to include ten expenses in your list.

Net profit

Net profit is the amount of money left when all expenses are deducted from the gross profit figure. Net profit is also referred to as the 'bottom line', because it is the actual profit that can be returned to the owners of the enterprise or reinvested to help the enterprise grow.

The formula for net profit is:

$$Net\ profit = Gross\ profit - Expenditure$$

Table 3.10 lists the impact of gross and net profit on an enterprise.

■ Table 3.10: The impact of gross profit and net profit

Gross profit and its impact	Net profit and its impact
When gross profit is positive, its revenue is greater than cost of sales.	When net profit is positive, gross profit is also positive and expenditure is within budgeted levels.
When gross profit is low or negative, action should be taken to: • increase sales revenue (maybe increasing sales volumes or prices) • reduce the cost of sales (e.g. using cheaper raw materials, buying in bulk, changing supplier or negotiating discounts).	When net profit is low or negative, this could be because gross profit is too low and/or expenses are too high. Action should be taken to: • increase gross profit • reduce expenses by checking to see where savings can be made.

Try to remember this formula:

$$Revenue - Cost\ of\ sales = Gross\ profit - Expenses = Net\ profit$$

> **DID YOU KNOW?**
>
> Expenses are also referred to as overheads – costs that an enterprise must pay in order for it to run. In the previous lesson, expenses (overheads) would be categorised as fixed costs. However, strictly speaking, overheads are not always fixed. For example, the heating bill at a company's head office is an overhead and can also be referred to as an indirect cost (as it is not directly linked to output), but it will vary between seasons. As a general rule, though, most overheads are fixed costs.

> **CHECK MY LEARNING**
>
> Write down all the terms you have learned about in this lesson that relate to money – e.g. 'turnover'. Although the words you have written down refer to money, how are they different?

Financial terminology: assets and liabilities

Remember, the basic concept of how finance works is:

Money in (Total revenue) – Money out (Total expenses)
= The reward for running an enterprise (Profit)!

In the last lesson, you looked at some financial terms enterprises use to understand their performance. Here are a few more.

Understanding terminology

Here are a few more key financial terms that enterprises will use:

- fixed assets
- current assets
- current liabilities
- long-term liabilities
- capital
- net current assets.

Try to memorise the definitions below.

Assets

An asset is something that an enterprise (or the owner of an enterprise) owns. Assets are usually broken down into two categories:

- fixed assets
- current assets.

Fixed assets

A fixed asset is something that:

- does not change in the short term
- the owner of an enterprise will use to make money.

For example, a vehicle used to deliver goods is a fixed asset. So is a factory or a piece of machinery.

Current assets

A current asset is an item that will change with every transaction, such as:

- stock
- debtors (people who owe the enterprise money)
- cash in the bank.

Current assets can usually be turned into cash quickly.

 Why might this pottery kiln be a fixed asset?

Liabilities

A **liability** is something an enterprise owes – including all the money:

- an enterprise owes to other enterprises
- that needs to be returned to customers
- borrowed from a bank.

Liabilities are broken down into:

- current liabilities
- long-term liabilities.

Current liabilities

A current liability is money that must be paid back within a year. Current liabilities include:

- trade credit to suppliers
- a bank overdraft.

These are short-term debts.

Long-term liabilities

Long-term liabilities include loans that can be repaid over a longer period of time. They might might also include the initial investment (sum of money) put into the enterprise by its owners. An enterprise or person who is owed money is known as a creditor.

Figure 3.9 provides an easy-to-remember summary of how some of the financial terms you have read about here relate to each other.

Capital

Capital refers to the money put in to start up or grow a business. Capital can generally come from one of three sources:

- a loan (which is a long-term liability)
- money invested in the enterprise by its owners (generally known as 'share capital')
- capital linked to profit – if an owner of an enterprise decides to use net profit to help the business grow, this is known as **retained profit**.

ACTIVITY

In a pair, discuss which of the following sources of capital you think has the lowest risk for the owner of an enterprise (try to justify your choice):

- loan capital
- share capital
- retained profit.

Net current assets

Net current assets are the value of current assets minus current liabilities.

Net current assets = Current assets – Current liabilities

This calculation shows the working capital of an enterprise. The working capital is the funds an enterprise has to pay for its day-to-day expenses.

KEY TERM

A **liability** is an amount of money an enterprise owes (debts).

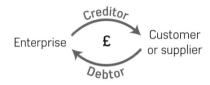

■ Figure 3.9: The relationship between creditors and debtors, enterprises and suppliers

KEY TERMS

Retained profit is profit earned and accumulated from previous trading reinvested back into the enterprise.

Net current assets are the difference between current assets and current liabilities. They show the value of the enterprise.

CHECK MY LEARNING

Create a table with two columns – one headed 'Assets' and one headed 'Liabilities'.

1 In the 'Assets' column, list everything you can think of that could be classed as an asset for an enterprise.

2 In the 'Liabilities' column, list everything you can think of that could be a liability for an enterprise.

3 Label the assets and liabilities you have listed as fixed assets (FA), current assets (CA), current liabilities (CL) or long-term liabilities (LT–L).

Statement of comprehensive income

Financial statements, such as a statement of comprehensive income, show how well an enterprise is doing. This kind of information is interesting to a range of people because it shows how well an enterprise is being managed.

The purpose of a statement of comprehensive income

A statement of comprehensive income can tell you how a business has performed financially over a period of time – usually a year. It shows:

- how much revenue has been received from sales of goods and services
- how much of this money was spent
- how it was spent.

LINK IT UP

To remind yourself about revenue, look back at the lesson 'Sources of revenue and costs' earlier in this learning aim.

Figure 3.10 shows an example of a statement of comprehensive income.

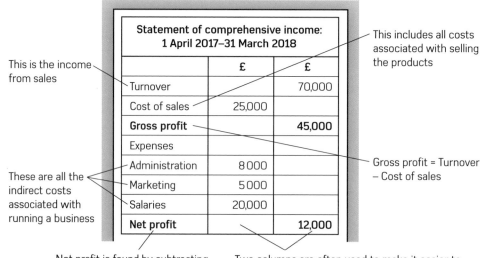

This is the income from sales

This includes all costs associated with selling the products

Statement of comprehensive income: 1 April 2017–31 March 2018		
	£	£
Turnover		70,000
Cost of sales	25,000	
Gross profit		**45,000**
Expenses		
Administration	8000	
Marketing	5000	
Salaries	20,000	
Net profit		**12,000**

Gross profit = Turnover – Cost of sales

These are all the indirect costs associated with running a business

Net profit is found by subtracting total expenses from gross profit

Two columns are often used to make it easier to:
- read additions and subtractions in the accounts
- separate out key information

◨ **Figure 3.10:** Why do you think the statement of comprehensive income here covers the period April to March?

ACTIVITY

Write out a statement of comprehensive income using the following information. Remember to calculate the gross profit and net profit.

- Rent £5000
- Raw materials £12,000
- Packaging £2000
- Wage costs (indirect) £1000

- Salaries £10,000
- Utilities £900
- Sales: 3000 units at £9.50 each
- Interest costs £500

GETTING STARTED

Draw a mind map with 'Stakeholders' at the centre, and these stakeholders (people with an interest) around the outside:
- shareholders
- managers
- customers
- employees
- suppliers
- government.

Annotate each stakeholder, explaining why they might be interested in the financial statements of an enterprise.

DID YOU KNOW?

In accounting, negative numbers – such as a negative cash flow or a loss – are shown in brackets ( ). This is to make it easier to interpret because a minus sign can easily be overlooked on a page of numbers.

From the example in Figure 3.10, we can see that the enterprise has made a gross profit of £45,000 and a net profit of £12,000. This is a positive position, but it may depend on:

- how the enterprise performed in a previous financial period
- how similar enterprises have performed.

We can also see that the expenses are made up of administration, marketing and salaries. A summary of the calculation used in a statement of comprehensive income is:

(Turnover – Cost of sales = Gross profit) – Expenses = Net profit

If costs are greater than revenues, however, then the enterprise will make a loss instead of a profit.

☐ Comparing your statement of comprehensive income with that of another similar enterprise will show you how well your enterprise is doing compared with others in that market

ACTIVITY

Reconstruct the statement of comprehensive income you created in the first activity, using the following information.

Price per unit falls from £9.50 to £9.00.

Salaries increase by £5000.

CHECK MY LEARNING

Analyse the two statements of comprehensive income that you have produced. Provide three pieces of advice to the owner of this enterprise, advising them on how they could improve the financial performance of their enterprise.

Statement of financial position

All enterprises have money invested in them. Even a window cleaner must have a bucket and a ladder. A statement of financial position shows how much money has been invested in an enterprise and what it has been spent on.

The purpose of a statement of financial position

An enterprise will normally produce a statement of financial position once a year, usually on the last day of the financial year. The statement is a snapshot of the enterprise's financial situation on that particular day, but summarises the activity from the whole year.

DID YOU KNOW?

A financial year is the trading period for which an enterprise collects information for its financial accounts. An enterprise's financial year doesn't have to start in January and end in December. It can start at any time, as long as it covers a 12-month period.

The statement of financial position shows:

- the value of all assets and liabilities in the enterprise
- the sources of capital used to finance the enterprise.

Figure 3.11 shows an example of a statement of financial position.

These are fixed assets that are unlikely to change within the next 12 months

These are current assets likely to change on a regular basis

This is the value of the enterprise

Statement of financial position as of 1 April 2018		
	£	£
Fixed assets		
Vehicle	1000	
Equipment	500	1500
Current assets		
Stock	1000	
Debtors	400	
Cash in bank	300	1700
Current liabilities		
Creditors	900	
Net current assets		800
Total assets less current liabilities		2300
Shareholders' funds		
Share capital	2000	
Retained profit	300	**2300**

These are debts that a business must pay within 12 months

The difference between current assets and current liabilities is also known as working capital

This is the source of income invested by the owners in the enterprise. This sum should always balance with total assets less current liabilities.

■ Figure 3.11: What other annotation would you add this statement of financial position to help you remember everything on it?

ACTIVITY

Using the following information, construct a statement of financial position.

1 Calculate net current assets and shareholders' funds.

2 Categorise assets and liabilities:

- van £1000
- creditors £600
- cash in bank £1100
- debtors £600
- computer £800
- stock £800
- overdraft £500
- retained profit £0.

ACTIVITY

Reconstruct the statement of financial position that you created in the first activity, using the following information.

The owner of the business buys machinery worth £1000.

Trade creditors increase by £400.

Cash at bank falls to £50.

Debtors fall to £150.

Statement of Financial Position

	Year Ending	
Dec. 31	Dec. 31	
5.621.456	5.963.548	5.74%
3.856.987	3.965.214	2.73%
561.248	621.547	9.70%
325.687	411.258	20.81%
125.487	131.487	4.56%
425.698	411.547	-3.44%
91.258	92.547	1.39%
11.007.821	11.597.148	5.08%
1.254.789	1.354.789	7.38%
258.697	259.147	0.17%
1.478.587	1.547.874	4.48%

▣ Who would be most likely to take an interest in an enterprise's statement of financial position?

CHECK MY LEARNING

Analyse the two statements of financial position you have produced. Provide three suggestions to the owner of this enterprise, advising them on how they could improve their financial performance.

Profitability and liquidity

Have you come across the terms '**profitability**' and '**liquidity**' before? They are words used to describe the 'health' of an enterprise – whether it's good or poor.

Cash vs. profit

Do you know the difference between cash and profit?

Cash is the money an enterprise actually has. This could include:

- cash in a till
- money in the bank.

For example, the sale of a product to a debtor will increase profits but the cash may not arrive for a few weeks.

LINK IT UP

To remind yourself about revenue, variable and fixed costs, look back at the lesson 'Sources of revenue and costs' earlier in this learning aim.

Calculating profit

Once all costs have been deducted from all revenue, the amount left is the profit.

Profit is an absolute calculation that is made at the end of a period of time. Businesses generally calculate one set of profits each year. However, monthly calculations can show whether the business is:

- solvent (has more money than it owes)
- on target to make a profit by the end of the year.

The key difference between cash and profit is time. Cash is the money a business has *at that moment* to pay bills and expenses. If an enterprise runs out of cash it will not be able to make a profit.

ACTIVITY

Read this scenario, then answer the questions that follow.

Leona is an artist who sells her paintings through a local gallery. She believes she can produce and sell up to six paintings each month. The average cost of producing a painting is £250 and Leona knows she can sell her paintings for £800–£1000. Leona has £850 in the bank and needs to buy new art supplies for the month. The gallery has let Leona know that they can display her paintings at the end of the month.

1   Is Leona going to make a profit if she sells six paintings this month?
2   Will Leona have enough cash this month?

Here are some simple formulas to help with cash vs. profit.

Cash balance = Cash inflow – Cash outflow

Profit = Revenues earned – Expenses incurred

The cash balance is the flow of money into and out of an enterprise at any given point. Profit is all revenue minus expenses over a period of time.

GETTING STARTED

Why do some profitable enterprises still fail? Discuss the following options in a small group and decide which ones you think are the main reasons.

1   Poor management
2   Economic factors
3   Cash flow
4   Too much competition.

KEY TERMS

Profitability is the ability of an enterprise to create a profit.
Liquidity is the ability of an enterprise to pay its debts.

Profitability

Profitability refers to an enterprise's ability to turn revenue into profit. This is known as a profit margin. It refers to the difference between:

- the amount an enterprise can sell its goods or service for
- what it costs to produce them.

Some enterprises sell products with very small margins – where the difference between the price and the cost is small. Others sell products that have a high profit margin. An enterprise will increase its profitability if it is able to:

- raise its prices without lowering demand
- lower its costs without lowering the quality or customer experience.

Take a look at Figure 3.12, which shows the profit margin of two enterprises. What do you notice?

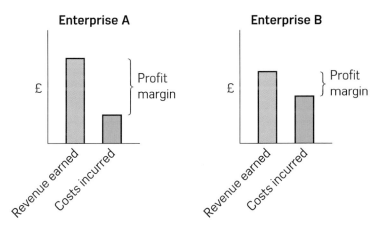

◘ Figure 3.12: Which of these enterprises is the most profitable?

Liquidity

Liquidity is the ability of an enterprise to pay its debts.

- If an enterprise has good (positive) liquidity, then it has sufficient working capital to pay any creditors.
- If an enterprise has poor (negative) liquidity, then it may struggle to pay its debts. If this happens, the enterprise is in danger of becoming insolvent (unable to pay its debts) and could have to close or cease trading.

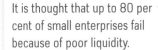

LINK IT UP

To remind yourself about working capital, look back at the lessons 'Financial terminology: assets and liabilities' and 'Statement of financial position' earlier in this learning aim.

DID YOU KNOW?

It is thought that up to 80 per cent of small enterprises fail because of poor liquidity.

CHECK MY LEARNING

Answer the following questions relating to cash and profit.

1 What is the calculation for profit?

2 Why is cash important to an enterprise?

3 What is meant by liquidity?

4 Why do some enterprises run out of cash?

Profitability ratios

Profit alone tells you very little about how an enterprise is performing financially. One enterprise might have made more profit than another, but they might not have performed as well. To evaluate the financial performance of enterprises, managers use a series of **ratios**.

KEY TERM

Ratios are financial tools that compare two pieces of information.

Understanding ratios

A ratio is a comparison of information often expressed as a percentage. Two important profitability ratios that managers use are:

- the gross profit margin ratio (GPM)
- the net profit margin ratio (NPM).

KEY TERMS

Gross profit margin is the gross profit as a percentage of sales revenue.
Net profit margin is the net profit as a percentage of sales revenue.

ACTIVITY

Using the example statement of comprehensive income which you first encountered earlier in this learning aim, calculate the gross profit margin and net profit margin.

Statement of comprehensive income: 1 April 2017–31 March 2018		
	£	£
Turnover		70,000
Cost of sales	25,000	
Gross profit		**45,000**
Expenses		
Administration	8 000	
Marketing	5 000	
Salaries	20,000	
Net profit		**12,000**

Gross profit margin

Gross profit is the difference between sales revenue and the cost of sales. The GPM helps an enterprise to measure its gross profit as a percentage of its sales.

Gross profit margin (%) = (Gross profit ÷ Sales revenue) × 100

For example, a GPM of 30 per cent means that for every £1 of sales revenue, 30p becomes gross profit.

Net profit margin

Net profit is the difference between sales revenue and total costs. The NPM helps a business to measure its net profit as a percentage of its sales:

Net profit margin (%) = (Net profit ÷ Sales revenue) × 100

For example, a NPM of 15 per cent means that for every £1 of sales revenue, 15p becomes net profit.

Using the information below, calculate profitability margins for the two years of financial information. In which year did the company perform best?

	2017	2018
Gross profit	£2.9 million	£3.1 million
Sales revenue	£4.7 million	£5.35 million
Indirect costs	£1.1 million	£2.4 million
Net profit	£1.8 million	£700,000

The average net profit margin for UK service industries is 18 per cent. For UK manufacturing the average is 12 per cent.

Look at the financial information below. In which year did the enterprise perform best? Explain your answer clearly using appropriate calculations. What other information might be necessary to analyse the company's performance?

	2017	2018
Gross profit	£2.7 million	£3 million
Sales revenue	£4.4 million	£5.6 million

■ Focusing only on profits will just tell you part of an enterprise's financial story

Liquidity ratios

Look at the statement of financial position below. Shareholders' funds represent the money that shareholders are entitled to. Comment on the liquidity of this enterprise. Is it in a good position or a bad position? Explain why.

	£
Fixed assets	50,000
Current assets	22,000
Current liabilities	(12,000)
Net current assets	10,000
Total assets less current liabilities	60,000
Shareholders' funds	60,000

As you have seen, ratios compare one piece of information to another. Liquidity refers to an enterprise's ability to pay its expenses. The two pieces of information used to assess this are the current assets and current liabilities.

LINK IT UP

To remind yourself about current assets and current liabilities, go back to the lesson 'Financial terminology: assets and liabilities' earlier in this learning aim.

DID YOU KNOW?

If an enterprise has more current assets than current liabilities, then it is unlikely to run out of cash.

Current ratio

The current ratio is the most basic of liquidity ratios. Unlike some financial ratios, this is expressed as a ratio – for example, 2:1. This ratio would suggest that for every £2 of current assets the enterprise has £1 of current liabilities. The ratio is calculated by:

Current assets ÷ Current liabilities

Liquid capital ratio

The liquid capital ratio is similar to the current ratio, except for one key difference. The liquid capital ratio discounts (removes) any inventories (stock) from current assets. It is calculated by:

(Current assets – Inventories) ÷ Current liabilities

Expressing current and liquid capital ratios

You may have noticed that the answer to the current ratio and the liquid capital ratio calculations is always a single number when it is shown on your calculator, for example 0.8. This number represents a ratio – 0.8:1 (for every 80p of current assets, the enterprise has £1 of current liabilities). If the number is greater than 1 then the enterprise has more current assets than it does current liabilities, e.g. 1.5:1 (£1.50 current assets to every £1 of current liabilities).

Removing inventories

The reason this formula removes inventories from the calculation is that it can be difficult for an enterprise to convert inventories into cash quickly. Therefore, it is not a very liquid asset – it cannot be used to pay off current liabilities in the short term.

For example, if a carpenter has inventories of timber, it cannot turn this timber into furniture and sell it quickly enough to pay off debts. Instead, it would be more appropriate for the carpenter to consider cash in the bank and debtors as the most relevant current assets. The liquid capital ratio might not be appropriate for enterprises that do not hold large amounts of inventory – for example, a hairdresser.

ACTIVITY

Below is a summary of financial information from the statement of comprehensive income and statement of financial position for BBT Trading Ltd.

Sales	£70,000
Purchases	£30,000
Opening stock	£10,000
Closing stock	£6000
Gross profit	£36,000
Net profit	£14,000
Creditors	£3000
Debtors	£8000
Cost of sales	£34,000
Capital employed	£160,000
Total current assets	£12,000
Total current liabilities	(£5000)

1 Using this information, calculate the current ratio for BBT Trading Ltd.

2 Calculate the liquid capital ratio for BBT Trading Ltd (assume that closing stock is the current stock held by the company).

3 Comment on the liquidity of BBT Trading Ltd.

CHECK MY LEARNING

1 Note down why current assets are important to an enterprise.

2 Give two examples of current liabilities.

3 Explain why stock is removed from the liquid capital ratio.

◼ Why does it make sense to remove inventories from your assets when assessing liquidity?

Learning aim B: assessment practice

How you will be assessed

You will be assessed on Component 3 of your course by a written examination. This component builds on the knowledge, understanding and skills that you have acquired and developed in Components 1 and 2. In your exam you will be presented with a short case study of a small to medium enterprise (SME) and a series of activities to complete. These tasks will relate to the nature of the enterprise in the case study and the products or services it sells. The examination will be completed under supervised conditions.

This assessment practice gives you an opportunity to practise a part of what you will encounter in your examination.

The activities in this assessment practice are based on this scenario. You should read the scenario carefully before you start the activities. Complete all the activities.

CHECKPOINT

Strengthen

- List the things a statement of comprehensive income shows.
- Explain what is meant by the term 'capital'.
- Outline why liquidity is important to an enterprise.

Challenge

- Explain how a business might improve its profitability.
- State the most important financial document an enterprise will produce. Justify your answer.
- Explain which is more important: cash or profit. Give reasons for your answers.

SCENARIO: THE CUSTOM BEAR COMPANY

The Custom Bear Company is a family-run enterprise specialising in high-quality personalised teddy bears that can be designed to resemble their owner. The managing director of the company is Brian.

To order a personalised teddy bear, customers submit a photograph and provide information via the website to choose a highly customisable bear. The Custom Bear Company has personalised teddy bears for several celebrities and this has generated lots of publicity via social media. The company now employs seven highly skilled bear makers and sells its bears via its ecommerce website.

The owner of the company has estimated the following financial information:

Financial information	£	
Average price per teddy bear	70	
Average variable costs per teddy bear	15	
Statement of financial position as of 1 April 2018		
	£	£
Fixed assets		
Bear production machinery	8000	
Warehouse fixtures and fittings	1000	
Computers	2000	11,000
Current assets		
Stock	4500	
Cash in bank	600	5100
Current liabilities		
Creditors	2500	
Net current assets		2600
Total assets less current liabilities		13,600
Shareholders' funds		
Share capital	10,000	
Retained profit	3600	**13,600**

Activity 1:

1 Brian has started to draw a diagram to show the flow of financial documents. The diagram shows the order in which documents are sent when The Custom Bear Company buys from a supplier. Each arrow shows who sends the document and who receives it. Copy and complete the rest of the diagram showing the order of documents sent and received. In each blank box, write one of these documents and draw the direction arrow:

- payment
- delivery note
- purchase order.

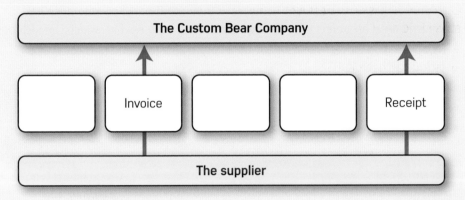

(6 marks)

2 Using the financial information in the scenario, calculate the gross profit that The Custom Bear Company would make if it made and sold 29 teddy bears this month. **(2 marks)**

Activity 2:

1 Using the information from the statement of financial position in the scenario on the opposite page, calculate:

- current ratio
- liquid capital ratio. **(4 marks)**

2 Brian has provided the following information on liquidity for the year ending 1 April 2017.

	2017
Current ratio	1:1.4
Liquid capital ratio	1:1.1

Comment on each ratio, comparing 2017 to 2018. **(4 marks)**

3 Using the information provided from Question 2, recommend how Brian could improve the financial position of The Custom Bear Company in 2018. **(4 marks)**

TAKE IT FURTHER

The best way to develop your understanding of financial records is to continue to study and annotate them, so that you fully understand the purpose of each. Look at a range of financial records and evaluate how they are useful to learn about different businesses and for businesses to keep track of their own financial information. Consider how real enterprises could improve the way they use financial documentation and keep track of their financial situation.

TIPS

Before completing this activity, plan the diagram and consider the flow of communication that takes place and the information each party requires to complete the transaction.

TIPS

The formula for gross profit is:
Sales revenue – Cost of sales
In this example, the variable costs are the cost of sales. The sales revenue is calculated by average price × quantity sold.

TIPS

You will require the following formulas to complete this task:
Current assets ÷ current liabilities and *(current assets – inventory) ÷ current liabilities*
Remember that 'inventory' means 'stock'.

TIPS

Make sure you start by clearly identifying the change between 2017 and 2018. Try to explain why the change might have occurred using examples.

TIPS

Compare the two liquidity ratios and look at the statement of financial position. Which of the two ratios is more important to Brian's business? How could he change the working capital position within his company?

Cash inflows and outflows

Think about the money you are given each week or month, and the money you spend in the same period of time. This is your cash flow – and it's exactly the same for an enterprise. **Cash inflows** and **cash outflows** are literally money coming into and going out of a business.

Cash

Cash does not always refer to the actual cash (notes and coins) an enterprise has at any given time. Cash refers to *all* the **liquid assets** a business has, which can include:

- money that an enterprise has in the bank and is able to spend (this could also include an overdraft)
- debtors who are expected to pay within the next few days
- products that can quickly be sold
- actual cash – notes and coins.

KEY TERMS

Cash inflows are the amounts of money entering a business's bank account.
Cash outflows are the amounts of money leaving a business's bank account.
Liquid assets are any assets that can be used in the short term to pay for things.

LINK IT UP

To remind yourself about assets, look back at 'Financial terminology: assets and liabilities' in Learning aim B of this component. To remind yourself about positive and negative liquidity, look back at 'Profitability and liquidity' in Learning aim B of this component.

ACTIVITY

Study this list of cash inflows and outflows for a manufacturing business:

- staff wages
- consumables
- sales income
- utility bills (gas and electricity)
- window cleaning
- rental on a sub-let office
- production materials
- loan from bank
- telephone and internet bills
- ingredients for the staff coffee machine
- cash from the staff coffee machine
- interest on bank loan
- sale of shares.

Separate the items on this list into two columns: one headed 'Cash inflows' and the other 'Cash outflows'.

Cash inflows

For most enterprises, the main cash inflow is payments by customers for goods and services they have bought. However, there are other possible sources of income, such as the ones shown in Table 3.11.

◘ Table 3.11: Other sources of income (cash inflows) to a business and why they are used

Source of income	Why it is used
Capital from investors (shareholders) who buy shares in the enterprise and receive dividends for those shares	• To help set up an enterprise • To buy more shares if extra capital is needed
Loan from a bank	• To help start up a new business • To help an existing business expand • To help when the business is facing financial difficulties
Property rental (for example, part of a building to other enterprises)	• To provide extra income

Cash outflows

Here are the most common forms of cash outflows from a business. What others can you think of?

LINK IT UP

To remind yourself of some of the things a business needs to spend money on, and what it might need to pay interest on, look back at Learning aim B of this component.

- *Staff wages*: this is one of the main forms of expenditure for most businesses that employ people.
- *Utilities*: this covers services such as gas, electricity and internet, which all have to be paid for by the business.
- *Materials for manufacturing*: if an enterprise is a manufacturer, then it will buy raw materials in order to make its products.
- *Insurance*: enterprises will legally insure against fire, damages to property and injuries to customers and employees.
- *Interest on loans*: this is a charge placed on top of the loan repayments an enterprise will pay for borrowed money.
- *Dividends*: these are paid to shareholders if the enterprise makes a profit.

Take a look at Figure 3.13, which may help you to visualise what happens when money flows into and out of a business.

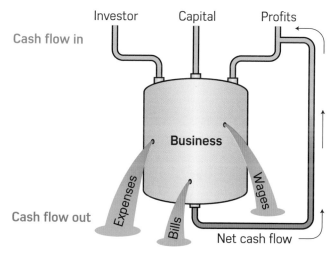

▢ Figure 3.13: It can be helpful to think of cash flow as water flowing through an enterprise – if the water runs out too quickly, the enterprise will run out of cash

CHECK MY LEARNING

1 Explain why cash is important to an enterprise.
2 Identify three types of cash inflow for an enterprise.
3 Identify three types of cash outflow for an enterprise.

Cash flow statements and forecasts

GETTING STARTED

Take a look at the cash flow statement in Figure 3.14. Then take a look at the calculation of the statement beneath it. With your calculator, double-check the calculations in the figure. This will help you to remember how these statements are constructed.

KEY TERMS

Cash flow statements are statements of actual cash inflows and outflows over a period of 12 months.
Cash flow forecasts are cash flow statements that predict the cash inflows and cash outflows for an enterprise over a period of time.
Net cash flow is the difference between the cash inflows and cash outflows over a particular time period.

DID YOU KNOW?

When a financial document shows a figure like £'000 at the start of it (see Figure 3.14), it means the figures in columns are in thousands. So, for example, 15 in Figure 3.14 really means £15,000.

LINK IT UP

To find out more about working capital, look at the lesson on 'Financing an enterprise' later in this learning aim.

A **cash flow statement** shows the actual cash inflows and outflows over a period of 12 months. These are produced by limited companies.

A **cash flow forecast** is a financial document that calculates the cash flow position of an enterprise. A cash flow forecast shows the *anticipated* cash inflows and outflows over a period of time and the **net cash flow**.

£'000	Jan	Feb	Mar	Apr	May
Cash inflows					
Sales	46	67	73	36	80
Cash outflows					
Production materials	15	18	22	14	25
Wages and salaries	18	30	30	25	30
Marketing	6	1	5	3	5
Other overheads	12	4	5	13	5
Total cash outflows	**51**	**53**	**62**	**55**	**65**
Net cash flow	**-5**	**14**	**11**	**-19**	**15**
Opening balance	25	20	34	45	26
Closing balance	20	34	45	26	41

◩ **Figure 3.14: A typical cash flow statement. How else might negative numbers sometimes appear in financial documents such as this?**

Why forecast?

Enterprises need to be able to forecast cash flow to enable them to make business decisions. This allows enterprise owners to determine their net current asset (funds available to them) requirements. This is important to monitor in order to make sure all expenses will be covered. Net current assets are also known as working capital.

Calculation for a cash flow statement

Take a look at this calculation for a cash flow statement. Try to remember it for future work.

> *Cash inflows (receipts) – Cash outflows (payments) = Net cash flow + Opening balance = Closing balance*

Now you can take a closer look at the details.

The information in a cash flow forecast

A cash flow statement shows the following information.

- *Receipts* – the total flow of cash into the business. In Figure 3.14 the total flow of cash into the business for April is shown as £36,000.
- *Payments* – the total flow of cash out of the business. In Figure 3.14 the total flow of cash out of the business for February is shown as £53,000.
- *Net cash flow* – the difference between the cash coming into the business and the cash flowing out. In January this was £46,000 – £51,000 = £-5000. The net cash flow can be positive or negative.

- *Opening balance* – the money carried forward from the previous month or what was left last month. In March this was £34,000. This was the money carried forward from the closing balance in February.
- *Closing balance* – the net cash flow plus the opening balance is what is left in the business at the end of the month. This will also be the opening balance for next month. In May this was £15,000 + £26,000 = £41,000.

Sales and purchases

- *Sales* are one of the most common sources of cash inflows for a business. This is because inflows from sales are normally quite regular.
- *Purchases* are all expenditures for the business. A purchase might include stock or equipment to help the enterprise function.

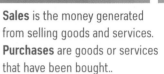
KEY TERMS

Sales is the money generated from selling goods and services. **Purchases** are goods or services that have been bought..

◘ What might happen if an enterprise makes too many purchases?

ACTIVITY

With the information below, construct a cash flow statement using the template as an example for a gardening company.

May

The company generates an average of £190,000 in sales each month. Its regular expenses include mortgage payments of £35,000 per month. May's wages were estimated at £55,000. Loan repayments were £8000 and stock ordered was £45,000.

June

All payments remained the same, although one of the garden centres had an extension built, costing £160,000.

July

Sales in July were particularly good, rising to £240,000. The company also sold of some of its land this month, raising a further £40,000. All expenses remained unchanged from June (except there was no extension to pay for).

	May	June	July
Income			
Total income			
Expenses			
Total expenses			
Net cash flow			
Opening balance	£10,000		
Closing balance			

CHECK MY LEARNING

1 Give examples of two things a business will use working capital for.

2 Explain what negative cash flow means.

3 Outline the difference between a business's opening balance and its closing balance.

The importance of cash flow forecasting

GETTING STARTED

Fill in the missing numbers for (a), (b) and (c) from the cash flow statement below.

	Sept (£)	Oct (£)	Nov (£)
Cash inflow	12,000	(b)	8000
Cash outflow	19,000	22,000	24,000
Net cash flow	(a)	(8000)	(16,000)
Opening balance	20,000	13,000	5000
Closing balance	13,000	5000	(c)

ACTIVITY

Fergus runs a floristry business. On 1 July, he decides to carry out a cash flow forecast for the month ahead. He does some calculations and notes the following figures:

Cash inflows   £2400

Cash outflows   £2100

Opening bank balance   £1200

He then does the following calculations:

Net cash flow = £2400 – £2100 = £300

Closing balance in bank = £1200 + £300 = £1500

Study his calculations and work out what would happen if the outflow figure was £2600 and all of the other figures remained the same.

Think about your own cash flow (your money coming in and your money going out). Do you ever try to forecast how much money you will have at certain times of the year? Enterprises use calculations that help them to do this, so that they can plan ahead.

The purpose of a cash flow forecast

The purpose of a cash flow forecast is to:

- identify the possible inflows
- identify the possible outflows
- add together the amounts in each category and work out the difference, which is known as the net cash flow.

When the net cash flow amount is added to money already in the bank, this is known as the cash balance (shown as closing balance on the statement).

Net cash flow + Money in the bank = Closing (cash) balance

The closing (cash) balance is the amount of money an enterprise has available.

An enterprise needs to be able to forecast its cash balance at any point in time, because it could face difficulties if it is unable to pay its debts.

Benefits and risks of cash flow forecasts

Take a look at Table 3.12, which outlines:

- some of the benefits for the owners of an enterprise in producing a cash flow forecast
- some of the risks of not using a cash flow forecast.

◘ Table 3.12: Cash flow forecasts – benefits of using one vs. risks of not using one

Benefits of cash flow forecasts	Risks of not using cash flow forecasts
• The timings of all expected revenue (cash inflows) are known • Reminders can be sent for any debts that are owed/overdue	Revenue may be received late or not at all
• The timings of all expenditure (cash outflows) are known • Payment dates can be renegotiated if there is a problem	• Payments may be delayed • Suppliers may become frustrated and could refuse to trade with the enterprise in the future
If there is likely to be a deficit, the owner has time to take action to delay payments, or obtain a temporary loan if necessary	The enterprise may have to pay high interest charges on an unauthorised overdraft or emergency loan
The owner has warning if there is a long-term problem, which means costs can be reduced and/or revenue increased to help the enterprise to survive	The enterprise may not be able to pay its bills and eventually might have to cease trading

▣ What might happen to a small enterprise that spins, dyes and sells its wool at specialist events if it doesn't undertake regular cash flow forecasts?

ACTIVITY

Copy out and complete the cash flow for Leigh's decorating services.
Leigh discovers that her van is in need of repair and will be off the road for two weeks in July.

1 How do you think she will react to this information?

2 What would you advise her to do?

Leigh's cash flow forecast			
	June (£)	July (£)	August (£)
Total receipts	1000	400	1200
Total payments	500	1200	1500
Net cash flow			
Opening balance	200		
Closing balance			

CHECK MY LEARNING

Imagine Fergus (in the first activity) chooses not to construct a cash flow forecast.

1 List the problems this might cause.

2 Outline the impact it could have on:
• his relationship with his suppliers
• his relationship with his bank
• his ability to pay his bills.

Cash flow problems

All businesses can have cash flow problems. A key point to remember is that an enterprise can be profitable but fail because it does not manage its cash flow effectively.

GETTING STARTED

What do you think the difference would be between a cash flow forecast prepared in advance to set budgets and a later version that contains the actual figures? What sort of factors might account for this variance?

Why do some enterprises have poor cash flow?

There are several reasons why an enterprise can have poor cash flow. Some of these are listed below.

- It may not use statements or forecasts. Therefore, it will not be aware of its cash balance now or at any point in the future.
- It might overtrade, which means it might try to grow too quickly without enough funds. For example, it might take orders for products without being able to source the raw materials to make them.
- Debtors (people or organisations who owe money) may not pay on time. In fact, some may not pay at all! This is referred to as 'bad debt'. Bad debt can occur if a customer or business cannot afford to pay you.
- All of its bills may come in at the same time. Most enterprises do not have the luxury of spreading their bills throughout the year.
- It may have unexpected payments. Sometimes a business will have things to pay for that it could not predict – for example, a broken machine might need to be fixed or a customer might want their money back because the enterprise wasn't able to deliver what the customer wanted.
- It may have poor cash flow management – for example, its record-keeping is poor and it does not chase its debtors.

ACTIVITY

Study the cash flow forecast below and list any problems the enterprise might be facing. Be specific and identify the exact inflows or outflows that might be causing the problem.

What advice would you give the owners of this enterprise?

	Jan	Feb	Mar	Apr	May	Jun	Jul
Income (receipts)							
Sales	236	300	240	470	560	420	380
Bank loan					200		
Total income	236	300	240	470	760	420	380
Expenditure (payments)							
Rent	70	70	70	70	70	70	70
Wages	140	140	140	140	140	140	140
Raw materials	140	105	84	165	106	147	133
Overheads	30	30	30	50	50	30	30
Other	12	18	11	10	5	3	4
Total expenditure	392	363	335	435	371	390	377
Net cashflow	(156)	(63)	(95)	35	389	30	3
Opening bank balance	210	54	(9)	(104)	(69)	320	350
Closing bank balance	54	(9)	(104)	(69)	320	350	353

Cash flow in different enterprises

Cash flow is not the same in all enterprises, as the examples below show.

- Some enterprises have very steady and easily predictable cash flows. Others might have a very long and unpredictable cash flow cycle – for example, if customers take months to pay.

- Some retail businesses sell to customers on cash terms (which means payment is instant and available to pay for expenses). Others offer customers **trade credit** terms (which makes it hard for an enterprise to manage its cash flow).

- Some manufacturers and enterprises have to pay for raw materials and production costs before sales are made. For example, a construction business will have to pay for its materials long before the houses are ready to be sold.

- Some enterprises are seasonal. This means that demand for their products or services changes throughout the year. For example, camping equipment is far more popular during the summer and sales will generally peak between April and August.

KEY TERM

Trade credit allows a customer to 'buy' things from a business without paying for them at the time. The money is paid back later in instalments (regular payments).

DID YOU KNOW?

Some furniture stores use trade credit for their customers. That means you could buy a sofa or a bed today, but not pay back any money for, say, another 90 days. Then, after that time, you would begin to pay back the money on a regular basis over a fixed period of time – say, 24 payments over two years.

ACTIVITY

Look at the list of cash inflows and cash outflows. Create a line representing a spectrum such as the one below. Place each outflow and inflow on the line to represent how easy/accurate it is for the owners of an enterprise to forecast:

- **easy/accurate**
- debtors
- sales
- fixed costs
- raw materials
- repair costs
- recruitment costs
- loan capital
- **difficult/inaccurate.**

CHECK MY LEARNING

1 Explain why some enterprises might have positive cash flows while others struggle to pay bills.

2 List the things an enterprise needs to be able to produce accurate cash flow forecasts.

3 Decide which of the following is most likely to cause an enterprise to have cash flow problems:

a) late payments from debtors

b) an unforeseen cost.

Solving cash flow problems

There are generally solutions to most problems – and that includes the cash flow problems an enterprise may have. It's all about making the right decisions, based on the right facts, at the right time.

Improving cash flow

Healthy cash flow, as you will remember, ensures there is enough working capital in a business at any point to pay for expenses. But if cash flow isn't so good, an enterprise may struggle to pay its employees and suppliers. There are a number of solutions that can improve cash flow. Here are a few.

- *Cutting costs*: an enterprise could look at its fixed and variable costs to see where savings could be made.
- *Increasing revenue*: an enterprise might consider raising its prices or doing promotions to increase its sales.
- *Reducing stock levels*: having stock, which is not easily converted to cash, means that an enterprise's money is tied up. Reducing stock levels can help to increase working capital.
- *Delaying payments*: delaying payments means cash stays in the enterprise longer. However, this approach could damage relationships with suppliers.
- *Reducing credit periods*: an enterprise could cut back on trade credit (see the previous lesson 'Cash flow problems') offered to customers.
- *Making an early payment bonus*: an enterprise could give its customers a discount for paying their invoices early.
- *Selling off assets*: an enterprise could sell **unused assets** to create extra cash.
- *Managing debt*: an enterprise could invest time in chasing debtors (people and businesses that owe it money) to ensure they pay.
- *Finding short-term cash flow solutions*: this might involve an enterprise agreeing a bank overdraft, a short-term loan or moving its payment periods with suppliers.
- *Delaying expansion plans*: an enterprise could decide to wait until there is a sufficient cash surplus before increasing its size.

Figure 3.15 may help you to remember the basic idea of solving cash flow problems, which is to increase cash inflow and slow down cash outflow.

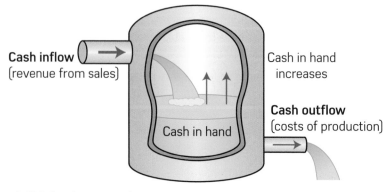

Cash inflow (revenue from sales)

Cash in hand increases

Cash outflow (costs of production)

Cash in hand

◘ **Figure 3.15: What happens when an enterprise speeds up its cash inflow and slows down its cash outflow?**

Analysing cash flow forecasts

When you analyse a cash flow forecast, the most important figure is the closing bank balance. This is the actual balance of cash the enterprise will have.

- Unless the enterprise has an overdraft it cannot have a negative balance.
- A small but positive figure means the enterprise can pay its bills and continue to trade.
- A large positive figure means there is money available for investment or expansion – for example, new products or new equipment.
- A small but negative figure means that money may have to be borrowed, at least for a short time. But borrowing money means more will have to be paid out next month to pay back the loan.
- A large negative closing balance means the enterprise cannot pay its way and may have to close unless action is taken to increase inflows and/or reduce outflows.

It is possible to identify the cause of cash flow problems by analysing inflows and outflows. For example, a business might ask itself the following questions.

- Are sales falling?
- Is there a month when outflows peak?

When analysing a cash flow forecast you should:

- always try to be specific
- try to identify exactly where (what month) and what (inflows or outflows) the problem might be.

LINK IT UP

To remind yourself about cash flow forecasts, look back to the lesson 'Cash flow statements and forecasts' earlier in this learning aim.

◘ **What are the positive and negative aspects for an enterprise of taking out a loan?**

ACTIVITY

Look at the two cash flow forecasts below for Ivy Home Interiors for a two-month period.

Forecast 1: Ivy Home Interiors' cash flow forecast, September 2017

£'000	Week 1	Week 2	Week 3	Week 4
Cash inflows	20	15	32	24
Cash outflows	25	27	20	30
Net cash flow	(5)	(12)	12	(6)
Opening balance	10	5	(7)	5
Closing balance	5	(7)	5	(1)

Forecast 2: Ivy Home Interiors' cash flow forecast, October 2017

£'000	Week 1	Week 2	Week 3	Week 4
Cash inflows	10	10	15	55
Cash outflows	22	20	20	25
Net cash flow	(12)	(10)	(5)	30
Opening balance	(1)	(13)	(23)	(28)
Closing balance	(13)	(23)	(28)	2

1 Analyse the two forecasts and identify the issues Ivy Home Interiors may face.
2 Identify possible causes of cash flow problems.
3 Provide three pieces of advice to the owners of Ivy Home Interiors for how they could improve their cash flow.

CHECK MY LEARNING

Create a flow chart showing the order of solutions an enterprise with cash flow problems should use. For example, the first solution on the list might be the easiest and most obvious. The last solution might be the one that causes additional problems or long-term instability.

Introduction to break-even

Have you ever used the term break-even for anything? It describes a balance point where nothing has been lost, but nothing has been gained. Businesses commonly use this as financial terminology.

Defining break-even

Break-even occurs when an enterprise has made enough money through product sales to cover the cost of making or producing them. There is no profit and no loss. Take a look at Figure 3.16.

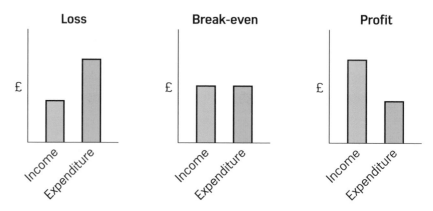

Figure 3.16: What other formats could you use to show break-even?

Calculating break-even

There are two ways of calculating the **break-even point**.

- The first is using a formula.
- The second is creating a chart.

This lesson will focus on calculating the break-even point using a formula.

Calculating break-even point using a formula

You will need to know three pieces of information to calculate a break-even point:

- price per unit
- variable cost per unit
- total fixed costs.

The formula used to calculate the break-even point is:

Break-even point = Fixed costs ÷ (Selling price per unit – Variable cost per unit)

When calculating the break-even point, what you really need to know is how many units an enterprise will have to sell (and produce) in order to cover all of its costs. If the enterprise makes and sells one more unit, then it will start to make a profit. Here's an example.

Fluffy Toys Ltd

Fluffy Toys Ltd manufactures soft toys and is able to sell all that can be produced. The maximum factory capacity is 700 toys each month. The variable costs (direct materials and direct labour) for producing each toy (one unit) are as follows:

Labour	£4
Raw materials	£3
Production costs	£2
Packaging	£1

The selling price is set at £20. The fixed costs of running the business are £5,000 per month.

Break-even point = 5,000 ÷ (20 – 10) = 500

ACTIVITY

A pet food company operates several shops across the UK. The owners estimate the running costs for one shop to be in the region of £60,000 per month. The average value of sales per customer who visits the shop is £55, with variable costs per sale of £12.

How many customers does the pet food company need to visit its shops each month to break even?

The importance of break-even

Break-even is an important calculation. This is because it tells the owners of an enterprise exactly how many products they must produce and sell before they can start to make a profit.

The benefit of using a break-even analysis is that it allows the owner to answer 'What if...' questions. Possible questions an owner could consider are shown below.

- What if we were able to sell an extra 200 units?
- What if rent went up by £80 per month?

ACTIVITY

1 If a product sells for £5, the variable cost is £3 and the fixed cost is £300, what is the break-even point? Use the formula to calculate it.

2 Without recalculating your answer, what do you think would happen to the break-even point if the fixed cost rose to £350 and the price rose to £6, but variable costs stayed the same? Have a guess and then calculate the new break-even point.

CHECK MY LEARNING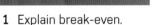

1 Explain break-even.

2 Give the formula for the break-even point.

3 Discuss how the owner of an enterprise might use break-even information.

4 Explain what would happen to the break-even point if the price of the product fell.

Interpreting break-even charts

In the last lesson, you learned about using a formula to calculate the break-even point. This lesson will look at break-even charts, and how they can be interpreted.

Break-even charts

The break-even point can be identified by drawing a chart. A break-even chart shows three main pieces of information (the lines). These are:

- total revenue (TR)
- fixed costs (FC)
- total costs (TC).

The point where total revenue meets total costs is the break-even point. This can be interpreted in:

- sales value
- units sold.

However, the number of units sold is the most common way to express break-even.

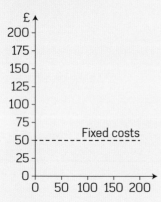

Chart 1

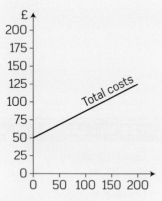

Chart 2

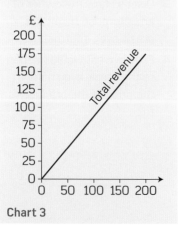

Chart 3

ACTIVITY

1 Study the break-even chart below. Then read the explanations underneath linked to the labels on the chart. You can ask your teacher about anything you do not understand.

2 Now, close your books and, in a pair, try to recall as much of the information you can that appears on a break-even chart.

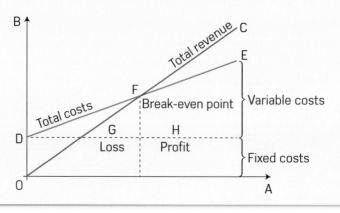

Examining a break-even chart

Take a look at the chart in the activity box. Compare the labels on the chart with their explanations below.

A is the X (horizontal) axis. On a break-even chart it shows the number of units. You will read off this axis when finding out the break-even point.

B is the Y (vertical) axis. On a break-even chart it represents costs and revenues (£).

C is the revenue line. It shows the total revenue the enterprise will make at various levels of output. The revenue line starts at 0 (zero) because if the enterprise sells nothing then its revenue will be £0.

D is fixed costs. The line is horizontal because it stays the same at all levels of output. Even if the enterprise sells no products, fixed costs still have to be paid.

E is total costs. This line starts at the fixed costs point (D). Total costs are plotted by adding fixed costs to variable costs. The variable costs line is not required on a break-even chart.

F is the break-even point. This is where the total revenue line and the total costs line meet (cross over). It drops down as a dotted line to show the break-even point in number of units. All sales *up to this point* will incur a loss (G) and all sales *beyond this point* contribute towards profit (H).

G To the left of the break-even line, sales revenue is less than expenditure and a loss is being made.

H To the right of the break-even line, sales revenue is greater than costs, which means a profit is being made.

DID YOU KNOW?

If the real costs and revenues were plotted on a break-even chart the lines would seldom be straight. This is because variable costs and revenues often change at different points. For example, raw materials might be cheaper the more an enterprise buys. As a result, variable costs per unit will fall the more a business produces.

ACTIVITY

Study the break-even chart below then answer the questions that follow it.

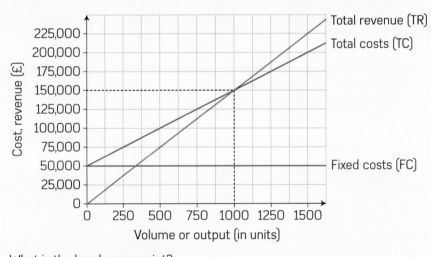

1. What is the break-even point?
2. What is the value of fixed costs?
3. What are the total costs at 500 units?
4. What is the value of sales if 750 units are sold?
5. What is the profit/loss if 1250 units are sold?

CHECK MY LEARNING

1. Close your books and try to recreate a break-even chart from memory.
2. Use a ruler and attempt to label all parts of the chart, including the break-even point.
3. Next to your chart, write down the formula to calculate break-even point (without looking!).

Putting together break-even charts

So far in the learning aim, you have examined what break-even is, learned how to calculate it using a formula and understood how you can use charts to find break-even. Now it's your turn to have a go, using the step-by-step guidance below. Good luck!

Break-even step by step

A break-even chart consists of three lines:

- fixed costs
- total costs
- revenue.

To draw a line on a chart you only need to have two points (first point and second point). Here is an outline of the chart you will need, based on the table in 'Getting started' for Picnics with Style. Copy out the chart, then try to complete it as you work through the following steps. Remember, you will already have calculated the variable cost per unit and the price per unit in 'Getting started'. Check your answers with others to make sure they are correct.

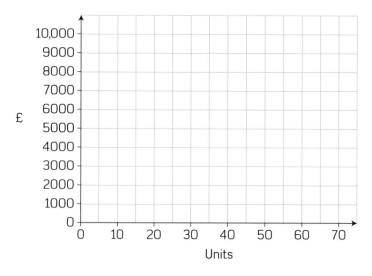

Step 1: Add the fixed costs line

Start by adding the fixed costs line to your chart. Fixed costs are constant across all levels of output so you will be drawing a horizontal line. For Picnics with Style Ltd, the fixed costs are £4000.

Step 2: Draw the total costs line

First point: The total costs line will always start where the fixed costs line meets the Y (vertical) axis.

Second point: This will be the variable costs per unit multiplied by any unit of output, plus fixed costs.

For example, at 30 units of output the total costs line will run through:

(30 units × £50 variable costs per unit) + £4000 fixed costs = £5500

Therefore, where 30 units (X axis) and £5500 (Y axis) meet is the second point through which the total costs line should run.

Step 3: Draw the revenue line

First point: Revenue will always start at 0 (zero).

Second point: This will come from multiplying any unit of output by the price per unit. So, using the same example of 30 units:

30 units × £150 per unit = £4500.

Therefore, where 30 units (X axis) and £4500 (Y axis) meet is the second point through which the revenue line should run.

Step 4: Clearly label your break-even chart

Make sure that you clearly label each line on your chart. You will need to show the break-even point, both axes and the margin of safety (see below).

ACTIVITY

In a small group, compare your charts. Note any differences and discuss why they might have occurred. Then check your chart against the correct version below.

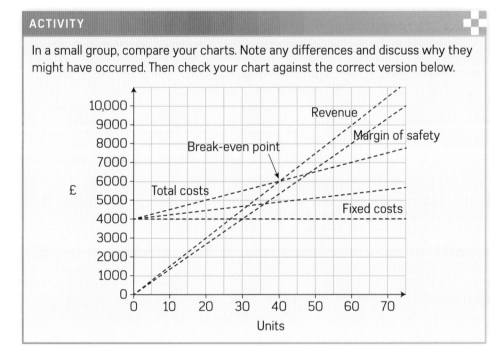

Margin of safety

The margin of safety is the difference between the level of output and the break-even point. It is the amount by which sales would have to fall before the break-even point is reached. See also p. 103.

The margin of safety is simply identified as a range beyond break-even, as shown in the chart in the second activity box.

ACTIVITY

Some of the variables from the break-even chart you have been working on have changed.

1   Construct another break-even chart, fully labelled, using the following information.
   Fixed costs £3000
   Variable costs per unit £70
   Price £180

2   Note down the profit or loss Picnics with Style Ltd would make if it produced and sold 60 picnic chairs.

DID YOU KNOW?

You can check that your chart is accurate by using the formula for the break-even point. If your chart is accurate, the break-even point should correspond to where the revenue and total costs lines meet.

CHECK MY LEARNING

1   Outline what the axes on a break-even chart show.

2   List the three lines drawn on a break-even chart.

3   State which line starts at zero.

4   Explain how you can check the break-even point on a chart is correct.

Using break-even analysis to plan

GETTING STARTED

Discuss which of the following can be understood/identified from a break-even chart.

- The profit an enterprise will make
- Variable costs
- The margin of safety
- The profit margin
- The efficiency of an enterprise.

LINK IT UP

To remind yourself about margin of safety, go back to the previous lesson 'Putting together break-even charts'.

As you discovered from the final activity in the last lesson, break-even points can change when other things change – for example, sales or costs. This lesson will help you to understand how you can analyse the break-even when figures change.

Why figures change

There are a few reasons why figures may change – for example:

- an enterprise's costs may increase, which will increase the break-even point
- an enterprise may raise its prices, which means it will reach break-even sooner.

Table 3.13 summarises these changes and how they impact on the break-even point.

◼ Table 3.13: Types of change of figures and their effect on break-even

Type of change	Effect on break-even
An increase in sales	The margin of safety increases
A decrease in sales	• The margin of safety decreases • If sales fall below the break-even point, the enterprise will make a loss
An increase in price	• The break-even point falls • The enterprise reaches break-even through fewer sales
A decrease in price	• The break-even point rises • More sales are needed to break even
An increase in costs (fixed or variable)	• The number of sales required to break even increases • Profit levels are likely to fall
A decrease in costs (fixed or variable)	The break-even point is lower, so the enterprise makes more profit

ACTIVITY

Draw three break-even charts. The first should be a standard break-even chart with three lines: fixed costs, total revenue and total costs. Identify where the break-even point is. The second and third charts should show:

- two changes to break-even
- a short explanation of the changes
- their effects on the break-even point.

The new lines on the break-even charts should be demonstrated as dotted lines – for example:

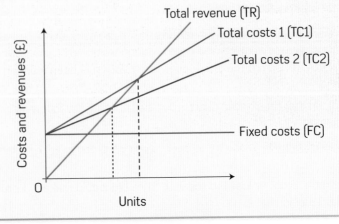

Benefits of break-even analysis

Break-even analysis is a useful planning tool for an enterprise. Break-even analysis helps enterprise owners to identify key financial information. It also helps them to set appropriate targets. The benefits of break-even analysis are listed below.

- Both the fixed and variables costs can be identified.
- Projected sales revenue is calculated.
- The owner knows how many items must be sold to make a profit.
- The owner can make adjustments to try to make a profit sooner – for example, reduce costs by obtaining cheaper materials or increase selling price.
- The margin of safety is known.
- The best goods are stocked and sold in order to maximise profit.

ACTIVITY

Discuss the actions a business might take if sales started to fall – ideally without adding too much to costs. Remember to relate your answer to the concept of break-even.

CHECK MY LEARNING

1 List which costs are combined to make the total costs line on a break-even chart.
2 Explain what is represented by the space between the total cost line and the sales income line above the break-even point.
3 Identify three benefits the owner of an enterprise gains from carrying out a break-even analysis.

■ What difference would it make to the break-even if a shop raised its prices?

The limitations of break-even analysis

You have seen the benefits of break-even analysis, but it can have its limitations and we will look at these in this lesson. First, however, you need to consider the risks of *not* completing a break-even analysis.

The risks of not completing break-even analysis

As you have already learned, break-even analysis is a useful financial planning tool for the owners of an enterprise, and there could be a number of risks if it is *not* used.

- Cost are not known or are too high.
- The selling price is too high or too low.
- The owner has no idea how many items need to be sold to make a profit.
- The enterprise makes a loss over a long period of time without any action being taken.
- The margin of safety is unknown.
- Stock costs too much, is sold at the wrong price (maybe at less than cost price) and, thus, the enterprise fails.

▣ How might a business be affected if its owner doesn't really know what's happening with the figures?

The limitations of break-even analysis

A break-even chart is an easy visual way of analysing an enterprise's financial position at different levels of output.

- Decision-makers can see at a glance the amount of profit or loss that will be made at different levels of production.
- The chart can be used to convince financial providers to lend money.

However, this assumes that:
- all output is sold
- no stock is held.

Assumptions

Break-even assumes all conditions will stay the same in the short term – for example, all wages and rent will stay the same over all levels of output. But this is not always true. For example:

- workers may be getting paid for overtime because they have worked extra hours
- the enterprise has had an increase in rent because it is now using extra floor space.

Changes in output

Break-even also assumes that revenue and total costs are linear (they travel along a straight line). However, this can also be untrue because prices and costs often change at different levels of output. For example, the price of stock often falls if it is bought in bulk (large amounts).

Break-even analysis can often be simple when an enterprise sells one type of product. However, most enterprises sell a wide range of products, all with different costs and prices. Figure 3.17 shows what happens when this is the case.

The effectiveness of break-even analysis

Whether or not break-even analysis is effective depends on the accuracy of information used. If the owner's calculations for costs and revenues are inaccurate, the conclusions drawn from the break-even analysis will be flawed.

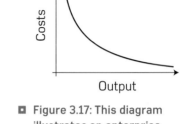

■ Figure 3.17: This diagram illustrates an enterprise selling a wide range of goods. Explain what you think is happening here

ACTIVITY

Below are three charts, each showing a different line from a break-even chart. These lines are not straight, which is often the case for lines on a break-even chart.

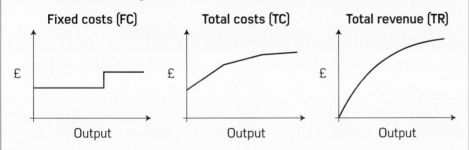

Fixed costs (FC)   Total costs (TC)   Total revenue (TR)

1 Try to explain what is happening with each line
2 What might be causing it?
3 Why might the answers to Question 2 cause problems for owners of an enterprise when using a break-even analysis?

CHECK MY LEARNING

Match the statements below so that they relate to break-even analysis.

A	Increase capacity...		i	while maintaining capacity and productivity
B	Increase selling price...		ii	while maintaining demand for your products
C	Lower fixed costs...		iii	while maintaining quality
D	Lower variable costs...		iv	while maintaining costs

Financing an enterprise

There is no escaping the fact that enterprises need finance (funds) in order to run. They need these both in the short term and in the long term so that they can operate, expand or, simply, survive.

The importance of finance

An enterprise will have a continuous flow of money. This money will flow:

- into the company – income
- out of the company – expenditure.

Expenditure can be classified as either capital expenditure or revenue expenditure.

- Capital expenditure includes the purchase of fixed assets and spending on items held by the business in the long term. These will be accounted for in the statement of financial position.
- Revenue expenditure relates to the purchase of goods and service that will be consumed or have already been consumed in the day-to-day operations of the business.

Sources of finance

The main sources of finance can initially be divided into those that are:

- internally available to the business
- externally available to the business.

Enterprise owners need to be fully aware of all sources of finance available to them – especially in the early stages of an enterprise's development. They need to be aware of finances that help them to start up, grow and run on a day-to-day basis.

ACTIVITY

Organise the following sources of finance into two categories: internal and external (look back at earlier lessons to check on definitions you are not sure of):

- owner funds
- credit cards
- retained profit
- overdraft
- leasing
- sale of assets.

Start-up finance

The money that enterprise owners will use to create their business is known as start-up finance. Some people will finance the start-up costs using their own money. Others will use a source of external finance – for example, a bank loan – to help create their business.

Starting an enterprise can be very expensive and it may take some time before the initial start-up costs are repaid.

Finance for growth

If an enterprise is successful, the owners may decide to expand. Expansion might involve, for example:

- producing and selling more products
- opening a new branch of the enterprise
- moving into new markets.

The sources of finance required for enterprise growth are similar to start-up sources. However, successful enterprises might be able to use retained profit to finance growth.

Working capital: day-to-day finance

Working capital is the money an enterprise needs to function from day to day. This money will be used to pay for things such as:

- stock
- bills
- wages.

Working capital is closely linked to cash flow. An enterprise must have sufficient working capital to keep the enterprise running.

Figure 3.18 gives more examples of start-up, growth and working capital.

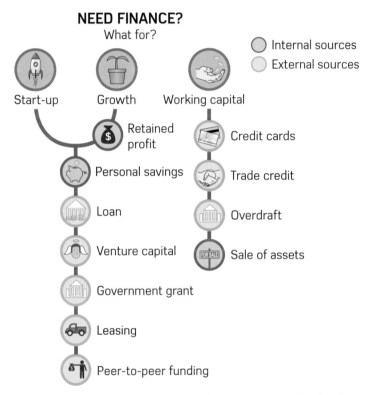

NEED FINANCE?
What for?

Start-up   Growth   Working capital

◯ Internal sources
◯ External sources

Retained profit   Credit cards

Personal savings   Trade credit

Loan   Overdraft

Venture capital   Sale of assets

Government grant

Leasing

Peer-to-peer funding

☐ Figure 3.18 Try to provide definitions for all of the things listed in this figure

CHECK MY LEARNING

1 Explain why an enterprise would require finance.
2 List the external sources of finance.
3 Give three examples of working capital costs.

Internal sources of finance

Finance that is internally sourced is money that comes into a business. Internal sources include retained profit, owner funds and sales of assets. They can be short term and long term.

Retained profit

Retained profit is a major source of long-term finance for a business.

Generally, the shareholders of a business will share between them most of the profit that the business earns during its financial year. Retained profit is the amount of profit that is *not* shared out. It stays (is retained) within the business. The amount of profit retained by a business can be seen in its statement of financial position.

Advantages of retaining profits

This form of internal finance has some advantages over external sources.

- It costs far less. This is because external finances, such as loans, often mean the business has to pay back interest on the loan in addition to the loan itself.
- The business does not have to explain to any external organisations what it will use the profits for.

Retained profit is only available to successful businesses; therefore, it is suitable for growth.

LINK IT UP

To remind yourself about the items on a statement of financial position, look back at the lesson 'Statement of financial position' in Learning aim B of this component.

ACTIVITY

Cameo is a small high street clothing brand with an outlet in Peterborough. The company has been very successful over the past few years and has developed a loyal customer base. The owners of the business would like to expand their current store into an unused unit next door. Builders believe the expansion would cost £6000.

Write an email to the owners of Cameo explaining why they should put off the expansion for six months in order to use retained profit to finance the expansion.

Owner funds

When starting a new enterprise, many entrepreneurs invest their own money. Although this can be a risk, they hope their investment will be repaid in time with a profit.

Owner funds are low risk, because they do not generally affect working capital (day-to-day costs). However, if an owner had taken out a bank loan, they would need to make regular repayments with the additional cost of interest.

DID YOU KNOW?

Banks are more willing to offer a loan to an enterprise if they can see the owner has also risked their own funds.

GETTING STARTED

Copy and complete this statement using the words below it.

Three reasons businesses may need finance are to ____ a business, ____ a business or help a business ____.

New businesses find it difficult to raise finance because they have no evidence that their ____ or ____ will succeed. The business may not have any ____ which the bank could use as ____ against the loan and sell if the business struggled to make repayments.

assets

run

product

start

collateral

service

grow

Sale of assets

As an enterprise grows, so will the products it produces and the assets it requires. Furthermore, assets depreciate (lose value).

To raise additional funds, an owner may choose to sell these assets to raise money. At times when funds are low, an enterprise can sell off assets in order to free up cash to pay off debts and purchase stock.

Weighing up advantages and disadvantages

Take a look at Table 3.14, which outlines the three methods of internal finance you have just learned about.

◻ Table 3.14: Internal sources of finance, their benefits and drawbacks

Finance method	Explanation	Benefits	Drawbacks
Retained profits	• Money kept in the business by the owners • Known as retained profit on the statement of financial position	No need to pay interest on the money	• Could have been invested elsewhere, earning a higher profit • The business may not have enough retained profit to meet its needs • Shareholders may become unhappy if this means lower dividend payments (their share of profit)
Owner funds	Money put into the business by the owner	• There is no interest to pay • Banks are more willing to lend money if the owner has put their own money into the enterprise	• Could have been invested elsewhere, earning a higher profit • Owner may not have enough funds to meet the needs of the business
Selling assets	Items owned by the business are sold and the money made is used to finance business growth or working capital	The business is using money it already has – so it won't need to take on loans or pay interest charges	• The business has to have something worth selling for this to be an option • The business may sell something it later needs

ACTIVITY

Faraz was made redundant (lost his job) in August and was given a redundancy payout of £3000. Over the past few months he has been working for his father, but has decided it is time to start a new career. Faraz has been considering starting a golfing supplies business and needs £5000 to cover the start-up costs. He believes the bank would be able to offer him an £8000 business loan.

Write an email to Faraz explaining why it would be better for him to invest his own money, rather than take out a bank loan.

CHECK MY LEARNING

Outline one scenario where the owner of an enterprise might use the following sources of finance. In each case, explain why it might be the most appropriate option:

• owner funds
• retained profit
• selling assets.

External sources of finance: short term

GETTING STARTED

External sources of finance can be categorised into short term and long term.

What do you think distinguishes short-term from long-term sources?

Remember that internal sources of finance are those that come from within an enterprise – for example, retained profits, money paid in by the business owner and money raised from selling assets. External sources come from outside an enterprise, and can be short or long term. Here, you will look at short term.

Overdrafts and credit

A short-term source of finance is generally an amount of money that will be paid back within one year of trading. These sources include:

- bank overdraft
- credit cards
- trade credit.

Bank overdrafts

A bank overdraft facility is often used by start-ups and small businesses. An overdraft is really a loan facility.

- The bank lets a business 'owe it money' when its bank balance goes below zero.
- In return, the bank charges the business interest – which can often be at quite a high rate.
- An overdraft is a flexible source of finance because it is only used when needed.

Support with cash flow

Bank overdrafts are excellent for helping a business when it:

- has seasonal fluctuations in cash flow (for example, if it produces products that are not needed at certain times of year)
- runs into short-term cash flow problems (for example, if a major customer fails to pay on time).

Credit cards

A credit card is a common source of finance for small enterprises.

- A credit card has an assigned credit limit, such as £3000, which the owner of an enterprise can spend up to.
- The owner only pays interest on the balance of the credit card (the amount that has been spent). If the total credit is paid within the month then no interest is charged on the balance.
- Each month, the owner will pay off a proportion of the credit.
- When a credit card is used to pay for large expenses, the balance might be paid off over a number of months (or even longer). In this scenario, interest is charged.

■ When wouldn't you pay interest on a credit card statement?

Trade credit

One of the main sources of short-term finance for a business is trade credit.

Current assets, such as raw materials, are purchased on credit with payment terms normally varying from between 30 to 90 days. Therefore, trade credit:

- represents an interest-free short-term loan
- allows a business to receive the revenue from goods sold before having to pay suppliers.

Advantages and disadvantages

In a period of high inflation there are clear advantages to purchasing using trade credit. However, these advantages must be weighed against the discount incentives (reductions in cost) suppliers offer for early payment.

Table 3.15 outlines the advantages and disadvantages of these three types of short-term external sources of finance.

ACTIVITY

For each of the scenarios below, choose whether a bank loan or credit card would be the most appropriate source of finance. Make sure you justify your choice.

1 A supplier needs paying £1500 by the end of the week and there are not sufficient funds in the business bank account.

2 Your company is looking to invest £7000 in product development. You are hoping the new product will be ready to market in 18 months, time.

3 Your enterprise has the opportunity to purchase fixed assets from a similar enterprise that is closing down. The assets are being auctioned-off today and you believe you could purchase them for £5000.

◻ Table 3.15: Examples, advantages and disadvantages of short-term external sources of finance

Example of short-term external source of finance	Advantages	Disadvantages
Overdraft	• Very quick to arrange • Good short-term solution to a cash flow problem	• Only suitable for small amounts • Has to be repaid within a short amount of time • Interest or charges are paid
Credit cards	• Flexible access to credit as required • No interest to pay if balance is settled within the month	• High rates of interest • Limit on the amount of credit
Trade credit	• Gives the business more cash to use in the immediate future	• Can only be used to buy certain goods • Bills usually have to be settled within 30, 60 or 90 days

---

ACTIVITY

Nadia has been struggling over the past few months to generate enough income to cover the running costs of her business. She knows her camping shop is very seasonal and believes trade will pick up by April.

Write an email to Nadia explaining how she could use a bank overdraft facility and trade credit to improve her financial position.

DID YOU KNOW?

Many credit card companies give customers an introductory offer of 0 per cent APR (annual percentage rate, or interest rate) for a set number of months before the rate rises. In some cases, credit card companies charge customers anything between 18 per cent and 50 per cent APR.

CHECK MY LEARNING

Below is a cash flow statement for Nadia's camping shop. Explain how she could use the sources of finance discussed in this lesson to improve her working capital position.

£'000	Week 1	Week 2	Week 3	Week 4
Cash inflows	20	15	32	24
Cash outflows	25	27	20	30
Net cash flow	(5)	(12)	12	(6)
Opening balance	10	5	(7)	5
Closing balance	5	(7)	5	(1)

External sources of finance: long term

As you learned in the previous lesson, short-term sources of finance are generally paid back within one financial year. Long-term sources of finance, therefore, last longer than that, but could also cost an enterprise more money in interest rates.

Loans, leases, grants and venture capital

Long-term sources of finance are debts that are repaid over a long period of time – often more than a year. Long-term sources of finance include:

- bank loans
- enterprise leasing
- hire purchase
- government grants
- venture capital
- peer-to-peer lending.

Bank loans

A bank loan is an agreed amount of money that will be paid back over a period of time. This might be anywhere between one and ten years. Interest is paid on the loan, which is added to the monthly repayments.

Owners of an enterprise will need to:

- apply to a bank for a loan
- show evidence that their business will be successful
- prove that they can repay the loan.

Leasing equipment

Leasing enables a business to use expensive assets, such as machinery and other equipment, without having to buy them. It works like this:

- a business leases (borrows) the equipment it needs from the company that owns it
- the business pays regular amounts of money to the company
- the business returns the equipment to the company when it has finished with it
- the company that lends the equipment remains the owner of the equipment.

Hire purchase

Hire purchase is an agreement that allows a business to:

- purchase equipment, such as machinery, from a supplier without having to pay the whole cost up front
- pay for the equipment in instalments (agreed amounts of money each month).

When the purchaser (the enterprise) has paid all the money owed, the equipment then belongs to them. It is now a company asset.

Government grants

Grants from local or national governments are incentives to support the growth and development of enterprises that have a positive impact on the economy. Some are only available in certain areas of the UK.

Government grants to businesses can take a number of forms. Grants might be available to enterprises that:

- provide a social benefit
- create jobs in high unemployment areas
- have a positive environmental impact.

Saeed Mustaq is a timber merchant. He operates as a sole trader from a yard in Birmingham. Most of his sales are credit sales to builders in the area, but some customers pay in cash. In March 2017, one of his larger customers went out of business, leaving him with a bad debt of £2200. As a result, he is likely to have problems paying day-to-day expenses. For example, he needs £4000 immediately or he will run low on timber stocks. Saeed identifies three possible sources of finance.

- His bank agrees to extend his overdraft to £2500 at a rate of 13 per cent APR.
- The bank also offers Saeed a loan of £5000 over a three-year period at a rate of nine per cent APR.
- A new timber supplier has offered Saeed favourable credit terms, but has insisted the first three months' purchases be made in cash.

Using examples from this case, explain the factors Saeed should consider before deciding which option to take.

Venture capital

A venture capitalist is an individual or enterprise that seeks to invest in new business ventures. The venture capitalist will offer capital for an agreed percentage return on their investment and share of the enterprise's profits. A venture capitalist may also have conditions over the control of the enterprise, such as a say in business decisions.

Peer-to-peer lending

This gives the general public and enterprises an opportunity to invest in business start-ups through an online portal.

Copy out the table below and, using the descriptions, identify the relevant sources of finance in order to complete it.

Source of finance	Description
	Money is put into the business by the owner
	The bank allows the business to draw more money from its bank account than it actually has in it
	An amount of money is borrowed from the bank, then repaid (with interest) over a set period of time
	Money is given to the business by the government, which is used to help finance new projects – especially those that create new jobs
	Finance is invested in a small, risky business – for example, a new business start-up – by experienced and wealthy entrepreneurs
	Long-term loan is provided by a bank in order to buy property

Learning aim C: assessment practice

How you will be assessed

You will be assessed on Component 3 of your course by a written assessment. This component builds on the knowledge, understanding and skills that you have acquired and developed in Components 1 and 2. In your assessment you will be presented with a short scenario of a small to medium enterprise (SME), and a series of activities to complete. These tasks will relate to the nature of the enterprise in the scenario and the products or services it sells. The assessment will be completed under supervised conditions.

This assessment practice gives you an opportunity to practise a part of what you will encounter in your assessment.

CHECKPOINT

Strengthen
- Explain the difference between cash and profit.
- Write out the formula for break-even.
- Identify three external sources of finance suitable for growing an enterprise.

Challenge
- Outline the quickest way for an enterprise to resolve cash flow problems.
- Explain the circumstances in which a bank loan might be a better source of finance than retained profit.
- List the consequences of having a small margin of safety.

The activities in this assessment practice are based on this scenario. You should read the scenario carefully before you start the activities. Complete all the activities.

SCENARIO: THE PORTABLE PIZZA COMPANY

Jo is the owner of the Portable Pizza Company, based in Lincoln. The company makes authentic pizza and homemade food cooked from a portable pizza oven that provides catering at outdoor events. The Portable Pizza Company can be hired for a variety of events including festivals, corporate days, parties and weddings. Jo started the Portable Pizza Company with £2000 of her own money and a bank loan of £5000.

The Portable Pizza Company only uses the finest ingredients, which are either grown locally or imported from Italy. Jo only requires a small space to set up the oven, food preparation and service area. At full heat, the oven can cook a pizza in just two minutes, meaning delicious, fresh food can be provided with a fast and simple service.

Jo has produced the following break-even chart illustrating the costs and revenues for a typical one-day event. The average price of a pizza sold at an event is £6. The variable cost to produce one pizza is £2.

TAKE IT FURTHER

The best way to develop your understanding of financial forecasting techniques is to practise constructing your own cash flow forecasts and break-even charts.

Activity 1

a) Using Jo's break-even chart, identify:

- the break-even point
- the margin of safety if Jo sells 65 pizzas
- the profit/loss if Jo sells 30 pizzas.

Remember to show your workings. **(4 marks)**

b) Jo has produced a table to help her produce this break-even chart. Complete the missing figures in the table for A, B and C.

Pizzas sold	Fixed costs (£)	Total revenue (£)	Total costs (£)
20	A	120	190
40	150	B	230
60	150	360	270
80	150	480	C
100	150	600	350

(3 marks)

c) Outline one way that Jo could lower her break-even point. **(2 marks)**

Activity 2

Jo has produced a cash flow forecast covering three months of trading.

The Portable Pizza Company: cash flow forecast			
	June (£)	July (£)	August (£)
Pizza sales	4200	3400	4800
Expenses			
Ingredients	1700	1400	1300
Fuel	120	140	250
Overheads	900	2800	900
Wages	400	600	600
Total payments	3120	4940	3050
Net cash flow	1080	(1540)	1750
Opening balance	50	1130	(410)
Closing balance	1130	(410)	1340

a) Comment on the cash flow situation of The Portable Pizza Company between June and August. **(4 marks)**

b) Using the information provided, recommend how Jo could improve the cash flow position of her pizza company. Justify your recommendation. **(4 marks)**

Activity 3

Jo is considering upgrading the pizza oven she uses to a bigger and more efficient model.

Recommend one of two sources of finance that The Portable Pizza Company could use in order to purchase the new equipment. Your recommendation should include:

- the benefits of the chosen recommendation
- how the source of finance would impact on the enterprise's cash flow
- the reasons why it is better than other sources, giving specific examples. **(6 marks)**

Component 3: practice assessment

Your assessment for this Tech Award will take place under supervised conditions. You will be able to find out in advance how long you will have and the maximum number of marks that can be awarded. Calculators are allowed in the assessment.

So that you can prepare yourself, you will have the opportunity here to complete a full practice assessment. All of the activities are based on the following scenario. You should read this carefully before you begin, then complete all the activities.

SCENARIO: LISTEN & GROOVE

Sam and Drew (cousins) had a passion for music and had played in bands since they were teenagers. They had always collected vinyl records, which they bought from around the world. In 2016 they decided to set up their own record store, Listen & Groove, specialising in vintage records and music memorabilia. They invested £20,000 of their own money from their short-lived success in bands to rent premises and purchase stock.

The store they rented was on the old high street in Derby, which suited the retro nature of their business. They had anticipated their main customers would be men aged 35-plus. However, they found that the average age of customers was mid-twenties and included both men and women, and typically university students. Sam and Drew believed that, as well as buying records and memorabilia, customers also visited the store for the shopping experience and to meet other enthusiasts. At the back of the store, they set up a small café, which was always busy.

Sam and Drew knew that they would need to have an online presence if their business was going to succeed, so they set up a website with an online blog, stock inventory and ecommerce facility. Within weeks they found that their website was receiving a lot of hits, especially for the vinyl record blog. By the end of 2017, the website accounted for 60 per cent of all sales.

Activity 1

Sam and Drew have started to draw up the statement of financial position for their enterprise. Use the information below to complete the shaded cells in the financial statement. **(6 marks)**

Share capital	£15,250	Retained profit	£5500
Furniture	£10,000	Stock	£8500
Debtors	£500	Creditors	£2000

Statement of financial position as of 1 April 2017		
	£	**£**
Fixed assets		
Café equipment	£3000	£13,000
Current assets		
Cash in bank	£750	
		£9750
Current liabilities		
Net current assets		£7750
Total assets less current liabilities		£20,750
Shareholders' funds		
	£5500	

Activity 2

Sam and Drew have received a purchase order from a local hotel that is looking to buy a range of classic vinyl records that customers can use with the record player in the hotel's lounge area.

The following financial documents have been used to complete the order. Identify the purpose of each financial document used in the transaction.

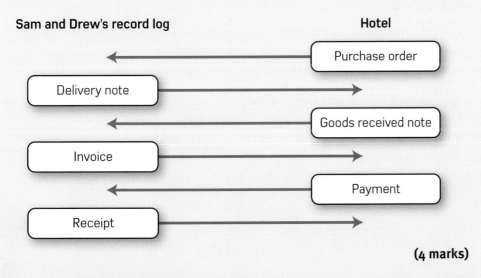

Sam and Drew's record log   **Hotel**

Purchase order
Delivery note
Goods received note
Invoice
Payment
Receipt

(4 marks)

Component 3: practice assessment (continued)

Activity 3

Sam and Drew are considering the promotional mix they could use to attract new customers to their website and record store. They have identified two methods they would like to use:

- sales promotions
- direct marketing.

   a) Outline **one** advantage of sales promotions.   **(2 marks)**

   b) Outline **one** advantage of direct marketing.   **(2 marks)**

   c) Using your understanding of promotion and the context of Listen & Groove, write a note to Sam and Drew recommending which of these two promotion methods would be the best for increasing the number of customers visiting their record store and website. Justify your recommendation.   **(4 marks)**

Activity 4

Sam and Drew are looking at their estimated costings and revenues for an average week at the record store in order to draw up a break-even chart.

Forecasts	
Variable costs per record	£10
Total fixed costs per week	£450
Average price per record sold	£20

Sam and Drew's records show that, on average, they sell 85 records per week.

   a) Draw a break-even chart for one week's trading at Listen & Groove on graph paper. Remember to label it fully.   **(6 marks)**

   b) What is Sam and Drew's margin of safety if they are able to sell 85 records per week?   **(1 mark)**

   c) What profit would Sam and Drew make from one week's trading at the record store if they sold 60 records?   **(3 marks)**

Activity 5

Sam and Drew have drawn up the following cash flow forecast for the rest of the month.

   a) Complete the cash flow forecast by calculating the missing values in the shaded boxes.

Listen & Groove: cash flow forecast			
	Week 2 (£)	Week 3 (£)	Week 4 (£)
Total receipts	900	1200	1250
Total payments	450	1900	610
Net cash flow		(700)	640
Opening balance	200		(50)
Closing balance	650	(50)	

   (3 marks)

   b) Explain how Sam and Drew can resolve their cash flow problems in Week 3.   **(3 marks)**

Activity 6

a) Outline **two** methods of segmentation that Sam and Drew could use to identify the characteristics of their customer base. **(4 marks)**

b) Outline why it is important for Sam and Drew to have a target market for their enterprise. **(2 marks)**

c) Sam and Drew are reviewing how they could create a greater awareness of their record store in the local area. They have considered using:

- **advertising**: an advert in a local newspaper
- **public relations**: album launch events at the record store.

Recommend which one of the two options they should use. Your recommendation should include:

- the benefits of your chosen method
- how it will attract customers
- the limitations of the other option. **(6 marks)**

Activity 7

Below is the statement of comprehensive income for Listen & Groove for the years 2016 and 2017. Sam and Drew are interested in how their enterprise performed.

Statement of comprehensive income				
	2016		**2017**	
	£	£	£	£
Turnover		75,000		77,000
Cost of sales	25,000		22,000	
Gross profit		50,000		55,000
Expenses:				
Administration	2000		8000	
Marketing	5000		1000	
Salaries	20,000		25,000	
Net profit		23,000		21,000

Ratio	Calculation
Gross profit margin	Gross profit ÷ Turnover × 100
Net profit margin	Net profit ÷ Turnover × 100

a) Calculate the gross profit margin and net profit margin for Listen & Groove in 2016 and 2017. **(4 marks)**

Gross profit margin	
	2016 _____ per cent 2017 _____ per cent
Net profit margin	
	2016 _____ per cent 2017 _____ per cent

b) Comment on each ratio, comparing 2016 and 2017. **(4 marks)**

c) Provide recommendations to Sam and Drew on how they could improve the gross profit margin at Listen & Groove. **(4 marks)**

Glossary

Assets are items that an enterprise owns – including property, machinery and cash. Assets can also be conceptual things that have a value, such as a brand.

B2B (business to business) is a market in which one company sells products to another.

B2C (business to consumer) is a market in which companies sell products directly to consumers.

Break-even is the point where income and expenditure (total money spent) are equal.

Break-even point is the number of units (goods or services) an enterprise must sell in order to break-even.

Budget is the amount of money designated for a specific activity or period of time.

A **business plan** is a formal document used to outline the details of a business start-up. Your micro enterprise pitch will include much of the information found in a business plan.

Capital is the money, buildings and equipment that an enterprise uses in order to trade.

Cash flow forecasts are cash flow statements that predict the cash inflows and cash outflows for an enterprise over a period of time.

Cash flow statements are statements of actual cash inflows and outflows over a period of 12 months.

Cash inflows are the amounts of money entering a business's bank account.

Cash outflows are the amounts of money leaving a business's bank account.

Chains are groups of businesses, such as hotels or coffee shops, owned by one parent company.

Characteristics are features that are typical of a particular enterprise.

Competitive advantage is the advantage gained by offering superior goods or services to those of competitors or offering cheaper prices.

Competitors are businesses that sell similar goods or services to your enterprise. You should take their products into consideration when deciding things like pricing and target markets.

Consumers are the people who buy and use goods and services.

A **contingency plan** is a back-up plan for when things go wrong for an enterprise.

Cost of sales is the cost of producing a product.

Customer needs are the wants or requirements a customer has for goods or services.

Demand is the amount of customers, or potential customers, actively wanting your goods or services.

Demographic relates to the way that a population, or market, can be divided up, including by age, ethnic background or educational level.

Digital advertising is done online or using a device such as a mobile phone.

Economy is the system by which a country's money and goods are produced and used.

Enterprise is an organisation that provides goods or services.

Entrepreneurs are people who set up a new enterprise in order to make a profit.

Ethical means avoiding harm to others, animals or the environment.

Feasibility means how easy or practical it will be to do something successfully.

Features are aspects or elements of a service or goods.

Financing is finding funding for something.

Fluctuation is variations such as rises and falls in prices or costs.

Focus groups are group interviews during which people are asked for their views and opinions about different ideas that are suggested to them – for example, a proposal for a new product or enterprise.

Gaps in the market are when an enterprise identifies an idea that no other business is offering, but for which there is likely to be a demand.

Goods are physical products that can be purchased.

Gross profit is the money made from selling a product (sales revenue) after the cost of sales has been deducted. It is calculated before tax has been taken off – profit after tax is called net profit.

Gross profit margin is the gross profit as a percentage of sales revenue.

Growth is when the number and value of goods and services produced in an economy is going up. This usually results in consumer confidence.

HMRC is Her Majesty's Revenue and Customs – the agency that works to collect taxes from individuals and businesses in the UK.

Image is people's opinions of goods or a service and what they associate it with.

Independent businesses are those that are not part of a larger chain or organisation.

Industry means an area of goods or services that are being sold – for example, the computer repair industry.

Innovation is when a new product or process is introduced to a market.

Innovative means coming up with new ideas.

Interest is a percentage of the total amount of money lent, which is added to the amount that must be repaid.

Junk mail is promotional material, either printed or digital, that the receiver regards as unwanted.

Legibility is the quality of handwriting. Being clear and easy to read.

Legislation relates to the laws of a country, which everyone must obey.

A **liability** is an amount of money an enterprise owes (debts).

Limited liability partnership is a partnership that is entered into with limited liability so that the partners are not responsible for each other's debts and cannot have their own assets taken away, as the amount that they would owe if the enterprise fails is limited.

Liquid assets are any assets that can be used in the short term to pay for things.

Liquidity is the ability of an enterprise to pay its debts.

A **liquidity ratio** shows how easily an enterprise can pay its bills through cash, or other things it owns that can easily be turned into cash, as a ratio, compared to how much it owes (debts) in the next year. Cash and debts should be at least equal or, ideally, there should be more cash available than debts; for example, 2:1.

A **loan** is a sum of money borrowed that is expected to be paid back to the lender, usually with interest added on.

Loyalty is when a customer returns to an enterprise to continue buying goods or services because they like that enterprise or will gain additional rewards.

A **market** is the type of customers an enterprise sells to.

Market research is the process of gathering information about customers, including what they want and what they need – for example, the number of people who might wish to buy a product.

Market segment is a section of the market with common characteristics.

Market share is the proportion of all the sales of a group of related goods or services that an enterprise makes when calculating the total 'market' for that group of products. The total market is calculated by adding together the sales made by the enterprise and all of its competitors.

Media is the general term used to describe all of the following collectively: newspapers, magazines, books, television, radio, websites and the internet. The media is a form of mass communication, which can be used to reach large amounts of people.

A **medium** is how an enterprise chooses to communicate with and advertise to its market.

Negotiating is having a discussion with others with the aim of reaching an agreement.

Net cash flow is the difference between the cash inflows and cash outflows over a particular time period.

Net current assets are the difference between current assets and current liabilities. They show the value of the enterprise.

Net profit is the money made from selling a product after all costs have been deducted from gross profit.

Net profit margin is the net profit as a percentage of sales revenue.

Non-verbal communication is communicating with individuals without speaking. Non-verbal communication includes body language, gestures, facial expressions, proximity and touch.

Open-ended questions are structured to encourage a long answer based on the interviewee's opinion.

Perseverance is not giving up and continuing to work at something, despite difficulties encountered along the way.

A **pitch** is the presentation made by an entrepreneur about the nature and details of an idea or start-up to persuade a person or business to invest in the enterprise, or loan capital to start up the enterprise.

Point of sales displays are sales promotions found next to or near the checkout counter.

Political pressure is the influence that government and local councils have on the way enterprises carry out their business.

Pop-ups are temporary physical shops or retail events that set up only for a short amount of time.

Primary research is research carried out directly with existing or potential customers.

Private sector enterprises are owned by individuals, as opposed to the government or local authority, and are run for profit.

Private shares are a stake in a company, from which the shareholder receives a share of the profits (known as a dividend).

Professionalism is the competency, skill and behaviours expected of someone who is a professional.

Profit is the amount of money earned minus the costs paid out.

Profitability is the ability of an enterprise to create a profit.

Promotional materials are things like flyers and brochures, that help to increase sales or gain business.

The **promotional mix** is the range of techniques and mediums an enterprise could use to communicate with potential and current customers. It would use the mix to inform and persuade people to buy its goods and services.

Public sector enterprises are, generally, owned by the government or a local authority.

Pull strategies are aimed at getting customers interested in a product to build demand, so that they will actively seek it out. They include advertising and other promotions.

Purchases are goods or services that have been bought.

Push strategies 'push' goods or services directly to the customer at the point of purchase, making them aware of your brand.

Qualitative research looks into people's opinions, ideas and thoughts – for example, by interviewing a customer.

Quantitative research creates statistics that can be used to compare or find patterns – for example, a survey or questionnaire with numerical ratings.

Ratios are financial tools that compare two pieces of information.

Recession is when the number and value of goods and services produced is going down. This may be followed by a lack in confidence and people buying less because they are concerned about the future.

Regulations interpret the law and state what people have to do to abide by the law.

Reputation is the opinions that customers have about an enterprise.

Resilience means not giving up after setbacks.

Retain means ensuring that a customer stays with an enterprise and does not take their custom to one of its competitors.

Retained profit is profit earned and accumulated from previous trading reinvested back into the enterprise.

Revenue is the money coming into the enterprise (income).

Risk averse is avoiding or being unwilling to take risks.

Running costs are the fixed costs and variable costs that have to be paid to keep a business trading.

Sales is the money generated from selling goods and services.

Sector is a part of the economy – for example, the IT sector, which consists of several related industries.

Services are acts or tasks carried out by an enterprise that can be purchased.

A **skill** is the ability to perform an action well.

A **skills audit** is the process of identifying what skills are needed and matching them to current skills to identify training and development needs.

Slideshow/Slide deck is a presentation of a series of still images and text on a projection screen or electronic display to help a presenter to communicate information to an audience.

Small and medium enterprises (SMEs) are enterprises with fewer than 250 staff.

Social media includes websites and applications that enable users to create and share content or to participate in social networking.

Social pressure is the influence that communities, customers, business owners, employees and other enterprises have on the way an enterprise operates.

Start-up costs are the amount of money spent setting up a business before it starts trading.

Stock is another word for the amount of goods an enterprise has immediately available for sale, without having to order more from its supplier.

A **target market** is the section of the market the enterprise aims to supply.

Tastes are the trends or fashions that a consumer may follow, relating to what they like, dislike and are interested in.

Taxation is the amount of money an enterprise or entrepreneur must pay the government each year. Enterprises and entrepreneurs are taxed on the amount of money they earn by running their business.

Trade credit allows a customer to 'buy' things from a business without paying for them at the time. The money is paid back later in instalments (regular payments).

Unique means that something is one of a kind, so if an enterprise is unique it is the only one.

Unique selling points (USPs) are features that make one product different from any other products.

Unused assets are items a business might have (such as motor vehicles) that it doesn't use or need.

Verbal communication is the sharing of information between individuals through speech and the written word.

Wages are usually calculated hourly to pay for work that has been done.

Appendix 1: Key formulae for enterprises

Break-even point (page 170)

Fixed costs ÷ (Selling price per unit − Variable cost per unit) = Break-even point

Cash balance (page 152)

Cash inflow − Cash outflow = Cash balance

Cash flow statement (page 162)

Cash inflows (receipts) − Cash outflows (payments) = Net cash flow
+ Opening balance = Closing balance

Current ratio (page 156)

Current assets ÷ Current liabilities = Current ratio

Gross profit (page 144)

Turnover − Cost of sales = Gross profit

Gross profit margin (page 154)

Gross profit ÷ Sales revenue × 100 = Gross profit margin (%)

Liquid capital ratio (page 156)

(Current assets − Inventories) ÷ Current liabilities = Liquid capital ratio

Net cash flow, for closing balance on cash flow statement (page 164)

Net cash flow + Money in the bank = Closing (cash) balance

Net current assets (page 147)

Current assets − Current liabilities = Net current assets

Net profit (page 145)

Gross profit − Expenditure = Net profit

Net profit margin (page 155)

Net profit ÷ Sales revenue × 100 = Net profit margin (%)

Profit (page 152)

Revenues earned − Expenses incurred = Profit

Revenue (page 142)

Number of sales × Price per unit = Revenue

Statement of comprehensive income (page 149)

(Turnover − Cost of sales = Gross profit) − Expenses = Net profit

Total costs (page 143)

Fixed costs + Variable costs = Total costs

Appendix 2: Examples of financial records

Goods Received Note

XYZ Holdings Ltd

Date: 7th July 2018

Supplier: ABC Trading Ltd
Order Number: 00123765

PO number: 000123
Date received: 4th July 2018

	Description	Quantity	Comment
1	Small Box	3	
2	Large Box	1	
3	Medium Box	4	Two items not matching catalogue description

Recieved by: _____ Date: _____

Checked by: _____ Date: _____

ABC
Trading Limited

Delivery Note

ABC Trading Ltd
1 Leeming Street
Tidchester
TD1 5WP
Phone: 01265 555238
Email: orders@ABCTrading.co.uk

XYZ Holdings Ltd
Borough Bridge Ave
Townsville
Brigtonshire
B1 7PT
Phone: 07611 555 437
Email: purchases@XYZHoldingsd.com

Delivery note number: 238445
Order number: 00123765

Date: 1st July 2018
Delivery date: 4th July 2018

PO: Number: 000123
Delivery method: 48 HOUR COURIER

ID	Description	Quantity	Checked
100023	Small Box	3	
100045	Large Box	1	
100077	Medium Box	4	

Notes
Two Medium boxes packaged in old style packaging. Same contents and features as new models.

Recieved in good condition

For and on behalf of:

Signature:_____ Date: _____

Purchase Order

Date: 1st July 2018

PO number: 000123

Vendor

ABC Trading Ltd
1 Leeming Street
Tidchester
TD1 5WP
Phone: 01265 555238
Email: orders@ABCTrading.co.uk

Ships To

XYZ Holdings Ltd
Borough Bridge Ave
Townsville
Brigtonshire
B1 7PT
Phone: 07611 555 437
Email: purchases@XYZHoldingsd.com

	Description	Quantity	Unit Price	Line Price
1	Small Box	3	£10	£30
2	Large Box	1	£50	£50
3	Medium Box	4	£25	£100
4				
5				
			Subtotal	£180
			Tax (20%)	£36
			Total	**£216**

Signature:_____ Date: _____

ABC
Trading Limited

Invoice

XYZ Holdings Ltd
Borough Bridge Ave
Townsville
Brigtonshire
B1 7PT

Date: 8th July 2018

Invoice Number: 00123765

Please send payment to: _____
ABC Trading Ltd
1 Leeming Street
Tidchester
TD1 5WP
Phone: 01265 555238
Email: orders@ABCTrading.co.uk

Description	Quantity	Unit Price	Line Price
Small Box	3	£10	£30
Large Box	1	£50	£50
Medium Box	4	£25	£100
		Subtotal	£180
		Tax (20%)	£36
Thank you for your business		**Total Payable**	**£216**

Please make payment within 14 days of receipt of invoice

Cheques should be made payable to ABC Holding Ltd

BACS Payments Account Number 99875234 Sort code 40-22-01

Credit Note

XYZ Holdings Ltd
Borough Bridge Ave
Townsville
Brigtonshire
B1 7PT

Date: 16th July 2018
Credit note number: C0038562

Description	Quantity	Unit Price	Line Price
Partial refund - Medium Box	2	£25	£50
		Subtotal	£50
Thank you for your business		Tax (20%)	£10
		Total Refund	**£60**

Your refund will be credited to your account within the next 10 days

Receipt

XYZ Holdings Ltd
Borough Bridge Ave
Townsville
Brigtonshire
B1 7PT

Date: 8th July 2018
Invoice Number: 00123765

Please send payment to
ABC Trading Ltd
1 Leeming Street
Tidchester
TD1 5WP
Phone: 01265 555238
Email: orders@ABCTrading.co.uk

DATE PAID: 12th July 2018
CHEQUE NUMBER: 000341
THANK YOU

Description	Quantity	Unit Price	Line Price
Small Box	3	£10	£30
Large Box	1	£50	£50
Medium Box	4	£25	£100
		Subtotal	£180
		Tax (20%)	£36
Thank you for your business		**Total Payable**	**£216**

Please make payment within 14 days of receipt of invoice

Cheques should be made payable to ABC Holding Ltd

BACS Payments Account Number 99875234 Sort code 40-22-01

Statement of Account

XYZ Holdings Ltd
Borough Bridge Ave
Townsville
Brigtonshire
B1 7PT

Date: 25th July 2018
Account Number: XYZ00235

Please send payment to: ───────────────────
ABC Trading Ltd
1 Leeming Street
Tidchester
TD1 5WP
Phone: 01265 555238
Email: orders@ABCTrading.co.uk

Date	No.	Description	Amount	Balance
15.6.18	00126722	Sale	£250	
19.6.18	00126722	Payment	-£250	£0
26.6.18	00129476	Sale	£340	£340
1.7.18	00123765	Sale	£216	
12.7.18	00123765	Payment	-£216	£0
16.7.18	C0038562	Credit	-£60	-£60
Thank you for your business			**Total Due**	**£280**

Payment due by 1st August 2018

Cheques should be made payable to ABC Holding Ltd

BACS Payments Account Number 99875234 Sort code 40-22-01

Index

Page numbers in **bold** indicate where the term is defined as a key term. Page numbers in *italics* indicate figures.